Developing Democratic Character in the Young

DEVELOPING DEMOCRATIC CHARACTER IN THE YOUNG

Roger Soder

John I. Goodlad

Timothy J. McMannon

Editors

Institute for Educational Inquiry

JOSSEY-BASS
A Wiley Company
San Francisco

Jossey-Bass books and products are available through most bookstores. To contact Jossey-Bass directly, call (888) 378-2537, fax to (800) 605-2665, or visit our website at www.josseybass.com.

Substantial discounts on bulk quantities of Jossey-Bass books are available to corporations, professional associations, and other organizations. For details and discount information, contact the special sales department at Jossey-Bass.

 Manufactured in the United States of America on Lyons Falls Turin Book. This paper is acid-free and 100 percent totally chlorine-free.

Library of Congress Cataloging-in-Publication Data

Developing democratic character in the young / Roger Soder, John I. Goodlad, Timothy J. McMannon, editors.
    p. cm.—(The Jossey-Bass education series)
    Includes bibliographical references and index.
    ISBN 0-7879-5685-6
    1. Education—Aims and objectives—United States. 2. Democracy—Study and teaching—United States. 3. Moral education—United States. I. Soder, Roger, date. II. Goodlad, John I. III. McMannon, Timothy J. IV. Title. V. Series.
LA217.2 .D48 2001
372'.01'14—dc21   00-012919

FIRST EDITION
HB Printing   10 9 8 7 6 5 4 3 2 1

CONTENTS

FOREWORD

WHETHER ALEXANDER HAMILTON ever really said so, he certainly considered the people, collectively, to be "a great beast."[1] Like many other political theorists of the late eighteenth century, he equated democracy with unthinking, emotional mob rule. Hamilton favored "the rule of gentlemen"—as Charles Mee Jr., put it, "a strong central government directed by men of wealth, . . . a well-buttressed system of senators elected from among the better sort and for life, a president elected for life and armed with powers that the king of England would have envied," and, most telling, "a popular house of limited powers and tenure."[2] Clearly, Hamilton worried that democratic government in the United States might end in disaster.

It nearly did, most spectacularly over the issues of slavery and states' rights in the Civil War, but also over such matters as taxation, ownership of western lands, trade policies, and a national bank. The early history of the United States—indeed, the history of the United States at any time— reveals sharp divisions among competing interests. By the time Lincoln spoke at Gettysburg, the four-score-and-seven-year-old nation had weathered any number of storms.

But Lincoln's Gettysburg Address raised once again the specter of failure. His closing sentence, often portrayed as a rousing guarantee that democratic republicanism will endure, is rather a warning. If the supporters of the Union did not dedicate themselves to "the great task remaining before [them]"—that is, if the Union did not put down the insurrection, as Lincoln insisted on calling it—"government of the people, by the people, for the people" might indeed "perish from the earth."[3] Lincoln, more than anyone else, realized that maintaining popular government is no simple task when some of the governed perceive it to be a threat to their interests.

How, then, do we avoid self-destructive self-rule when we do not always share the same interests? The chapters in this book offer suggestions: attend to civil relationships as well as civic institutions, adopt an ecological outlook that recognizes the need to preserve our habitat in order to preserve ourselves and our institutions, ensure that all citizens have the opportunities and knowledge to participate effectively in an evolving social and political democracy. What all of these chapters have in common is the admonition that building and maintaining a democracy is hard work that requires an educated citizenry.

Schools, as the institutions given the task of enculturating young people into society, must play a major role in educating children and youths to do that work. This point is implied in some of the chapters in this book and stated more overtly in others. But schools are not the only educational institutions in modern society, and young people are not the only ones continually being educated. The news media, advertisements, friends, relatives, coworkers, churches, coffee shops, even our declining bowling leagues educate all of us in one form or another.

To ensure that the people's government does not become perverted to mob rule, however, we cannot rely on haphazard education. The preservation of democratic government and democratic character requires our giving conscious attention to the best thinking on the subject. The chapters in this book provide a good starting point. The companion book, *The Last Best Hope: A Democracy Reader,* edited by Stephen John Goodlad, carries the subject further. Selections by Neil Postman, Robert Putnam, Wendell Berry, Noam Chomsky, and many others explore the meanings of democracy, the connections between democracy and education, and the role of schooling in educating a democratic citizenry. The next and most important step is infusing that democratic thought into our schools, our relationships, our political structures.

Toward the end of John Steinbeck's masterpiece, *The Grapes of Wrath,* Ma Joad insists that the people will survive. Despite the loss of their home, deaths in the family, unemployment, mistreatment by authorities, and a very uncertain future, she observes: "We ain't gonna die out. People is goin' on—changin' a little, maybe, but goin' right on."[4] This thought would not have been reassuring to Alexander Hamilton, but those of us who have faith in the people and their government hope that Ma Joad was right and that the people will endure. Our task is to ensure that government by the people does not end in mob rule, that competition between different interests does not lead inevitably to conflict, and that our changin' and our goin' take us toward greater democracy.

Seattle, Washington   TIMOTHY J. MCMANNON
January 2001

Notes

1. *Bartlett's Familiar Quotations,* 16th ed. (Boston: Little, Brown, 1992), will only go so far as to say that the statement, "Sir, your people is a great beast," is *attributed* to Hamilton. See p. 97, note 4. If Hamilton did say it, he is in good company. Plato, Erasmus, Machiavelli, and Shakespeare, among others, used similar words. In fact, the scholarly Hamilton may well have been intentionally or unconsciously quoting one of these writers.

2. Charles L. Mee Jr., *The Genius of the People* (New York: Harper & Row, 1987), p. 79.

3. See Garry Wills, *Lincoln at Gettysburg: The Words That Remade America* (New York: Simon & Schuster, 1992), pp. 133–137.

4. John Steinbeck, *The Grapes of Wrath* (1939; reprint, with an introduction by Robert DeMott, New York: Penguin, 1992), p. 577.

PREFACE

AT A VERY GENERAL LEVEL, there appears to be considerable agreement in the United States on what the nation's schools are for. Several large-scale surveys have revealed that parents are unwilling to give up on any one of the four major domains of traditional purpose: academic, social, vocational, and personal. They grow uneasy when any one of these domains appears to be neglected in their children's schools. Yet in national policy and local practice, the struggle over specifics is intense. The common good seems always to be at risk of being overbalanced by the multitude and intensity of private interests.

One area of agreement has so come to the fore that it has narrowed debate to matters of implementation to the exclusion of all other views: the mission of the schools is to prepare the young for work and for the enhancement of the economy. Hence, presumably, both private and public purpose will be served. A busy populace is lulled into believing that all else will be taken care of by the workplace and the Internet—an updated, streamlined version of education through *paideia,* that is, the teaching of the surrounding community. The trouble is that the guiding ethic of the workplace is profit, as Milton Friedman has unequivocally proclaimed. The Internet has no ethic.

An ethic has meaning only when it moves beyond words to implementation in practice. In our comprehensive studies of schooling and teacher education, we found ample evidence of an ethic in practice: an ethic of educators' caring about their students and about one another. Teaching, like medicine and nursing, is a caring profession. But, as with medicine and nursing, one finds instances of noncaring. What we found all too rarely—and probably would find all too rarely in other occupations and professions—was the presence of an all-encompassing ethic embracing the well-being of humankind and its nourishing habitat. In effect, we found no guiding ethic—or mission, if you will—comparable in power and pervasiveness to the guiding economic ethic of the workplace. Is there any possibility for such?

We thought so back in the late 1980s when we were collating the data of our Study of the Education of Educators and contemplating the findings, and we still think so today. We found ourselves inquiring into what this ethic might be. Clearly, it could not and should not be a fixed precept to which all schools and educators would adhere. Equally clearly, it would be moral, because schools presumably exist to educate, and education is a moral endeavor.

We independently wrote and together discussed short position papers—extended memos in essence. Because learning is a large part of what it means to be human, we discussed learning, with special attention to the critical inquiry and deliberation that educators so often favor when they address learning from the standpoint of better rather than worse. Since teaching is intentional, we found our focus turning from learning toward teaching, and we were quickly in the classic quagmire of differentiating good intentions from all others. Nonetheless, this proved to be a productive shift. There comes a time in practical affairs when ideology is necessarily blunted by existing circumstances. Schooling is a practical, political affair. Leave it to languish while the philosophical edges of debate are endlessly sharpened, and the vacuum in mission is quickly filled by instrumental purposes considered too unworthy for serious deliberation. The god of economic utility smiles once more.

Not surprisingly, because most of our attention was still taken up by the data we had gathered, this pragmatic shift turned us to the missing mission of teacher education. Surely those whose good work is preparing teachers for the nation's schools should have a guiding star and a clear fix on what the journey toward it entails. Furthermore, they should have created a work environment of ongoing attention to conditions necessary to the success of the journey—those likely to advance its health and those likely to be pernicious. A guiding ethic is not "out there"; it is ubiquitous in the surround. The many faculty members with whom we conducted interviews and discussions agreed on both the omission and the need to fill the void.

In reflecting in the late 1980s on the experiences behind us and the data before us, we were struck by the disturbing significance of the dual omission: of mission and of a deliberate process of defining and sustaining it. The dominant program-planning process consisted of a faculty group (or, occasionally, just the director of teacher education) putting together the courses thought necessary to comply with state credentialing requirements. Participation by the arts and sciences departments, where future teachers engage in the bulk of their studies, or by personnel from the schools used for the highly important student teaching component was rare. With the programmatic pieces so scattered among little-communicating educational sectors, what were the chances for achieving some common sense of direction for the teacher education enterprise? We were too caught up in our inquiry to be derailed even by this daunting question.

Thinking about teaching directs attention to such questions as "Teaching what?" and "What for?" Teaching in our schools appeared to us to be a special case of teaching that demands attention to public as well as private purpose. Sustaining the delicate balance between collective responsibility (public purpose) and individual freedom (private purpose) is the work in progress referred to as democracy. We found ourselves visiting familiar ground, therefore, when we focused on enculturating the young in a social and political democracy as the first major part of schools' mission. For this enculturation to occur, one needs a broad, general education that sets one free to roam widely in the human and natural surrounds. We referred metaphorically to this education as preparation to participate in the human conversation, and thus we had the second part of the mission for schooling.

The mission of teacher education, we concluded, is to prepare people to advance this mission of schooling, and so the education of the schools' stewards must embrace it. Teachers of teachers must acquire a repertoire of deeply caring teaching skills and a comprehensive understanding of what the stewardship of schools in a democratic society requires. This dual mission of teacher education, thus linked to the twofold mission of schooling, is not exclusively the ethic of colleges of education. It constitutes the moral grounding of all who take on the risk-laden venture of preparing people to teach in our schools.

We constructed a three-part agenda for those who so venture: a mission comprising the elements of democracy, the human conversation, caring pedagogy, and moral stewardship; conditions necessary to the mission expressed as nineteen propositions we call postulates (to which a twentieth has now been added); and a strategy of collaboration for renewing the component parts of teacher education programs: general education, pedagogy, and guided experience. We then spread the word that we were interested in having teacher-preparing settings join us in advancing this agenda, now known as the Agenda for Education in a Democracy. We were gratifyingly overwhelmed by the response, which presented us with the logistical and political problem of selecting just a few from many applicants interested in joining our National Network for Educational Renewal (NNER). We have thus far kept membership limited while engaging in a process of ensuring implementation of the Agenda to a visible, tangible level.

During the first two or three years of experience with the Agenda, member settings of the NNER are typically preoccupied with implementation—

and especially with the strategy we refer to as simultaneous renewal, in which school and university people (from both the arts and sciences and the colleges of education) struggle with the unique demands of collaboration. But almost invariably, a shift in concentration occurs. References to the moral grounding and questions about it become more frequent. What is meant by and involved in enculturating the young in a social and political democracy? What school practices fall within a framework of moral acceptance? Where and how in a teacher education program is the Agenda's mission to be addressed?

The necessary conditions embraced by the postulates are quite general. One of the three books generated by our Study of the Education of Educators and published in 1990, *The Moral Dimensions of Teaching*, addressed some very practical moral issues at the school and classroom levels. It initially attracted more attention than we had anticipated and continues to have a modest, steady sale (double that of the other two books combined in 1998). The additional books on the Agenda produced during the 1990s (all published by Jossey-Bass) have dealt more with major components than with the specifics of teacher education programs and school practices: education and democracy, educational renewal, developing leaders for advancing the Agenda, educating the professional teacher, partner schools, and centers of pedagogy. Interest in and demand for learning more about the implications of the moral grounding for the conduct of both teacher education and schooling are increasing.

This book grew out of our interest in building a bridge from the general to the more specific, from unpacking the meaning of the Agenda's mission to articulating the issues and problems for which this mission is relevant. Future work will locate and explore these issues and problems in specific educational contexts. We have found ourselves using a kind of shorthand for the mission—"developing democratic character"—and have endeavored to translate this concept into the dispositions to be developed in the young and into the preparatory curriculum and pedagogy of those who will educate the young. The operational aesthetic of the Agenda is in what emerges when the onion is peeled back just a little more.

One of our most gratifying experiences in working with colleagues in the NNER has been how school-based colleagues in the NNER have identified with the Agenda's mission, particularly the elements embedded in enculturating the young into a social and political democracy. They come to have a kind of *aha!* experience of recognition regarding what the so-called common school is for. This is less the case with our colleagues in higher education, who more readily identify with the constitutional and political implications of democracy. The university is much less an institution of "the people." Nonetheless, some of our colleagues in the arts and sciences quickly saw the potential of the Agenda for drawing together in a common mission the largely separated academic disciplines. We decided to expand the common ground of school-university collaboration in teacher education by capitalizing on this perspective. If both school and university people saw the Agenda as relevant to their own work, they might well see it as relevant to their common work of educating future teachers.

Consequently, we at the Institute for Educational Inquiry—a nonprofit organization located in Seattle—decided to convene a small group of scholars in a variety of disciplines to unpeel the democratic enculturation component of the Agenda. Over a three-year period, the Working Group on Developing Democratic Character attended to this difficult and complex task; the results of its work are reflected in this book.

What Follows

The core of Chapter One, by John I. Goodlad, is an unpacking of the concept of democratic character. The necessary dispositions embrace the social, the political, and the environmental: how we are with one another, how we conduct the symbiotics of civic life, and how we are with our habitat. The well-being of our environment is so neglected and abused that perhaps an adjective should be added to the mission of developing democratic character so that it reads "developing ecocentric democratic character."

In Chapter Two, Robert W. Hoffert takes on the complex task of unraveling the symbiotics of political democracy from how they are addressed in the two documents that are building blocks in our understanding of and commitment to the work in progress that is this nation's experiment with democracy. The moral grounding is the equal value of each human being. Hoffert then builds a bridge from this conceptual orientation to the critical work of the schools in advancing understanding and commitment in the young.

Chapter Three, by Kathleen Staudt, reminds us that democracies are not perfect. There is often differential representation in the political process based on gender, class, age, and other characteristics. We need to attend to and reduce such differential participation. Democratic educational renewal, with its focus on critical thinking, can help ensure the authentic involvement of all groups of citizens.

In Chapter Four, Stephen John Goodlad tackles the largely missing but increasingly critical ecological take on the democratic landscape. Democratic character must encompass understanding of and sensitivity to the natural environment that supports humankind as it must encompass humankind itself. Fortunately, the young tend to be curious about—indeed, fascinated by—their habitat, and so it offers almost unparalleled opportunity for the experiential learning advocated for but not commonly provided in schools. The prospects for new curricula and multimedia instructional materials are unlimited.

Chapter Five emphasizes the economic issues that bear not only on the ways we use and abuse our natural environment but also on making changes in our commitments and behavior that are necessary to sustain it. Paul Theobald and Clif Tanabe argue for a deliberative democracy, one that goes beyond procedural or even traditional constitutional democracy. Extending the argument in Chapter Four, Theobald and Tanabe advocate a central role for schools in encouraging critical deliberation.

Mary Catherine Bateson invites us in Chapter Six to consider the desirability of—indeed, the strong need for—entertaining multiple and even conflicting points of view while avoiding the attractions of demonizing opponents (an argument similar to that Alexander Hamilton expressed in the Federalist No. 1). Change in human institutions is an inevitable process that is tempered by the need to value resistance and viability. Bateson concludes with a description of participant observation as a way of understanding and rising above dogma.

The insights into learning provided by Benő Csapó in Chapter Seven remind us that it is easy but dangerous to assume that academic learning transfers readily to real-life situations. Indeed, we must be cautious (as suggested, too, in Chapter Six) in assuming that behaviors learned and applied in one context will be practiced in another even if it is only a little different. This thoughtful, research-based analysis of cognition and the uncertainty of transfer is timely given today's confidence that there is a close correlation between successful academic performance in schools and virtuous dispositions such as those we connect with democratic character. Even if democratic character were to become the guiding mission of schooling, there would be little to show for it were there not an equally profound shift in the prevailing paradigms of school expectation and conduct.

Just as Chapter Seven draws our attention to the slippage from precept to practice in human behavior, Chapter Eight addresses the slippage from the general to the specific in regard to public agreement on the school's educational missions. This slippage is so great that one is led to question whether public schools can serve the public good to the extent of seeking to develop democratic character in the young. Nel Noddings uses the religious case against the schools to develop the critical issue of whether and how a common system of public schooling can successfully serve both the public and the private interest.

Chapter Nine deals with much of the same terrain as Chapter Eight, but with a focus on the rhetoric and claims of school privatization. Julie Underwood considers school-choice claims in the light of the public purpose of schooling and questions whether the virtues of democratic citizenship and respect for plurality can be met in other than the common public school.

In Chapter Ten, Roger Soder identifies a series of conditions necessary for the creation, sustenance, recovery, and improvement of a good democratic republic. Conditions do not exist in themselves; they must be created by people. Specific characteristics or dispositions must be developed to ensure the creation of each of the postulated conditions, and we must consider which societal agencies are to be responsible for their development.

Seattle, Washington   Roger Soder
January 2001   John I. Goodlad
                                         Timothy J. McMannon

Acknowledgments

THIS BOOK EMERGED FROM the lively and informed conversations of the Working Group on Developing Democratic Character, convened by the Institute for Educational Inquiry. To all of the members of the group, we extend our thanks for their hard work and willingness to engage with, argue about, and weigh and consider democratic character in the very best spirit of democracy.

The Longview Foundation provided generous support for the working group over a period of three years. We are grateful to the foundation for its steady commitment to furthering the understanding of democracy here and abroad.

Not for the first time and, we trust, not the last, Paula McMannon has rendered first-rate service in seeing the manuscript through all phases of production. Because of her consistently high standards of accuracy and cogency, the outcome is much the better. We thank her.

THE EDITORS

Roger Soder is a senior associate of the Center for Educational Renewal at the University of Washington and vice president of the independent Institute for Educational Inquiry. Soder is editor of *Democracy, Education, and the Schools* (1996, Jossey-Bass) and coeditor with John Goodlad and Kenneth Sirotnik of *The Moral Dimensions of Teaching* and *Places Where Teachers Are Taught* (both 1990, Jossey-Bass). His articles in professional journals center on education, politics, professionalization, and rhetoric. His research interests continue to focus on the ethics and politics of rhetoric, education, and democracy and on the role of the university in a free society. Prior to joining with Goodlad and Sirotnik in creating the Center for Educational Renewal in 1985, Soder was an administrator in the Cape Flattery School District on the Makah Indian Reservation at Neah Bay, Washington, and education director of the Seattle Urban League.

John I. Goodlad is president of the Institute for Educational Inquiry and professor emeritus at the University of Washington. Goodlad has taught at all levels and in a variety of institutions in Canada and the United States, including a one-room rural school. He has held professorships and administrative positions at Agnes Scott College and Emory University in Georgia, the University of Chicago, the University of California at Los Angeles, and the University of Washington. Goodlad has authored or edited over 30 books, written chapters and papers in more than 120 other books and yearbooks, and published more than 200 articles in professional journals and encyclopedias. His 1984 publication, *A Place Called School*, received the Outstanding Book of the Year Award from the American Educational Research Association and the Distinguished Book of the Year Award from Kappa Delta Pi. He also received the Outstanding Writing Award from the American Association of Colleges for Teacher Education for *Teachers for Our Nation's Schools* (1990, Jossey-Bass). For the past several decades, Goodlad has been involved in an array of educational renewal programs and projects and has engaged in large-scale studies of educational change, school improvement, schooling, and teacher education in the United States. His most recent books are *In Praise of Education* (1997, Teachers College Press) and *The Public Purpose of Education and Schooling,* coedited with Timothy McMannon (1997, Jossey-Bass).

Timothy J. McMannon is a senior associate of the Institute for Educational Inquiry and the Center for Educational Renewal at the University of Washington. He also teaches U.S. history at Highline Community College, Des Moines, Washington. He is the author of *Morality, Efficiency, and Reform: An Interpretation of the History of American Education* (1995, Institute for Educational Inquiry), coeditor with John Goodlad of *The Public Purpose of Education and Schooling,* and general editor of the Agenda for Education in a Democracy Series (four volumes to date, all 1999, Jossey-Bass). His interests include recent U.S. history, the history of American education and schooling, and the interrelationships of social trends and public policy.

THE CONTRIBUTORS

Mary Catherine Bateson is a cultural anthropologist who divides her time between teaching in Virginia and writing in New Hampshire. She is currently Clarence J. Robinson Professor in Anthropology and English at George Mason University in Fairfax, Virginia. Bateson's most recent book is *Full Circles, Overlapping Lives: Culture and Generation in Transition* (2000, Random House). Other books include *With a Daughter's Eye: A Memoir of Margaret Mead and Gregory Bateson* (1984, Morrow); *Composing a Life* (1989, Atlantic Monthly Press); and *Peripheral Visions: Learning Along the Way* (1994, HarperCollins).

Benő Csapó is a professor of education at the University of Szeged, Hungary. He has held a fellowship at the Center for Advanced Study in the Behavioral Sciences in California and received a Humboldt Fellowship for research work at the University of Bremen, German Federal Republic. Csapó is the author of several books and journal articles examining such issues as cognitive development, teaching thinking, inductive reasoning, and operational abilities in children. After the political changes in Central and Eastern Europe, he participated in several research projects that dealt with adolescents' perceptions of social transition.

Stephen John Goodlad is a writer and philosopher whose interests most recently have centered on the complex relationships among environmentalism, ecology, and democracy, and in turn, the implications of those relationships for education and schooling. One important facet of this research has been a focus on the connection between what is termed democratic character and the notion of ecological identity: their similarities, differences, and potentialities. He lives in Seattle, Washington, and divides his time among a variety of teaching, writing, and research projects.

Robert W. Hoffert is a professor of political science and dean of the College of Liberal Arts at Colorado State University. He is the author of *A Politics of Tensions: The Articles of Confederation and American Political*

Ideas (1992, University Press of Colorado), an exploration designed to recapture a greater awareness of the complexities and possibilities within American democracy. Hoffert has participated in several initiatives within a K-16 framework, including the development of state and district content standards, innovative courses to link high school and university students, National Endowment for the Humanities institutes for junior high and university faculty, and humanities institutes for pre- and postcertification secondary teachers and university faculty in education and the liberal arts.

Nel Noddings is Lee L. Jacks Professor Emerita of Child Education, Stanford University. She currently teaches philosophy and education at Teachers College, Columbia University. Her areas of special interest are feminist ethics, moral education, and mathematical problem solving. She is a past president of both the National Philosophy of Education Society and the John Dewey Society. Noddings was a Phi Beta Kappa Visiting Scholar for the year 1989–1990. She is the author of many books, among them, *Caring: A Feminine Approach to Ethics and Moral Education* (1984, University of California Press), *The Challenge to Care in Schools* (1992, Teachers College Press), and *Educating for Intelligent Belief or Unbelief* (1993, Teachers College Press), and more than 150 articles and chapters on topics ranging from the ethics of caring to mathematical problem solving.

Kathleen Staudt is a professor of political science at the University of Texas at El Paso (UTEP). She is also faculty coordinator for UTEP's Institute for Community-Based Teaching and Learning, which has multidisciplinary task forces that work with public schools, neighborhoods, and organizations. Staudt is the author or editor of many books, including *Free Trade? Informal Economies at the United States-Mexico Border* (1998, Temple University Press) and *The U.S.-Mexico Border: Transcending Divisions, Contesting Identities* (coedited with David Spener; 1998, Lynn Rienner). Her research interests address borders, immigration, and maquilas; development and international organizations; gender and women; and African and Mexican political affairs.

Clif Tanabe is an assistant professor at the University of Wisconsin–La Crosse and associate director of the Research Center for Cultural Diversity and Community Renewal. He began his career as an educator in the Hawaii public schools. His research interests are in political and educational philosophy.

Paul Theobald is dean of the Division of Education at Wayne State College in Nebraska. Theobald has published numerous journal articles and monographs, as well as two books. His more recent book is *Teaching the Commons: Place, Pride, and the Renewal of Community* (1997, Westview). His research interests continue to focus on democracy, schooling, and rural communities.

Julie Underwood is general counsel of the National School Boards Association. She is coauthor of five books, has published chapters in more than a dozen books, and has written numerous articles appearing in both education and law journals. She has written widely on religion in public schools, special education law, and school finance equity and is a frequent speaker at state and national conferences on education.

Developing Democratic Character in the Young

I

CONVERGENCE

John I. Goodlad

ON DECEMBER 30, 1999, Sarah Knauss died just short of having lived in three different centuries. Even at 119, her family reported, she still expressed amazement at humankind's ability to create new ways to hurt each other, heal each other, and explore the world. On that day and the next, the editorial and op-ed pages of virtually every newspaper in the United States commented on the struggle for primacy between two contradictory impulses of technological progress: its astonishing improvement of human life, on the one hand, and its simultaneous magnification of the horrible consequences of murderous tendencies, on the other. The twentieth was the bloodiest century in human history.

George Will viewed the first half of the century as belonging to physicists and the second half to biologists, and he observed that good physics and good biology without good philosophy would bring us calamity in the twenty-first century.[1] His theme was expressed in various ways by pundits worldwide, shaping for public attention the celebrations of human accomplishment that marked the end of the second millennium.

It was easy to miss among the endless lists of the millennium's warriors and thinkers, inventions, and natural catastrophes, as well as those of memorable personalities of the century, the annual report of the National Defense Council Foundation. At the close of 1999, a third of the world's 193 nations were embroiled in conflict. The 65 extant conflicts were up from the 60 reported in 1998. We do not do very well in translating these statistics into human misery. The media do a magnificent job of sanitizing the blood and guts of real war and are incredibly creative in making the brutality and violence of virtual reality bloodless, exciting, and even attractive.

With material comfort wide but inequitably spread, it is easy also to miss some close-at-hand statistics that cry out for "good philosophy": each day in the United States a child under age ten is killed by a gun; 6 children or youths commit suicide; 13 children or youths are killed by firearms; 78 babies die; 420 children are arrested for drug offenses; 2,162 babies are born into poverty; 5,388 children are arrested; 17,152 public school students are suspended. Are statistics such as these of war and family tragedy— on the rise rather than the reverse—to be the norms for the twenty-first century? Are a return to family values and the posting of the Ten Commandments on every classroom wall adequate remedies? The malaise appears to be beyond the domains of physics and biology that have contributed so much to our well-being.

We have difficulty identifying empathetically with the statistics of human tragedy. We have even greater difficulty translating into implications for the human race—for one another—the potential impact of rapid increases in the number of us sharing the world's resources. What are the limits to the earth's carrying capacity? Does the disappearance of whole species of living things have implications for the future of the human species? For many of us, these are tomorrow's questions, and since this tomorrow lies beyond most people's tomorrows, they are out of mind. To postpone such questions for tomorrow is to postpone them forever.[2]

Humans have accomplished amazing things. Nothing phenomenological and little mythological deters their imagination, creativity, and technological prowess. By taking advantage of their accomplishments, people everywhere can communicate with people everywhere in seconds and be face-to-face in hours. The life span has been doubled, most physical pain quickly relieved, body parts replaced, the brain cloned, and both the oceans' depths and outer space all but opened up to tourism. But in what pervades these wonders lurks an enemy: humankind itself. The malaise that humans have been unable to eradicate persists: the inhumane treatment of some humans to and by other humans.

This primitive condition, as old as civilization itself, is not the result of neglect. Some of the best minds in successive eras have inquired into what it means to be human and treat all others in the light of the meanings gleaned.[3] The principles derived rationally are markedly similar to those derived divinely by all the great religions.[4] It is a basic tenet of these religions that the young are capable of understanding and abiding by these principles at an early age. Punishment has been the dominant corrective mode for disapproved acts of humans directed at other humans. But there are and have been sweeping exceptions to this moral creed—in war, "ethnic cleansing," racial exclusion, caste systems, and more. Behavior considered wrong within a nation is considered right against another nation, wrong within one's religion is approved when against another religion, shameful for my race is appropriate against another, right for one caste is off-limits for another. Consistent adherence to a moral principle such as "thou shalt not kill" is twisted to make of killing a virtue under certain circumstances. Peace on earth is unlikely when the rules of peaceful coexistence embrace only some of its people.

Getting Beyond Rhetoric

In the writing of this book, my colleagues and I are under no illusions about coming up with a set of principles, akin to the scientific principles guiding so much human accomplishment, that at long last will resolve the malaise of humans' treating other humans inhumanely. Were such principles the wonder invention, the prognosis for humankind would be cheerily positive since, in composite, those we now have transcend the nations, religions, castes, languages, and colors of the world's people. But, with special identifying adornments added, they also are the possession, sometimes the obsession, of individual nations, religions, and castes, to the extent of turning against other nations, religions, castes, and races the very behaviors these principles prohibit. Clearly, principles as precepts are not for humankind harbingers of what the principles portray. With similar clarity, continued dependence on punishment suggests that reliance on principles as precepts falls far short of relieving even parochial constituencies of behavioral malaise. Something of greater substance and sustaining attention is required, and this something will bring with it no guarantees. The accomplishments of humans in all other areas of need and endeavor pale when compared with the challenges presented by seeking to bring human behavior several significant steps toward the ideals portrayed by profound thinkers in both the rational and the divine idiom.

Toward Education Writ Large

It has been said many times over the years that this "something of greater substance" is education, and we nod our heads in unison. Our thoughts go immediately to schools, the steps that might be taken to make them safer havens for children and youths, and the courses on character development that might be added to a bloated curriculum. Adult interests prevail, and it becomes increasingly difficult to differentiate schools from prisons. Increased security and more rules are constant reminders of the malaise.

Our instant equating of education and schools assures us that education so constrained will change little in the way we relate to one another and the habitat we all share. Indeed, even if some schools managed to become exemplary havens of mutual respect, caring, and democratic living together of teachers and their students, the rest of the daily surround would challenge or negate the in-school teaching.[5] Walk the few yards from school classrooms to city streets, and one is in a public classroom that turns upside down the narratives of belief that, ironically, many of us would envision for the exemplary school. The narratives of the marketplace teach that a Buick is something to believe in, that life's rewards go to the top guns (preferably but not necessarily within the law), and that material comforts bespeak God in his heaven and all's right with the world. These narratives have at their command all the teaching tools routinely denied our schools. Some school board members, in lapses of reason, rise to the bait of securing these tools in trade for "low dosages" of the marketplace narratives transmitted into the classroom. The issue of whether the tools that hammer home the economically driven lessons of the marketplace are well suited to the educational mission of the school is scarcely recognized, let alone addressed.[6]

No, if the something of substance necessary to making significant progress with humankind's most overwhelming problem—that is, with itself—is education, then at least five profound changes in our thinking and accompanying actions pertaining to education writ large and to schooling must take place. Since humans are virtually incapable of contemplating oblivion, what is necessary to avoid oblivion may not be feasible. Yet this inability to accept oblivion could turn out to be the necessary motivation for changing our thinking and redirecting our actions accordingly.

First, the thinking of scholars who have inquired deeply into the dim prospects for sustaining the present trajectory of our existence must rise to the forefront among the dominant narratives of the human conversation (even if their current projections are only half right). Second, the teaching (for which "humanitarian" comes to mind as the appropriate descriptive narrative) that we periodically propose to add to our schools in times of perceived behavioral crises among the young must become indigenous to the culture. Third, instead of becoming a curricular add-on, this humanitarian narrative must become the guiding mission of schools. Fourth, mental health must have a place of high priority in the human infrastructure supporting individual well-being. Fifth, although the humanitarian narrative must encompass the microsymbiotics of everyday interpersonal and civic relationships, it must also transcend these to embrace the macrosymbiotics of multiethnic, multiracial, multinational, and multiecological relationships on which the future of humankind depends. These themes are woven into the fabric of much of what follows in this chapter.

Converging and Diverging Narratives

The rhetoric and the functioning of technology are compatibly linked with the rhetoric and the functioning of capitalism. Technology is generative in that technology begets technology. The fuel is capital. Capitalist theory says that competition cuts profit margins, improves quality, and hence speeds—democratizes—benefits to the people. Producers are entitled to reasonable profits in return for their investment of capital, time, and human energy. However, this rather simple, commonsense principle is compromised by what appears to be further democratization: the people are encouraged to share in the profits through investing in ownership (stock) of the business. The bottom line for these new owners is more likely to be the return on their investments rather than the price and quality of goods made available to consumers. A whole new cycle is often put in motion wherein the name of the game is eliminating competition. The human motivation is commonly referred to as greed.

What appears, then, to be a sound democratic economic principle is corrupted by lack of moral principle and compassion for humankind. The penultimate corruption is that of equating economic success with virtue. The god of economic utility takes over and spins for us all an enticing narrative.[7] This abuse discredits capitalism as a potential companion of democracy, stimulating attacks on the system that tend to obscure consideration of the possibility that the problem lies with humankind. The human-induced flaw in the practice of capitalism is, of course, the driving concept of unlimited growth. This puts the economic narrative out of sync with those principles of democracy that stress the good of all and fuels excess claims for growth benefiting everyone.

Bill McKibben argues that "global capitalism has lifted living standards in many places, lengthened lives, improved nutrition, broadened education. It may have ended forever the argument between the moralist and the revolutionary, replacing them both with the logic of the cash register and the trading floor."[8] But then he sounds a caveat: "Sooner or later we will face the problem of stasis. Having grown as large as we can both in numbers and in appetites, we will need a different idea to balance our economies, our politics, our individual lives. *The thing that comes after growth is elusive.*"[9]

The educative surround—dominated in its teaching by the media—characterizing the United States at the end of the twentieth century invokes a markedly different sentence: *The thing that comes after growth is megagrowth.* But if one probes into thoughtful analyses of the time, what emerges as necessary for the future is less elusive in concept than in feasibility. It runs counter to the materialistic argument that laissez-faire capitalism requires no change in human dispositions. Rather, large-scale competition can be counted on to produce the good life for all. McKibben sees promise of a counterview in Gandhi's advice—"renounce and enjoy"—but fears that it may require too much of us.

I have observed the convergence of the rational and the divine in their bottom-line near-agreement on dispositions necessary to human well-being. Both the rational and the divine recognize the individual and collective discipline necessary to these dispositions' becoming virtually routine in daily behavior. All of the great religions stress renunciation and the need to routinize virtuous behavior but often have stressed ritual over substantive commitment. Similarly, the principles derived from rational inquiry are commonly intellectualized rather than practiced. Many people practice two codes: one for the commonplaces of human interaction and another for the abstractions of worship or philosophical discourse. Nonetheless, both lines of inquiry have fostered a considerable, growing attention to the hungry, the malnourished, the destitute, the ill, and the impoverished, particularly children, who mark humankind's malaise. But eliminating this malaise requires much more than charity and philanthropy.

There are emerging both a third domain marked by rhetoric that converges with the other two and a component of what has been at times a controversial educational movement: environmentalism and global education. Environmentalism has moved rapidly from primary interest in preservation of natural resources to an extraordinarily diverse array of themes that pertain to the preservation of the human race and the connections of this preservation to our habitat, and to the ecology of our interactions with one another and with our natural surround.[10] The bottom line becomes character, and the central question is how to ensure over time sufficient cultivation of the character largely agreed on by these domains of inquiry to ensure global stability, renewal, and continuity. This is an educational problem that transcends schooling. Character development will be an ineffectual curricular add-on, as it is currently in some schools, unless there is a strong educational narrative of mission emanating from the cultural surround. To date, this has not surfaced. But since the 1970s, religious belief and environmentalism have converged on some themes that have for many years drawn the attention of human rights scholars and activists. What few people noticed regarding the much-publicized conference of the World Trade Organization was the convergence that occurred in Seattle early in December 1999. Diana Butler Bass was one of those who noticed:

> Seattle proved that religious belief is not at enmity with the Earth. Those wanting to "dominate" the Earth were the politicians and economists. Among those wanting to save it were many thousands of religious people. . . . In Seattle they joined forces for human rights of all nature: for slaves, debt relief, humane labor conditions; for clear air, sea turtles and rain forests.
>
> Diverse groups laid aside theological difference for common cause: If we lose the Earth, we lose everything. . . . A new message has gotten through. All creation—humanity included—is connected. We are all part of a divine ecosystem.[11]

Many who agree would drop the adjective *divine*. The issue that arises is, of course, whether the common cause to which she refers will be permitted to transcend the differences in parochial belief that have brought about millennia of human suffering. To this obstacle must be added both the appeal and the marketing resources of multinational corporations over which national governments have only token control. What hope is there for worldwide convergence around a humanitarian, environmental narrative to guide the behavior of humankind?

Global Education

The somewhat bumpy ride of global education provides a microcosm of some of the difficulties involved. World War II gave birth to the same post–World War I sentiments that fueled creation of the League of Nations and a host of humanitarian ventures. The United Nations was the political parallel; the springing up in several countries of centers on world peace and international understanding was the social parallel. Veterans who had not before strayed far from their places of birth came home with new perspectives that included becoming better informed about other parts of the world and "other people." The Fulbright programs still in existence were set up precisely to satisfy these and related interests. Universities responded by establishing courses in comparative and global education, some of them embracing a period of travel or residence abroad. Many established campus centers to coordinate rapidly expanding connections with colleagues around the world.

The post–World War II domain of interest and study that emerged was amorphous, with ill-defined and easily penetrated boundaries. However, there were clustered under the general rubric of "global education" rather clearly defined groups and associations of people with identifying primary interests: peace, interculturalism, internationalism, human rights education, comparative education (which grew into a specialization in education offered by some universities), and others. All shared in the concept of a closely connected world. Programs joining schools and communities across international lines and revealing the global connections in supplying goods from everywhere to everywhere proved to be particularly popular with teachers. Increasingly, the connectedness of the world's social, political, economic, physical, biological, belief, communications, aesthetic, and religious systems opened up attention to both human and natural ecologies and their interdependence.[12]

The various groups shared an interest in improving a world torn by intolerance and strife and in awakening in the young awareness and appreciation of people, flora, and fauna beyond the normal encounters of daily lives—not exactly revolutionary or unpatriotic preoccupations. But such seemingly well-intentioned interests ran afoul of the fear of communism that plagued the country for years. The Soviet Union's launching of *Sputnik* in 1957 was as frightening to many people as would have been the dropping of an atomic bomb on New York City. The ill-defined boundaries of global education allowed an exceedingly diverse array of interest groups to claim identity with the field. Suspected as unpatriotic were any who even discussed a world court or global citizenship, pro or con. They and all others claiming an identity with global education were declared fellow travelers. The United Nations and its subsidiary, the United Nations Educational, Scientific, and Cultural Organization (UNESCO), were suspect in many quarters.

My years of representing the United States on the governing board of UNESCO's Institute for Education in Hamburg, Germany (1972–1979), opened my life to scrutiny by ardent isolationists, even though my appointment was by the Department of State. It is impossible to conceive of the full range of horrors conjured up in the minds of some people by the very words *global education*. Individuals and groups so categorized included some from whom serious global educators endeavored to disassociate themselves.

The post–World War II passion for peace and goodwill toward all was fueled by the Korean and Vietnam Wars abroad and the civil rights movement at home. Elsewhere I have written about books I encountered much earlier in my life that stimulated awareness of the commonalities among people everywhere in which flourish incredible uniqueness.[13] What is more fascinating than the journey we share? My various associations and travel from the 1960s into the early 1980s both fleshed out and focused this awareness. Significant were my membership on the board of directors of Global Perspectives in Education, supported primarily by the Mertz-Gilmore Foundation, which connected with many of the most influential leaders in global education, and the board of directors of the Longview Foundation, which, although small, supported a rich variety of school programs. Colleagues and I in the Kettering Foundation's Institute for Development of Educational Activities were successful in getting an array of key leaders in the field to share their ideas in a book.[14] We believed that getting the seminal ideals to educators in particular could make some contribution to changing human behavior.

I had the good fortune to become closely associated with an individual who believed passionately in the unity of humankind, in the necessity of getting the idea of mankind (as he stated it) into the public domain, and of the power of the idea to make a profound difference.[15] Gerhard Hirschfeld was not an academic, but the power of his words and person and the passion of his commitment resulted in his managing to convene from time to time a small group of distinguished scholars in such fields as anthropology, economics, history, and philosophy, mostly from the University of Chicago, near Hirschfeld's residence. He had no difficulty persuading me to join his embryonic Council for the Study of Mankind and its periodic discussions. In spite of his diligent efforts, Hirschfeld (who had left the business world to devote all of his time and modest family resources to the cause) was able to raise only very limited philanthropic support, all representing faith in him. The need for funds to bring the council together became more acute with the coincidental relocating of both the Hirschfelds and the Goodlads to the Los Angeles area, a move that intensified our association—indeed, so much so that I found myself chairing the council and caught up in Gerhard's mission. One of Hirschfeld's most successful visions was that of infusing each of the major fields of study with the idea of humankind, a vision aborted for lack of funds but not before we had produced several volumes.[16]

I have always been restless with restricting inquiry to ideas. John Dewey wrote much about the testing and refining of ideas in practice. Indeed he saw significant ideas rising out of practice and then, after further clarification and refinement, being applied to improving practice.[17] Intrigued by the idea of mankind, colleagues and I were motivated to carry it into the domain of schooling. In collaboration with the council and with some financial support from the Ford Foundation, we launched a three-part project focused on children and teachers. The first part was to extract and collate concepts we thought relevant to children from the written works of the council. The second was to work with several teachers in the laboratory school at UCLA to develop a curriculum unit designed to teach some of these concepts to young children. The third was to teach this unit to a summer session class of children aged nine to twelve and, simultaneously, introduce this activity and the idea of mankind to a group of teachers enrolled in a parallel summer workshop.

None of this was easy. Agreeing on concepts likely to resonate as universally applicable to humankind proved to be a profoundly difficult intellectual endeavor. Our search turned up few appropriate reading materials for the children. The teachers in the lab school wanted more specifics in pedagogical content and method than we were able to provide. But none of the work was dull, and our fears about children's not being interested in the material or able to connect it with their lives were unfounded. What kind of difficulties we might have experienced with parents of a typical public school can only be surmised. There were no lines of people in bookstores wanting to buy *Toward a Mankind School,* the book we wrote to describe the whole.[18] It passed into oblivion well before the first printing was sold out, and I have heard scant mention of it during the intervening quarter-century.

This does not mean that the concepts we were pursuing went the way of our book. One of our colleagues, Kenneth A. Tye, remained very active in the global education field, which he sees as connecting today with the democracy and education movement worldwide.[19] He believes, as I do, that the idea of humankind is at the very core of what is required to bring the people of the world together in what, for want of a better term, I refer to as a democratic relationship.

Democratic Character

A substantial body of thoughtful writing about the close and somewhat delicate relationship between democracy and education now exists. Some of this work addresses the concept of how we relate to one another—civility— or the concept of functioning political communities—*civitas*—and some the desired characteristics of both. More and more, the word *democracy* is used to embrace the entire compass of human beings living and working together in desirable ways. Perhaps a more definitive word will be coined, but *democracy* appears to be the placeholder until such emerges.

There is considerable convergence of divine and rational thought regarding human traits deemed virtuous, whether one studies the conclusions of the great religious thinkers, humanists, or environmentalists. The common and overlapping dispositions define exemplary human character just as an array of specialists might define exemplary human anatomical functioning. There is a wholeness that embraces the duality of the autonomous and the relational self, with *honesty* and *courage* suggesting the former and *compassion* and *love* suggesting the latter. These are dispositions commonly considered when we are asked to testify to someone's character.

Unfortunately, in formal educational contexts such as schooling, the word *character* and the concept of character development have come to carry some unfortunate baggage. For example, the proposed introduction of character education in our schools conjures up for many people a return to the Christian precepts in textbooks and syllabi characteristic of curricula until quite recently. And some postmodernists cringe over the prospect of character traits etched in stone serving as curricular building blocks in the school experiences of the young. Nonetheless, the word *character* is not likely to be expunged from everyday discourse. Satisfactory synonyms are hard to come by.

In our work in advancing what colleagues and I refer to as the Agenda for Education in a Democracy, we have become well aware that the word *democracy* carries considerable baggage. This becomes abundantly clear in the chapters that follow. But that has not deterred us from using the word over and over. Indeed, we have deliberately joined the conversation about democracy—its meaning, the endangered work in progress that is the American democracy, competing conceptions of democracy, and the like—with a view to ridding the word of some of its baggage.

As if contending with the two sets of baggage independent of each other were not enough, we have bundled them into the single concept of democratic character to encompass the dispositions so commonly set as desirable for the autonomous, relational human being simultaneously respecting of self and context. Together the two words embrace an incredibly wide range of discourse that ultimately pertains to the experience and meaning of being human.[20] Walter Parker sees the careful cultivation of this discourse as so crucial to civic virtue that he puts the process at the very heart of what he defines as deliberative democracy.[21]

To push the concept of democratic character aside because of the baggage it brings to the human conversation is only to create a vacuum to welcome its later return. I prefer to seek a measure of clarification through comprehensive engagement with it now. Indeed, teaming the two words removes some baggage from each. Much of the abstractness of "character" as part of what it means to be human is lifted. We are addressing "democratic" character, not character as it might be defined by sectarian or secular religion. Yet neither is excluded, given the convergence of the two in posing desired human dispositions. The word *democratic* forces attention to both the self's developing characteristics and the necessary transition of the self in acquiring the symbiotic arts of civility and civicness and, ultimately, identifying with the whole of humankind. What could be more fundamental to participation in the human conversation?

Democracy and Education

For years before school enters into a child's life, the child is exposed to a cacophony of teaching about whom to like, love, or hate; what to eat, crave, and believe; and how to behave and not behave in a variety of circumstances. By the time the child enters school, he or she is quite far advanced toward the adult who is to be. The child is mother or father to the woman or the man—a malleable harbinger of the private and public person and citizen in progress.

It follows, then, that the relationship between education and democracy is fashioned by this entire educative surround and not just the schools. Indeed, from a quantitative perspective and in the light of the school's relatively late arrival in the trajectory of a life, the school might well be regarded today as a minor educational player, a view now being massaged by inflated expectations for the Internet. If our society were inherently just, caring, hospitable to the diversity of its inhabitants, and neatly balanced in the interplay of freedom and authority—in other words, democratic—we would have less need to worry about the demise of public schools. But thoughtful people writing about education and democracy view the conditions of humankind as not inherently democratic and in dire need of the responsible moral stewardship that only a democratically educated polity can provide.

Unfortunately, the educative surround is not purposively oriented toward teaching democracy. We presume to have a democratic society; one assumes its values and ways through a process akin to osmosis. But in osmosis there is a source for what becomes pervasive. An examination of what is pervasive in our American society today draws us to a source that is anything but purposely democratic—a massive business enterprise driven almost entirely by economic purpose for which electronic media are, in the words of the late Marshall McLuhan, both the message and the massage. The result is aptly encompassed in the title of Robert McChesney's book, *Rich Media, Poor Democracy.*[22] There is not in the educative surround a ubiquitous narrative for democracy that is more than a whimper when compared with the power and pervasiveness of the narrative of economic utility.

As contemporary analysts increasingly point out, there are stirrings among the multinational corporations and the business world generally regarding the necessity for change, even if for the wrong reasons. Command of the media makes it easy to give a philanthropic twist to what is essentially self-serving necessity: there will be no natural resources without preservation; much-vaulted corporate efficiency breaks down when underrewarded workers cry "enough already" and endure a long strike; the fruits of economic success are soured when the infrastructure necessary to enjoyment is crumbling. To anticipate a change in the bottom line is to be naive. To seek to strengthen and embellish the democratic narrative is the route of hope and wisdom.

This narrative is three-pronged: interpersonal and social, civic and political, environmental and ecological. There is now a substantial literature on the characteristics of each but a much lesser one on educating for the desired symbiotics. Out of many writers and publications, I pick four who are representative of the several genres.

Donna Kerr writes movingly about relationships of mutuality—how we are with one another—connecting with Buber's thoughts on the education of character:[23] "The development and flourishing of the self, the soul, and character—necessary features of moral life, including democratic relationships—depend upon one's experiencing relationships of mutuality, upon what some would choose to call generosity, trust, and respect, and yet others (in whose numbers am I) would boldly term love. Yes, short of love—love free from domination—democracy is a failed project."[24] Discourse about interpersonal, social democracy commonly refers to civility, but Kerr moves this genre to a higher plane.

Robert Putnam builds a bridge from the social to the political in correlating robust social engagement with robust community political engagement (civicism).[25] Recently, he has become an activist, seeking to stem what he perceives to be decline in the former as endangering the latter.[26] He is skeptical of his critics' contention that new genres of socializing, as through electronic media, are adequate substitutions for face-to-face gatherings. Benjamin Barber penetrates to the very core of democratic civic culture in charging our country with turning away from its own future in attacking not only education but public education: "Public schools are not merely schools *for* the public, but schools of publicness: institutions where we learn what it means to *be* a public and start down the road toward common national and civic identity."[27]

The Worldwatch Institute provides a sweeping inventory of decline in the natural resources and diversity of flora and fauna in our habitat and a frightening diagnosis of the case for recovery, much of it already lost:

> The overriding challenges facing our global civilization as the new century begins are to stabilize climate and stabilize population. Success on these two fronts would make other challenges, such as reversing the deforestation of Earth, stabilizing water tables, and protecting plant and animal diversity, much more manageable. If we cannot stabilize climate and we cannot stabilize population, there is not an ecosystem on Earth that we can save. Everything will change. If developing countries cannot stabilize their populations soon, many of them face the prospect of wholesale ecosystem collapse.[28]

These are not the words of a single-minded zealot, a "tree hugger" as naysayers like to label such. The development of democratic character encompasses how we are with the environment as well as how we are with one another.

The word *democracy* conjures up in the minds of many people—probably most—only the political theme. Leaving partisan politics aside, a democrat is one who believes in a particular form of government. "What the democrat seeks," writes Robert Wiebe, "is a reaffirmation of the American heritage that draws people with all kinds of identities and loyalties into a collective self-governing process. A national gathering of these participating publics creates an exhilarating prospect: citizens divided by race and nationality, sex and sexual preference, social class and physical condition, sundry goods and many lifestyles, contributing equally to discussions that some win, others lose, but all accept as a fact of life. It is a civic affair."[29]

Whether we seek democracy as a civic affair, a civil affair, or an environmental affair, we need no "doomsday-comes-tomorrow" polemics to tell us that the necessary balance between freedom and responsibility is a delicate affair. Nor should we need strident reminders of the degree to which achieving and sustaining such balance is an educational affair.

Educating for Democratic Character

Earlier in this chapter, I wrote, "Our instant equating of education and schools assures us that education so constrained will change little in the way we relate to one another and the habitat we all share." The need is for a surround that puts the well-being of humankind first and infuses all of our ubiquitous educating media with this mission. I went on to write that it is naive to expect a sea change in the prevailing ethic of the marketplace. Barber sees hypocrisy in the dissonance between the values and the rhetoric of this surround: "We honor ambition, we reward greed, we celebrate materialism, we worship acquisitiveness, we cherish success, and we commercialize the classroom—and then we bark at the young about the gentle art of the spirit."[30] Panning for gold in the silt at the river's edge, I found a nugget in the probability that the "takers" will need to adopt some habits of the "leavers" (as Daniel Quinn's conversational protagonist, Ishmael [please see Note 2], differentiates between those who take and those who leave alone or give back) if even their perceived needs are to be satisfied. In other words, supporting the three-pronged ethic of democratic character will become a necessity rather than a rhetorical gambit.

But we cannot afford to wait for this realization to become manifest. Consequently, deliberate attention to the development of democratic character in the young becomes an imperative. And so, since the school as a proclaimed essential component of our democratic infrastructure is the most obvious locus for deliberate educational activity, it becomes the logical nurturing nexus. For the first half of the twentieth century, the school was closely, almost reverently, associated with our freedom, well-being, and both current and future prosperity. Its fall from grace has accompanied a growing dominance of individualism over concern for the common good. Ironically, the increasing dominance of economic purpose in the school's mission has not restored its earlier luster.

Panning for more gold flakes at the river's edge, I am emboldened to hypothesize that the time for another sea change in the school's mission is fast approaching. There are at least three harbingers. The first is a veritable outbreak of scholarly critique, much of it cited in succeeding chapters, that calls for the bolstering of our democracy and points to the role of education and schooling in this endeavor. The second is a fascinating potpourri of contemporary advocacy that reminds one of the increased frequency and intensity of ceremonial rain dances as those with propriety interest in their outcome became increasingly aware of growing tribal skepticism. Those who would "reinvent" the public school to serve their economic purpose better, under the ill-disguised rhetoric of advancing the disadvantaged through semiprivatizing it, are finding it necessary to invent the truth for want of convincing data and argument. The third development, fed by several rising streams, reflects the cyclical, twentieth-century history of the relationship between individualism and the common good. The god of economic utility always will have ardent followers, but some are finding the journey to be less than satisfying. My father was fond of saying that money is the root of all evil, but he would have liked to have had more of the root. However, the human spirit thrives on the nourishment of other roots.

The Schoolhome

Jane Roland Martin begins the prologue of her book *The Schoolhome* with Virginia Woolf's invitation "to stand with her on the bridge 'between the old world and the new' and watch the procession of men that moved from private home to public world each morning and back again each night." She repeat's Woolf's question, "How can women cross the bridge with the men and yet remain 'civilized human beings?'"[31] Martin then invites her reader to take another look:

> Come stand with me on the bridge and watch the procession go by. See, women are no longer just traipsing along behind as Woolf said they were in the 1930s. They have entered the procession en masse. Some are even marching at the head looking as solemn as the men and almost as confident. But what is wrong with that woman at the very front? She looks distraught. Her child is sick and she is wondering how to sandwich a trip to the doctor between clients. What about the young couple close to tears? They are so dismayed by the unrelieved grimness of their preschooler's daycare center that they do not want to leave her there another moment, but they have not been able to find a better facility they can afford. And why are these women carrying infants on their backs and dragging toddlers beside them? Welfare workers have directed them to find jobs, but there is no place to put their youngsters.[32]

Martin's proposal for small, homelike schools—the schoolhome—is not directed just at the plight of the indigent. It embraces all children. Those of the affluent need and often lack caring too. Stories of neglect are the stuff of many a psychiatric session later on. Many seeking solace are men and women who crossed the bridges from home to school and then to workplace, ultimately to become highly successful according to the narratives driving both sets of institutions.

A report of the Public Agenda Foundation supports other studies in the conclusion that the architects of recent and current instrumental school reform just do not get it.[33] Ms. Jones might be as strident as are some of her neighbors at a public meeting in expressing her view that the school is not doing an adequate job in the teaching of reading. But her primary concern the following morning is whether her child is safe, known, and cared for in the local school. The Columbine and other shooting tragedies did not create this priority; they serve, rather, to remind us sharply that all else in school function is secondary. No recent studies contradict the 1984 study of 17,163 students and 8,624 parents in thirty-eight representative schools regarding perceived problems: those pertaining to the schools' custodial function far overshadow the academic, even though "poor teaching" and "poor curriculum" are among the choices presented.[34]

Bits and pieces of Martin's idea of the schoolhome have been around in educational theory for years. Many of these even have been put together to resemble at least part of what she envisions. Regarding the unique domestic aspects of her concept, she draws extensively from Maria Montessori. But then she writes wryly:

> If Montessori had gained entry to the pantheon for herself and her school, would the critics of American education have responded with alacrity to the parental wish reported by Goodlad that "Teach my child with tender loving care" be posted on the school bulletin board side by side with "Knowledge sets the human spirit free"? I doubt that her inclusion would have been enough to contradict the scorn of "soft pedagogies" to which William James gave voice in his *Talks to Teachers*.[35]

Toward Balance in the Educational Narrative

It is important to remember in anticipating the possibility of an ideological sea change toward what President George H. Bush referred to as a "kinder, gentler nation" that alternating between the "hard-and-tough" and the "soft-and-tender" in James's description of the warp and woof in the fabric of American thought and practice is rarely other than a shift in balance. There usually is a readiness for the arts in schooling when the soft-and-tender is in fashion, but parental support is likely to be more forthcoming when the teaching of reading and mathematics appears to be in good shape. The end of the dominant educational narrative is near once its dominance begins to be celebrated. Consequently, one must be careful in anticipating the demise of what is now dominant.

At the time of this writing, there is a convergence of economic instrumentalism and what is commonly referred to as the standards/testing/accountability movement in school purpose and practice. This hard-and-tough theme brooks little counter and is so caught up in excess as to reveal its vulnerability. The furor over a computer in school for every child is blind to the fast-growing presence of computers in the home and to the history of how quickly public fascination with radio and then television sobered advocates' enthusiasm for the radio age and the television age in schools. And regarding the last-ditch equity issue of family ability to purchase, we need only remember driving through the rural countryside in the 1950s: nearly every house boasted a television aerial whether or not it had doors and windows. I am not with Clifford Stoll in thinking that computers have no place in schools, but crippling school budgets to ensure computer literacy in the young makes about as much sense as schools' purchasing bicycles to ensure competence in their use would have made when I was young.[36] It appears that school policies are frequently disconnected from their community surround no matter who is calling the shots.

But the subtle, deeply disturbing flaw beginning to come to the light in the currently dominant educational narrative is far more fundamental. The emerging debate, still quite muted, is over what education is. The debate one reads and hears about is how best to advance the dominant theme: whether the standards being set are sufficiently precise, whether teachers are adequately prepared to advance them, whether the tests are valid, whether the bar is set too high or too low, whether pupils who fail to clear it should be required to repeat the grade. To date, it appears, the question as to whether the intended and sometimes achieved outcomes have anything to do with the development of a thinking, wise, civil, caring, and responsible present and future citizen apparently warrants no response. And so the current era of narrow, linear, simplistic ends-means school reform, cloned from the model of all those eras that have preceded it, is doomed.

The goal now must not be to eradicate every vestige of this reform theme, not just because this is impossible but, more important, because such is not wise. Standards are a part of almost the whole of human existence; tests of some sort are indigenous to all cultures. Being responsible is, however, a much more uplifting and challenging concept than being held accountable (with all its connotations of compliance). The economic theme always will be with us, but the prattling of politicians about the jobs *they* created verges on the obscene, especially when such a large percentage of them provide incomes at or barely above the poverty level. The human need is for satisfying work. If technology lives up to its most uplifting promises, our reward surely will not be the many dull, routinized jobs it has spawned in the past, but the necessary income for all while good work in the human and environmental ecosystems of our planet becomes the norm.[37]

The concept of good work as a critical element in what it means to be human helps to foster convergence in the conflicting ideological themes of the American democracy. The aims set for our schools have provided rhetorical integration of the individual and the common good. In his effort to provide balance in the school's mission, Mortimer Adler weaves the economic into the whole without quite reaching the role of work in the development of democratic character: "Preparation for duties of citizenship is one of the three objectives of any sound system of public schooling in our society. Preparation for earning a living is another, and the third is preparation for discharging everyone's moral obligation to lead a good life and make as much of one's self as possible."[38] With good work a realistic expectation for composing a life that includes earning a living in a context of caring for one another, our institutions, and our habitat, an agenda for education in a democracy begins to take shape. If we did not have schools to advance this agenda, we would have to invent them. But since the schools we have are largely in service to other ends, a daunting adventure awaits us.

A Place for the Young

Pervading Martin's idea of the schoolhome is a concept profound in its implications for schooling. We are accustomed to hearing the words, "It's all for the children," from adults as they argue over their conflicting proposals for change. The results are always the same: schools are adult creations functioning to satisfy adult needs and interests. Operating schools to satisfy children's needs and interests is a profoundly radical and, for many people, disturbing idea. It is central to Martin's schoolhome.

Few who resonate to it are ready to carry the concept as far as does Martin. Figuratively speaking, she envisions a school site jutting out from the world of the private home: "A new kind of school is going to be constructed on this site, and youngsters of all ages, many of them dragging a parent along, have come here to make sure that their needs are met."[39] It is to be a place for children where the words, "It's all for the children," ring true.

Neil Postman argues forcefully for such a place.[40] Young people scattered about in the parentless home and the marketplace attending the school of virtual reality on the Internet are not for him. The schools that emerged in seventeenth-century Europe and were then carried in concept to the New World created childhood but were not for children. They were and largely remain the makers of adults. They are manipulated by and for adults to align with the value of adults in the dominant power structure. Since childhood has no identity of its own, it and its education become instrumental to sustaining the extant value of adults. Today, that value is economic.

Consequently, childhood is clothed in economic value: a consumer today, both consumer and producer tomorrow. The school becomes an instrument to economic human utility.

With no identity in its own right, childhood is readily abused and denied. I opened this chapter with some frightening statistics, but these are only symptomatic of a profound malaise: the instrumental use of childhood for adult ends and the accompanying downgrading of a fifth or more of the life span. Hence the need of a place for children, a place exclusively for educating the childhood self—a place called school, crafted in the image of the schoolhome. It is not too late to address the void created when both mother and father crossed the bridge to the workplace and when schools were invented to prepare children for adulthood without cultivating an identity for childhood.

Agenda for Education in a Democracy

In the late 1980s, colleagues and I conducted the last of three comprehensive studies that laid the groundwork for an agenda of simultaneously renewing schooling and the educational programs of those whose work is the stewardship of schools. These studies laid bare both the common absence of an articulated mission for either schools or educator-preparing programs and, glaringly apparent, of conceptual and operational linkages between the two.

Vacuums invite intrusions. Rapidly filling the vacuum in schools was the 1983 message of the National Commission on Excellence in Education: the schools must be mobilized for a genre of global economic warfare; the future of the United States depends on it.[41] The authors of that report, I believe, did not anticipate that successive interpretations and reinterpretations would in time push aside what presumably was intended to serve the common good in favor of private purpose.

Agendas of school "reform," with their accompanying accusations and implications of incompetent people doing misguided things, were rapidly filling the vacuum in school mission at the very time we were pondering the implications of our massive body of data on educational change, the conduct of schooling, and the condition of teacher education in the United States. Twentieth-century myopia regarding the relationship between the quality of teacher education and the quality of schools was faithfully repeated by the Commission on Excellence in Education. My colleagues and I chose to address the necessary connection.

In retrospect, our decision was a good one. But doubts hovered around contemplation of our work throughout the 1990s. Whereas our 1984 report on elementary and secondary schools received widespread and continuing public and professional attention (it is still in print), the publication life of our equally comprehensive 1990 report on teacher education has been in rapid decline for several years.[42] However, had the politically driven reform of teacher education been in high gear in the first half of the 1990s, as school reform had been during the second half of the 1980s, we probably would have experienced once more the time-and-energy-sapping frustration of reporting our findings to seemingly endless audiences of would-be reformers who closed their eyes, ears, and minds to our recommendations.

As Theodore Sizer wrote so pointedly, although the Commission on Excellence in Education had access to the findings and conclusions of the manuscript, *A Place Called School,* the report "reflected little either of the analysis or the findings."[43] But because teacher education was not yet the target of the still-ongoing school reform era, our relatively little-noticed report on its national condition saved us from several years of selective misuse and accompanying distraction. Instead, we were able to go about the business of laying the foundation for an initiative of considerable relevance to the substance of this chapter and, indeed, the rest of this book.

In 1990, we produced three books based on the inquiries of preceding years. One of these, *The Moral Dimensions of Teaching,*[44] addressed education as a moral endeavor, posed an ethical and moral mission for schooling and the education of educators, and in the words of Kevin Ryan and Karen Bohlin, challenged the teacher education community to fill "teacher education's empty suit" through teaching a core of ethical values.[45] Several scholarly critics with professional ties to teacher education viewed the book's message as more significant than the research findings and recommendations reported elsewhere. But, of course, the contemplation of teaching and teacher education in a near-spiritual light is far more uplifting and much less wearying than is assaying the task of designing and fashioning a coherent teacher education program. Nonetheless, when the word got out that we were interested in working with a clutch of teacher education settings in implementing an agenda of redesigning the enterprise in line with the mission and principles put forward in *The Moral Dimensions of Teaching,* the response was overwhelming. Nearly a quarter of the nation's teacher-preparing institutions responded; almost sixty went through a demanding application process that produced eight charter members of the National Network for Educational Renewal (NNER). Today, there are 17 NNER settings embracing 41 colleges and universities, some 115 school districts, and more than 700 partner schools. The settings collectively exhibit substantial implementation of the agenda.

The agenda, now known as the Agenda for Education in a Democracy, embraces a four-part moral mission for schools and teacher educators, twenty propositions referred to as postulates that identify about sixty conditions aligned with this mission, and a strategy of implementation and stewardship. The soft and tender and the tougher themes of America's expectations for schools converge in the mission statement to align with the admonition cited earlier: "Teach my child with tender loving care," and "Knowledge sets the human spirit free." The mission of the full agenda, described elsewhere by colleagues, aligns with much more, including the three-pronged delineation of democracy portrayed in this chapter.[46]

Most of the settings of the NNER are at the forefront in implementing what increasingly have become agreements on the conditions necessary to the nation's having a qualified, competent, caring teacher in every classroom: collaboration of schools of education and arts and sciences departments in strengthening both the general and professional education programs of prospective teachers, partnership between both of these groups and educators in maintaining professional development schools for student teaching internships, more careful selection and socialization of candidates for teaching, and more.[47] But what all of the participants want to talk about most when they come together for local and national meetings is what they refer to as the moral mission and grounding of the Agenda. This constitutes the heart of the curriculum for developing a corps of leaders for the settings. But they want this curriculum translated in considerable detail for their own use. What are the essentials of a teacher education program that educates teachers in creating learning environments for the development of democratic character in the young? What are the essentials of a school fashioned and conducted according to democratic principles? What might be the curriculum and pedagogy of schools imbued with a moral commitment to the development and enrichment of the childhood self? These are not the kinds of questions at the forefront of school reform, past or present.

They lead me back to the Preface of this book. Our experiences of the recent decade in particular tell us that major engagement in current debate and activity in regard to tightening up and privatizing our schools is an exercise in futility, if not stupidity. Both the debate and the activity are empty of the moral and ethical essence of what education is and our schools should be for. There is far more to be gained by addressing this void than by trying to stem the flow of politically driven school reform that will ebb inevitably with the changing of the tide (but not from counterargument).

We convened a small group of scholars whose interests connected with our own to pool their thinking on democracy, education, and democratic character. We will continue to plow this common ground. Meanwhile, we brought together other groups to check on the public and professional relevance of the direction and initiatives of the journey taking shape in our minds. The challenge now is to deepen the layers of understanding and implementation of the Agenda for Education in a Democracy: for teacher educators, stewards of our schools, and the educative community.

NOTES

1. George Will, "Triumphalist Mood Tempered by Reaction to a Violent Century," *Seattle Post-Intelligencer,* 30 December 1999.

2. Daniel Quinn's literary device for getting us to think about such questions is to make a gorilla the reader's interrogator and teacher. See his *Ishmael* (New York: Bantam, 1992).

3. One of the most comprehensive and optimistic (in spite of the challenges presented) is that of Alan T. Wood, *What Does It Mean to Be Human?* (New York: Peter Lang, 2000).

4. W. Warren Wagar, *The City of Man: Prophecies of World Civilization in Twentieth-Century Thought* (Boston: Houghton Mifflin, 1963).

5. Benjamin R. Barber, "America Skips School," *Harper's Magazine* 286 (November 1993): 39–46.

6. Clifford Stoll, astronomer and early participant in the development and use of computer technology, addresses head on, and with deep concern, the entry into classrooms of business interests tied to technology. See his *High-Tech Heretic* (New York: Doubleday, 1999). He writes: "Learning isn't about acquiring information, maximizing efficiency, or enjoyment. Learning is about developing human capacity" (p. 22).

7. Neil Postman argues convincingly that this is the narrative now driving our schools. See his *The End of Education* (New York: Knopf, 1995).

8. Bill McKibben, "The End of Growth," *Mother Jones* 24 (November 1999): 70.

9. McKibben, "End of Growth," p. 95.

10. For a comprehensive bibliography, see Stephen John Goodlad, *Democracy, Environment, and Education,* book manuscript in process.

11. Diana Butler Bass, "Religious Join Global 'Greens,'" *Seattle Post-Intelligencer,* 7 January 2000, p. A13.

12. See Kenneth E. Boulding, *The World as a Total System* (Thousand Oaks, Calif.: Sage, 1985); and John I. Goodlad, "The Learner at the World's Center," *Social Education* 50 (October 1986): 424–436.

13. For example, John I. Goodlad, *In Praise of Education* (New York: Teachers College Press, 1997), p. 44.

14. James M. Becker (ed.), *Schooling for a Global Age* (New York: McGraw-Hill, 1979).

15. Advanced in Gerhard Hirschfeld, *An Essay on Mankind* (New York: Columbia University Press, 1965).

16. Bert F. Hoselitz (ed.), *Economics and the Idea of Mankind* (New York: Columbia University Press, 1965); Robert Ulich (ed.), *Education and the Idea of Mankind* (New York: Harcourt, Brace, & World, 1964); and W. Warren Wagar (ed.), *History and the Idea of Mankind* (Albuquerque: University of New Mexico Press, 1971).

17. John Dewey, *The Sources of a Science of Education* (New York: Liveright, 1929).

18. John I. Goodlad, M. Frances Klein, Jerrold M. Novotney, Kenneth A. Tye, and Associates, *Toward a Mankind School* (New York: McGraw-Hill, 1974).

19. Kenneth A. Tye, *Global Education: A Worldwide Movement* (Orange, Calif.: Interdependence Press, 1999).

20. For an unusual perspective on discourse as an end in itself, see Alexander M. Sidorkin, *Beyond Discourse: Education, the Self, and Dialogue* (Albany: State University of New York Press, 1999).

21. Walter C. Parker, "The Art of Deliberation," *Educational Leadership* 54 (February 1997): 18–21.

22. Robert W. McChesney, *Rich Media, Poor Democracy: Communication Politics in Dubious Times* (Urbana: University of Illinois Press, 1999).

23. Martin Buber, "The Education of Character," in his *Between Man and Man* (New York: Macmillan, 1965).

24. Donna H. Kerr, "Toward a Democratic Rhetoric of Schooling," in John I. Goodlad and Timothy J. McMannon (eds.), *The Public Purpose of Education and Schooling* (San Francisco: Jossey-Bass, 1997), p. 79.

25. Robert D. Putnam with Robert Leonardi and Raffaella Y. Nanetti, *Making Democracy Work: Civic Traditions in Modern Italy* (Princeton, N.J.: Princeton University Press, 1993).

26. Robert D. Putnam, *Bowling Alone: The Collapse and Revival of American Community* (New York: Simon & Schuster, 2000).

27. Benjamin R. Barber, "Public Schooling: Education for Democracy," in Goodlad and McMannon (eds.), *Public Purpose of Education and Schooling*, p. 22. See also his *Aristocracy of Everyone: The Politics of Education and the Future of America* (New York: Ballantine, 1992).

28. Worldwatch Institute, *State of the World 2000: A Worldwatch Institute Report on Progress Toward a Sustainable Society* (New York: Norton, 2000), p. 16.

29. Robert H. Wiebe, *Self-Rule: A Cultural History of American Democracy* (Chicago: University of Chicago Press, 1995), p. 263.

30. Barber, "America Skips School," p. 42.

31. Jane Roland Martin, *The Schoolhome* (Cambridge, Mass.: Harvard University Press, 1992), p. 1.

32. Martin, *Schoolhome*, p. 2.

33. Jean Johnson and John Immerwahr, *First Things First: What Americans Expect from the Public Schools* (New York: Public Agenda Foundation, 1994).

34. John I. Goodlad, *A Place Called School* (New York: McGraw-Hill, 1984). See especially pp. 72–73.

35. Martin, *Schoolhome*, pp. 127–128.

36. Stoll, *High-Tech Heretic*.

37. Edward Tenner, *Why Things Bite Back: Technology and the Revenge of Unintended Consequences* (New York: Knopf, 1996).

38. Mortimer J. Adler, *We Hold These Truths* (New York: Macmillan, 1987), p. 20.

39. Martin, *Schoolhome*, p. 8.

40. Neil Postman, *Building a Bridge to the Eighteenth Century: How the Past Can Improve Our Future* (New York: Knopf, 1999).

41. National Commission on Excellence in Education, *A Nation at Risk* (Washington, D.C.: Government Printing Office, 1983).

42. Goodlad, *A Place Called School;* John I. Goodlad, *Teachers for Our Nation's Schools* (San Francisco: Jossey-Bass, 1990).

43. Theodore R. Sizer, "Back to a Place Called School," in Kenneth A. Sirotnik and Roger Soder (eds.), *The Beat of a Different Drummer* (New York: Peter Lang, 1999), p. 104.

44. John I. Goodlad, Roger Soder, and Kenneth A. Sirotnik (eds.), *The Moral Dimensions of Teaching* (San Francisco: Jossey-Bass, 1990).

45. Kevin Ryan and Karen Bohlin, "Teacher Education's Empty Suit," *Education Week,* 8 March 2000, p. 42.

46. Wilma F. Smith and Gary D Fenstermacher (eds.), *Leadership for Educational Renewal: Developing a Cadre of Leaders* (San Francisco: Jossey-Bass, 1999).

47. For a comprehensive list, see National Commission on Teaching & America's Future, *What Matters Most: Teaching for America's Future* (New York: National Commission on Teaching & America's Future, 1996).

EDUCATION IN A
POLITICAL DEMOCRACY

Robert W. Hoffert

JOHN GOODLAD'S MORAL INJUNCTION for public schools to enculturate youth in the life of a social and political democracy often has been
dismissed or ignored.[1] For some people, the notion of an essential, to
say nothing of a moral, link among education, public schools, and
democracy is baffling. For others, the relationship is satisfied through
patriotic mantras or by pedagogical recipes focused on forms of participation. In either case, the complex and subtle richness within the simple elegance of Goodlad's moral challenge is too frequently unrecognized
and unattended.

There are many ways to explore the "complex and subtle richness"
embedded in Goodlad's moral challenge. This particular discussion
focuses on the element of democracy, especially democratic concepts in
democratic contexts. Although many people do not understand Goodlad's
linking of educational renewal to democracy and may even regard such a
framing of educational renewal as misguided, the concept of democracy
itself is typically viewed as a rather straightforward affirmation of a familiar and normatively proper principle synonymous with American purposes
and experiences. Thus, democracy's relevance to an educational renewal
agenda may be unclear, but its meaning and goodness seem to be unam-
biguous and, for the most part, uncontested.

Perhaps these appearances are a reversal of the actual circumstances.
That is, only through a thorough and reflective exploration of the complexity of meanings and divergence of implications in modern democracy

does its significance for the renewal of education and public schools become clearer and the importance of Goodlad's moral challenge become fully salient. Unfortunately, there is little awareness that thorough and reflective explorations of democracy are needed, and consequently, they do not come easily.

A memorable bicentennial experience illustrates the difficulty. On the evening of July 4, 1976, in the shelter of an air-conditioned motel room in the Arizona desert, I listened to a newsman explain the historical significance of that day: "Today, America celebrated the 200th anniversary of its form of government." Not only was this claim incorrect, but I suspect that few listeners sensed that they had been misled. In fact, Americans had to wait another thirteen years until they could celebrate the two hundredth anniversary of their form of government.[2] This confusion is not based solely on theoretical and historical technicalities. It reflects a lack of understanding about democratic meanings and about the conflicting choices and purposes that have been part of the pursuit of democracy in the United States and throughout the rest of the world.

In more concrete terms, it reflects the dominant American state of mind in which democracy has an uncomplicated and fixed meaning that we cannot quite express, but "you know what I mean." Many Americans perceive no substantial differences of meaning, purpose, or consequence between, for example, the Declaration of Independence and the U.S. Constitution.[3] They are just keystones in the legacy of our "founding fathers"—those important guys who speak to their progeny with a common voice in a unified democratic tradition through key political documents that are conceptually undifferentiated.

This convergent understanding of America's democratic foundations is problematic, not primarily because it is at odds with historical and academic precision, but because it preempts the basis for an appreciation of democracy's rich diversity and the distinctive alternatives and choices that democracy brings to human life. Americans broadly feel a keen attachment to both documents and respond with deep affection to the principles and perspectives that both articulate. Consequently, if there is a recognition and exploration of the variety of ways in which the Declaration and the Constitution are differentiated from one another, the discovered distinctions are not as likely to lead to simplistic either-or oppositions, but to new and fuller understandings of the complexity and richness of democratic possibilities.

Exploring the differentiated meanings and possibilities in democracy through reading these two documents offers particular benefits. First, this gives a conceptual task (theories of democracy) a foundation in the specific, familiar documents of great political significance to the practical experiences of American life. And second, this exploration of diverse democratic meanings is tied to sources that quicken in most Americans a strong bond of sincere commitment. Therefore, my objectives are focused: to use the Declaration and the Constitution as reference points through which the kinds of conceptual tensions that are inherent in a committed pursuit of democracy can be identified and to appreciate the essential role of education in bringing these distinctions to life and guiding the choices and combinations we create within and among them. There is, however, an essential preamble or introductory preface to any discussion of distinctions and choices within democratic theories.

Democratic Theories

Modern democracy has within it an amazingly diverse spectrum of meanings and choices that must be understood and taken seriously. It also has a broadly shared coherence of meaning that is of great significance. This coherence of meaning is especially evident whenever democracy is contrasted with nondemocratic or antidemocratic social and political forms. Simply put, the coherence of meaning within modern democracy is centered on its affirmation of the fundamental value of every human being. Alexis de Tocqueville, in spite of his anxieties about democracy and his aristocratic inclinations, sensed that some form of democracy was virtually inevitable in the modern world. The key to this historical transformation was the political relevance and authenticity that democracy gives to every human being and the mobilization of human energy that is created by this ideal.

The seeming innocence of popular sovereignty—the idea that authority is founded in and comes from the people (the *demos*) and is legitimated by their consent—is misleading and hides its radically transforming powers. To be sure, modern democracy is not the first form of human meaning in which the value of every human has been affirmed. Christianity, as one example, claims such a position for every human being in relationship to God and his saving love. But democracy made this claim about human value with regard to our relationships with each other in this world. "In Christ" there may be neither male nor female, slave nor free, circumcised nor uncircumcised, said the Scriptures, but in the meantime, in this world, wives should obey their husbands and slaves their masters. In modern democracy, the equal dignity, value, and authenticity of every person is not metaphysical but temporal; it is not spiritual but social and political; it is not our hope beyond mortal life but our hope in this world.

Tocqueville wanted to examine this new human hope. He came to America not to study Americans but to study democracy *in* America. He scrutinized American social conditions for rather simple purposes: to determine what difference, if any, it makes to live in a society built on a principle of the full authenticity of every human being or in a society in which claims are made on behalf of every human being's equal relevance to the authoritative shaping of its public life. Are there manifestations of these differences in the everyday lives of people who have been authenticated by this principle? He did not focus his attention on the abundant evidence that not every human being actually is equally valued in American democracy. Rather, he sought a richer understanding of the human implications of life in a society that embraced the principle of universal human value as its articulated standard and highest aspiration.

Nothing denies the value of every human being more directly and unambiguously than does slavery. And as we know from the deformity of America's own historical experiences, modern democracy's propositional assertion of universal human value has never prevented the systematic and cruel denial of it. Thomas Jefferson, who gave inspiring life to the principle of human equality as the inherent condition of nature, owned slaves. By claiming the fundamental value of every human being, modern democracy does not exempt itself from the attitudes and practices that undermine and deny that claim. Rather, it exposes itself to a high and demanding standard by which it can be legitimately challenged and disciplined and to which it must be unrelentingly educated. That standard must be constantly exercised within every democratic society committed to transformations that quicken human potentialities. It is especially shameful to use the principle of universal human value as a deadening opiate that keeps people passive, enfeebled, and exploited. In short, modern democracy has created a noble and demanding human challenge: to create a world in which every human being has a fundamental value.

The principle of a sovereign people raises not only the practical challenges of living in concert with that ideal, but the equally practical challenge to interpret the specific form and meaning of that ideal. When the claim is raised that "the people" are sovereign, how are we to understand "the people"? Is "the people" a collective whole or a sum of parts? Is it a community or a collection of individuals? Is it singular or plural? Clarifying these issues is not just a housekeeping activity. How we give form and definition to "the people" structures how we will go about giving them value. For sure, humans can be valued as individuals with their own cherished and protected autonomy, or they can be valued as members of moral communities whose norms and purposes are honored and fully practiced.

However, if I see the democratic value of my life in my distinctive and quirky separateness and you value me communally, or if I see the democratic value of my life through my membership in a community of shared purposes and meanings and you value me individually, I am likely to feel unvalued in either case.

There is clarity in democracy's affirmation of our fundamental human value. There is significant ambiguity as well. Tensions of meaning within modern democracy have no single source but are significantly tied to the ambiguity within democracy's clearest claim: the fundamental value of every human being.

Tensions of Meaning in Concepts of Democracy

The clarity and ambiguity of popular sovereignty are evident in both the Declaration of Independence and the U.S. Constitution. These two political documents approach the challenges of democratic political formation differently, and they form different political objectives. The Declaration gives shape to the American nation—its "peopleness." The Constitution shapes the American state—its government.

Perhaps in America uniquely, the formation of the American nation (the American people) has been as politically significant as the formation of the American state. National identity for most peoples is not centered on a political identity. Germans, Chinese, Egyptians, Turks, and Spaniards, for example, have evolved national identities even as they have been politically divided and have experienced great swings in political moods and directions. Over many generations, they have created a shared sense of nationhood primarily through language, religion, food, and cultural rituals. In America, on the other hand, there was an urgent need to become a people, and the usual route to that goal was inaccessible. Language, religion, food, and cultural forms did not give Americans a basis for unity; they were impediments to the national project. Democratic politics provided an alternative: we became a nation or people by committing ourselves to a common political purpose and identity. This may explain America's pattern of focusing political controversies within a very narrow segment of the political spectrum. For Americans, political divisions are not just threats to governmental stability; they threaten cultural cohesion as well. Therefore, every effort must be made to moderate them to the fullest extent possible. This unique American pattern may be why for Germans and Chinese everyone is German or non-German, Chinese or non-Chinese, but for Americans everyone is American, non-American, or un-American.

Because of the political foundation of both the American nation and the American state, the Declaration and the Constitution generated separate, even contentious, dynamics that are especially relevant to the meanings of social and political democracy in America. The political formation of the American nation was centered on issues of legitimacy grounded in the creation of strongly integrative social bonds among what the Declaration referred to as "the good people of these colonies." The formation of the American state turned on strategies of competitive fragmentation—checks and balances, separations of power—designed to limit the dangers of excessive authority and personal power. America's democratic voices expressed the unifying confidence of trust in the Declaration and the segmenting anxiety of suspicion in the Constitution. In both, the valuing of the people was being pursued but understood differently.

Americans see themselves both as a virtuous people, who build only "defensive" bombs, and as aggressively self-interested individuals, who can be trusted only to maximize their own advantages. We need to educate for democracy in part to make certain choices between these alternatives. We need to educate for democracy even more to build the bonds of a unifying foundation that also protects the distinctions through which we express our unique and authentic selves. It is too easy to translate these tensions of meaning into mere polarities or contradictions. It is relentless work to weave them into a nurturing national fabric.

The real challenges of giving life to democracy in America reveal even more powerfully than the pure concepts the inherent ambiguity of the *demos,* the people. To whom do we give authority when we make "the people" sovereign? Specifically, is it the "good people" of Jefferson's Declaration or the self-driven individuals of Madison's Federalist No. 10? Is democracy better served through the Constitution's methods for expressing and protecting unique individuals and their self-referencing pursuits or by the Declaration's affirmation of the primacy of human solidarity, sociability, and community?

This ambiguous meaning of "the people" in America's two most fundamental political documents is reflected in the divergent understandings given to the practical expression of "the people" in everyday democratic practices, that is, the majority. Is the majority's will a guidepost to justice? Should we build a political order that facilitates the expression and authority of that majority? Or, because majorities are collective principles with unreliable implications for individuals, are they the most serious potential source of corruption and abuse in a democratic order? Should we build a political order that inhibits, diverts, and fragments majoritarian impulses? The Jeffersonian tradition of the Declaration associates the majority with possibilities for justice; the Madisonian tradition of the Constitution associates it with threats of tyranny.[4] How do they build their respective cases for democracy and the fundamental value of the people?

Both Jefferson and Madison, and the traditions of democracy they represent, turned to nature as the foundation for their new conceptual journey into democracy. For both, a reading of nature offered an opportunity to create a new, democratic political order free of traditional, nondemocratic principles. Nondemocratic political principles were typically based on transcendence or history, on the world beyond this world or the dominating forces within this world. The Greeks of antiquity claimed that politics properly formed needed the guidance of justice. Justice was a dimension of truth accessible through reason. And reason was reliably expressed only in the transcendent world of the immortal spirit. And so, for Plato, we need kings who are philosophers, that is, rulers who honor and pursue reason. Similarly, the Western religious tradition grounded politics on the will of a sovereign, transcendent God who either appointed his earthly agents or formed selective covenants with them. This is how we got the divine right of kings and God's chosen people, Israel.

When politics was not grounded on beings or criteria beyond this world, it typically authorized the dominant results of life within this world—the standard and patterns of history. Two examples of political orders grounded in history are those based on military conquests and hereditary monarchies. Often transcendence and history were woven together to create political authorizations. Conquests were given the blessings of Providence, birth lineages claimed divine right, and even the dominant patterns of worldly orders were authorized when transcendent reason and the perfections of God were unavailable. (Consequently the practical political guidance became "render unto Caesar that which is Caesar's, and render unto God that which is God's.")

"Nature" offered grounds for creating new political possibilities free of the inscrutability of perfection beyond this world and the fatefulness of dominating human events in this world. On the one hand, nature is about the structure of temporal life. On the other hand, nature is about the essential structure of life in the temporal order and not the accidental structure of mere historical events within it. For example, in history we confront a seemingly endless string of cases in which humans have dominated one another. This is so even if, in nature, there is no intrinsic principle or condition that authenticates that subjugation. However, in modern democracy, the claim is raised that we can access nature. Nature is not in the hands of forces beyond our capacity or understanding. It is self-evident or available for consultation through common sense and reflective introspection. As a result, it is also available to challenge the legitimacy of mere events and of standards that arbitrarily authorize and give dominating power to criteria that ultimately are accidental, not essential. Both Jefferson and Madison sensed the inventive possibilities of nature as a political criterion and used it in analogous ways to create a foundation for a new democratic social and political order. Nevertheless, their specific portraits of nature were virtually antithetical.

As Jefferson claims in the Declaration, nature presents no deficiency or inconvenience requiring the compensatory efforts of political authority. In fact, the troubling "course of human events" is the result of a kind of fall— "a long train of abuses and usurpations." Political action is required not by the pure conditions of nature but by the corruption of natural conditions in history and civil society. In fact, it is the "fall" of the order of nature in history that necessitates the redemptive political response of democracy to reorient the people back to proper natural principles. This implies that the emergence of civil society in history, and of political power within it, was based on various challenges to the natural community of equals. For example, Jean-Jacques Rousseau suggests multiple factors that contribute to the swindle of history through which the people were robbed of their natural, equal worth. However, when one man said, "This property is mine," and authority was established to protect his claim, the swindle was fully consummated. Given this historical corruption of nature, a new authority must be formulated to reconstitute society through the social and political revitalization of the natural principle of equality.

James Madison reads nature quite differently. As he argued in the Federalist No. 10 in explanation and defense of the Constitution of 1787, nature is in some respects deficient—what John Locke described as "inconvenient."[5] Specifically, it is deficient in providing individuals with a reliable orderliness sufficient for the effective pursuit of their own self-creation. Nature's deficiency arises because it is unable to provide any reliable enforcement of natural law's protection for persons and property. This results in insecure circumstances especially disorienting and damaging for self-interested individuals. Paradoxically, naturally autonomous individuals have been left to struggle with the damaging limitations imposed on themselves by their own absolute freedom. On this view, the movement from nature to civil society arises from a rational choice of self-interested individuals to replace their natural conditions of self-governance with contractually defined conditions in civil authority. In this new arrangement, it will be possible for individuals, now technically less free, nevertheless to enjoy greater practical benefits from their conditional autonomy than they ever were able to enjoy in their state of natural liberty.

This movement of individuals from nature to a contracted civil society defines the primary responsibilities of government: to establish and maintain a fair and secure order in which individuals can maximally pursue their self-defining activities. Mere order will not do. Mere order does not remedy the specific deficiency of nature, but threatens to create difficulties far more severe than those caused within the inconveniences of nature. Therefore, an order must be established that will define and enforce uniform rules and procedures and permit individuals, within these processes and criteria, to operate as they see fit and in pursuit of goals of their own choosing. Madison commends his constitutional design for our acceptance precisely because he claims for it such a properly limited order, centered on process, that preserves as much individual autonomy as is consistent with security and stability—"domestic tranquility."

Madison's and Jefferson's alternative uses of nature not only frame different political agendas but they also ground those agendas on the two primary political values of democracy: liberty and equality. Maximum, practical protections for individual freedom inhibit the expression of solidarities and the development of deeply significant social bonds, especially those that are presumed to be necessary to define a morally purposive community. Conversely, as the Declaration asserts, nothing builds the principled and practical bonds of a people more securely than equality. Our "equal station" not only puts us at the same level but gives us common interests and an integrating energy in the pursuit of those interests. Maximizing liberty legitimates that which is particular and differentiated—the individual—just as it undermines the unique claims of collectives; maximizing equality gives a foundation for the general and shared—the community—just as it undermines the unique claims of individuals.

A series of significant distinctions evolves out of these different strands of modern democratic thinking. When nature gives special validation to humanity's shared life in community, the expression of this condition often has a religious or spiritual voice. Covenant language, such as "chosen people," is used to reflect the homogeneous interests among associates. The act of covenanting or of being covenanted affirms intrinsic relationships of common purpose and commitment. Jefferson, for example, appeals to "the Supreme Judge of the world for the rectitude of our intentions" and pledges, within the protection of Divine Providence, "our lives, our fortunes, and our sacred honor."

Communities, especially covenanted communities, tell stories, powerfully moving forms through which they can express the uniqueness of their experiences, identities, and purposes: "When, in the course of human events, it becomes necessary for one people . . ." A community of purpose is not content with mere order and process (conditions that are essentially ahistorical and unstoried). It is concerned with the positive results of life together. Through this attention to outcomes, the equality and purposes of a community are achieved and preserved. If results are neglected, the community's shared meanings and conditions will fragment, and hierarchies of power and advantage soon will establish themselves and flourish. In settings of equality, law is the will of a properly constituted community discovered and expressed in the natural vitality of its members. Thus, the purpose and role of law are moral, establishing a basis for substantive justice over injustice, mere order, and process. This moral orientation casts government into a positive role. It is appropriate and necessary for government to specify its intended direction and outcomes. As the political expression of a purposive community, government must give positive leadership so that the proper essence of the people will prevail. Such a community's story expresses this essence and gives the community a practical tool by which it remains true to itself.

Not surprisingly, this democratic tradition presses for an enlargement of the public sphere. Government, law, and especially the general interactive life of the people have an expanded public role. This orientation has equally significant implications for personal life as well. Personal meaning and fulfillment are not viewed as matters of isolated experiments of self-discovery and expression; we are not natural voids scurrying around trying to create ourselves, guided by mere self-assertion. Instead, nature has given human life a form and an authenticity, often challenged and undermined by historical conventions, that can be reconstituted through the public life of a covenanted community. Consequently, private and public well-being are not antithetical in their pursuit or their ends.

Democracy, in the orientation of the Declaration, creates a political realm that expresses the shared aspirations of a people—"one people." There is no greater challenge to the popular will of a well-ordered community than the pressure or temptation to use authority on behalf of particular interests, especially when those particular interests conflict with or seek exemptions from the collective wisdom of the majority. In this tradition, the majority will is a qualitative principle, not just a quantitative one. It is qualitative because it expresses the dominant understandings of all citizens (or, as the Declaration calls them, "the good people") in communities properly organized for democratic choices ("free and independent states").

Madison's explanation of the U.S. Constitution provides a strikingly different approach to another kind of democracy and democratic life.[6] In his approach, politics protects particular rights and interests that are validated by the laws of nature. Obviously, this makes the creation of common authority a tricky business. The willingness of individuals to create a common authority is never a willingness to submit to the personal power of any other individual. Therefore, the contractual common authority must be as impersonal as possible. The contractual common authority must result in an apparatus that will permit competing individuals to continue their ongoing competitions under substantially improved conditions of reliability and security. This relates directly to Madison's characterization of the Constitution as "an order producing machine."

How exactly does this machine impersonalize political power? A number of techniques are used to achieve this result. One technique is to make power an expression of law, that is, to separate power from the expression of personal will and define it through processes of rule making. In this form, law is impersonal because it is abstract; it never comes from or expresses a specific will or specific circumstance. In fact, sufficiently complex governmental machinery ensures that laws will always be the negotiated results of conflicting wills. Politics and good government, then, are more consequences of technique and method than of commitment and purpose. Techniques for checking and processing individual interests are needed to construct impersonal standards and to prevent co-optations of the law's abstract standards.

Making legal content procedural further enhances the impersonal and abstract qualities of law. Law is not to designate outcomes (winners and losers) or determine specific substantive results (right faith and true morals). Rather, it is to define fair and uniform standards for competition—rules of the game—that provide the practical basis for order and freedom. Procedural conditions are the grounds for the predictability and security that make an agreement to "play the game" a rational choice for autonomous, free individuals. To reinforce the procedural character of law, this tradition clearly separates law from matters of fundamental meaning, especially religious and moral meanings. The contractual state is not designed to be an agent of moral or religious purposes. The individual is to be the agent of moral and religious choice and responsibility. The state must be committed to the limits of a practicability that ensures a secure and predictable process for voluntary interactions. The most profound expression of human liberty—moral responsibility—must never be preempted by the very artifice that free individuals have created to protect and effectively express their free choices.

Commonly, the expression of political authority in this approach is described as negative government. When this description is used, the essential point is that direction, priorities, values, and interests are not to be determined for individuals by governments; that is, governments are not to impose positive agendas onto their citizens. Rather, direction, priorities, values, and interests are to be the expressions of free individuals or the unintended outcomes of unfettered interactions among free individuals. Government may not intrude and usurp this area of choice and responsibility; to do so would be to negate claims that belong solely to individuals. Government's role is limited and practical: to fashion a legal process whereby individuals can more successfully define and pursue their own positive agendas. To preserve a proper relationship between the role of government and the opportunities for individuals, a secular realm is created for political life. This secular public realm requires a spirit of tolerance and habits of openness. Properly formed, this tolerance is not a reflection of indifference or hostility to fundamental political, religious, or moral choices and values. It is a reflection of the judgment that the considered differences among individuals on these questions are so fundamental and persistent that to establish public order on the basis of these principles is to jeopardize both common authority and individual liberty. Therefore, a political sphere that limits itself to matters of secular practicality has a dual role: to create the possibility for public order as well as the opportunity for individual responsibility within a free life.

Democratic life, in this orientation, must create a politics that speaks to and for the individual. "The people" rule and are most valued when individuals are free and when the government they have authorized provides an orderly protection for the pursuit and expression of their freedom. Correspondingly, the great threat to free individuals is most pronounced when collective principles directly impose themselves. For example, when majorities rule directly, the dangers can be enormous. The constituent members of a majority inevitably perceive themselves as acting in harmony with their freedom as individuals. They do not acknowledge their collective power and imagine that they are merely acting in relationship to their own individual preferences exactly in the manner of every other individual. This can be a dangerous misperception. Majority decisions are always based on a collective principle: the authority of numbers. They are not based on individual preference, reason, truth, justice, the will of God, or the order of nature. A majority rules solely because of the number of people who support a decision regardless of the inherent wisdom or folly of that decision. A majority can rule if there is no shared rationale, even if there is *no* rationale, for a decision backed by their numbers.

Majorities therefore must be checked. Madison's explanation of the Constitution's design identifies two prominent techniques for checking majorities. First, representational patterns must be engineered in ways that make the indirect and negotiated expressions of majority preferences unavoidable and the direct and spontaneous expressions of majority preferences impossible. For example, the Constitution, Madison explains, is specifically designed to ensure that all political groups joined in shaping the government are forced to act as minorities of the whole. Consider how the national government is currently constituted: the members of the House of Representatives represent 435 nonoverlapping districts, members of the Senate represent 50 nonoverlapping states, the president and vice president are selected by an electoral college formed on the basis of separate votes in each of the 50 states, and Supreme Court justices are not elected by anyone. Nowhere is the national government shaped or controlled by a direct majority of the whole. If a majority is not able to speak or rule directly, its voice necessarily will be "compromised" or "negotiated." Such a "manufactured" majority voice, in contrast to a directly expressed majority voice, is likely to be more limited in scope, less durable, and more internally unsettled. In short, it should be strong enough to construct a reliable social order yet weak enough to reduce significantly the risks of tyranny or abuses of power.

Second, the pattern of the extended but fragmented representation scheme that Madison built into his constitutional design creates a strong foundation for an antimajoritarian principle that acts to restrain the inherent majoritarian tendencies in all democracies. The practical application of this principle in the Constitution is found in its specific protections for individuals: prohibitions of bills of attainder and ex post facto laws, and habeas corpus rights.[7] Madison's constitutional commitment to protect minorities is not a choice to protect small groups over large groups or the vulnerable over the privileged. A commitment to protect the majority is always the assertion of a group principle over individual ones. A commitment to protect minorities is the basis for protecting individuals, the ultimate minority. In effect, Madison and the constitutional tradition argue that a healthy democratic process must include a certain antidemocratic bias. However, the Constitution's minoritarianism is not designed to give privileges to an elite, presumptuous, and cunning class or political group. It is to protect a stable political order from the excessive influence of any collective force—large or small, privileged or vulnerable—that can too easily damage or destroy individual liberty.

Democratic Concepts in Context: The Educational Challenge

Taken together, the Declaration of Independence and the U.S. Constitution reflect the rich variety of priorities and purposes incorporated into the building of American democracy. It is neither automatic nor easy to serve autonomous individuals and moral communities, to maximize equality and liberty, to protect procedures and results, and to build a vibrant public sphere of common purpose and an expansive market society of private interests. Yet I have suggested that a thorough and reflective exploration of the complexity of meanings and divergence of implications in modern democracy will contribute to clearer and more compelling understandings of the significance of education for democracy and of democracy for educational renewal and public schools. This claim—that clarity and purpose can arise out of a seemingly confusing impasse—will be considered in four interrelated contexts.

The Chaos of Democratic Meanings

An essential, even if traditional, relationship between democracy and education is based on the clarification of meanings and usage. The richness and complexity of democratic possibilities can come to life only insofar as we are educated about them. It is simply not the case that modern democracy, in the United States or anywhere else in the world, has a singular, coherent, and self-evident structure of meanings and implications. In fact, democracy has simultaneously given coherence to contemporary life and generated many of its greatest conflicts. That is, democracy has become a nearly universal aspiration made manifest through widely divergent, often deeply antagonistic forms and purposes. This chaos of democratic meanings cries out for educational examinations to clarify both common ground and real differences.

Education about democratic concepts does not create automatic or authoritative answers. It does not resolve or eliminate the chaos of democratic meanings. It does, however, clarify the challenges and provide a foundation from which to address these challenges. Education about democratic concepts provides the only basis on which we can pursue the building of a responsible democratic life and enculturate the young into the fullness of possibilities available through the pursuit of democracy. Merely to endorse "democracy" is either to expose a chaos of meanings and possibilities or to be imprisoned within the fated habits of parochial and unreflective worlds. There is nothing particularly noble or ennobling about being lost or being preempted. When we embrace "democracy," we do not make our lives easier or clearer; we take on an engagement of demanding responsibilities, perplexing possibilities, and paradoxical choices. We cannot meet these demands or resolve these complexities if we remain in a naive or ignorant state. The awareness and understanding necessary for both self-expression and the building of a social and political democracy require education in and of democracy's complexity of meanings and applications. In short, education is necessary not just for the goal of enculturation but for the actual forming of the social and political democracy into which we aspire to enculturate our young.

The Tensions of a Tradition of Mixed Democratic Concepts

A commitment to enculturate the young into the context of American democracy is especially challenging. In the United States, democratic concepts are not only expressed with conflicting differences, but the national preference has been to create mixed or synthetic understandings of democracy that weave together elements of these conflicting differences without acknowledging or resolving the tensions within their meanings. Typically, Americans reflect little self-consciousness or discomfort about their advocacy of both the autonomy of "self-made" individuals and "the virtue of the good people of this Christian nation," of their calls both to limit government and to expand it, of their insistence both on government's procedural roles (as in the economy) and positive roles (as in abortions and prayer), of both impersonal standards of merit and personal standards of loyalty, and of both "the magic of the marketplace" and public expressions of faith and moral life. Americans are the individualists who struggle to embrace a classical democratic formulation essential to individualism—"equal opportunity under the law"—for women and minorities. In short, we are the individualists who trust the impulses of communal majoritarianism, the communalists who often want nothing more than to be left alone.

In America, conflicting democratic concepts have been given vital expression, but the national preference is to embrace and absorb these conflicts within a mixed, synthetic, or hybrid democratic tradition rather than to isolate and resolve them within reasonably coherent traditions of differentiated democratic meanings.[8] Consequently, this mixed democratic tradition is the source of political consensus and continuity as well as the source of political conflicts and change. Americans experience both the frustrations and the satisfactions of a functional approach to democracy that soothes the wounds of conflict by placing differences within a setting of agreements and that confronts the power of conformity by placing agreements within a setting of conflicting tensions. Without the tensions of its hybrid democratic tradition, America would be a prime candidate for the ravages of unresolvable conflicts or for the atrophying sterility of uniformity. By mixing together opposing ideas of democracy into a shared national creed, American democracy has been saved from the twin extremes of its unique circumstances and attitudes. An isolated consensual society, lacking the diversity of alternative traditions and identities, has remained vital in part because of the complex tensions within its own democratic consensus. And a society continually at odds with itself, yet seldom willing to reach beyond itself, has found cohesion through the incoherent inclusiveness of its theoretical base.

This paradoxical context creates especially demanding challenges for an education committed to serve as an agent of democratic enculturation. Furthermore, the significance and difficulty of this educational challenge are considerably deepened if the goal is not to "resolve" or "purify" the tensions within America's mixed democratic tradition either by denying or camouflaging the reality of its conflicting parts or by becoming the champion of a single, consistent strand within the whole. The educational challenge is to enlighten a paradox: How do you make Americans more aware of the democratic tensions in their national life without insisting on the internal consistencies that would eliminate them? American democracy will never become more aware of its democratic tensions and will never appreciate the value of those tensions for the building of the nation if that educational challenge is not pursued with commitment and effectiveness.

The unique complexity of democracy in the United States must be better and more self-consciously understood. Perhaps the greatest impediment to an understanding of the paradoxes and tensions within American democracy relates to this lack of a sufficiently rich and invested appreciation for the conflicting possibilities that have been absorbed into the American democratic synthesis. In order to see and value the remarkable variety of ways in which the democratic traditions of the Declaration and the Constitution can and have been mixed together, the distinctions central to these two conceptual traditions must first be understood and articulated. Only then will educational engagements of American democracy be possible that appreciate the rich variety of possibilities and directions made available to national life through diverse democratic understandings.

Enlightened Democratic Possibilities

Alexis de Tocqueville raises another significant relationship between democratic concepts and democratic contexts that is especially significant for the educational enculturation of the young into a social and political democracy. Democratic concepts, he suggests, are pursued to their best consequences if they are "rightly understood."[9] Although he has clear and strong conceptual preferences of his own, this call for enlightened or rightly understood self-interest is not an attempt to prescribe "right" democratic choices from "wrong" ones. Instead, he is suggesting that the healthy pursuit of democratic concepts calls us to place our pursuit of these ideals and values in concrete time and space—in real, human contexts.

Absent human contexts in time and space, concepts of the individual are too isolated and too much captured by the moment, just as concepts of community are too undifferentiated and too much captured by abstract idealization. Specific contexts weave concepts into enduring patterns of practical life. For example, consider self-interest. If we wish to maximize self-interest, do we do so most effectively within a context or without regard to context—that is, is the "self" in whom each of us takes an interest an abstraction or a real person? If it is a real person, do we have an interest in it only now or as long as it exists? If we have an interest in our "self" as long as we exist, is that interest relevant only to already known interests or to possible interests that have not yet taken shape in our lives or been recognized by us? Tocqueville is not asking us to discard or reject self-interest. He is asking us to place our commitment to self-interest in context. The effect is that the practical pursuit of the things we value takes on a mixture of qualities it never possesses without the context. In fact, the joining of concepts to context has the effect of creating balanced, mixed traditions.

Education not only articulates and clarifies the meaning of democratic concepts and an awareness of intriguing combinations among these concepts, it is also essential to placing life effectively within healthy human contexts. Human culture and history are not biologically scripted, self-evident, or spontaneously available to guide us. Awareness of historical and cultural contexts is learned through the processes of education. Therefore, it is not possible to enculturate the young into a social and political democracy if the essential relationship between democracy and education is denied or ignored. Education does not merely shed light on democratic ideals. Education helps to clarify the best democratic possibilities achievable in actual settings of human life and purpose.

Democracy's Uniqueness

Two elements relevant to this discussion require reaffirmation. First, if democracy is a carrier of multiple meanings and possibilities, what is it that makes all of these diverse options "democratic"? Second, if there is an essential relationship between democracy and education, what makes this relationship uniquely relevant to the renewal of public schools? These two questions may seem to be disjointed or unrelated, but the answer to the former significantly informs the answer to the latter.

The unique, common characteristic of democracy in all of its voices and manifestations is a principled claim on behalf of the authenticity and public relevance of every human being—the fundamental value of every person. Democracy, in practice, does not perfectly embody its own principles any more than does aristocracy, in practice, ensure the rule of the "best." Nor does democracy, in practice or theory, aspire to manifest its principles in uniform ways or in accordance with a single evaluation standard.

Americans should understand this well. The clarion call for universal human dignity and popular sovereignty came from owners of slaves, and the document specially designed to protect individual liberty was made possible through a compromise to protect the continued enslavement of individuals. It is not the purity or unity of democracy in theory or practice that is unique and fundamental; it is democracy's universal claim of the value of every human life.

If democracy's unique claim regarding the universal authenticity of every human being is taken seriously and pursued with commitment, it is impossible to avoid the issues of education, public schools, and educational renewal. Human beings begin life incomplete but rich in potential. Paradoxically, humans are most incomplete in the development of their humanity, and our human development is neither easy nor automatic. It requires the commitment of a nurturing education. Contemporary fashion and ideologies to the contrary, education for humans can never be reduced to options, careers, or skill sets. Education is about the building of our humanity.

If the building of our humanity depends on a nurturing education and if the humanity of all people has an equal dignity and relevance, then it is irresponsible, if not immoral, not to make educational opportunities available for everyone. The pursuit of democracy and of democracy's most fundamental tenet transforms the nature of the setting in which we must educate. The democratic value of every person makes it unacceptable to educate selectively or accidentally, that is, to build the humanity of some and neglect the humanity of others. In democracy, education is no longer an optional, private matter; it is the guarantor of the effective human status that has been claimed for each of us. Education in a democracy requires public institutions that are responsible to serve well the building of every citizen. Public schooling in a democracy is not an educational strategy or option but a moral obligation.

This is the clarity of John Goodlad's vision and the simple elegance and compelling power of his moral challenge. If public schools are essential to the building of a democratic citizenry, then we cannot afford to be indifferent to the moral dimensions of the work that we do within them and for them. We must be responsible stewards of these schools, providing access to knowledge and to the building of humanity for all, and practicing methods of teaching that nurture students' richest potentialities. We must acknowledge the considerable extent to which public schools fail to build the humanity of every youth they are asked to serve, just as we must celebrate the extent to which public schools serve so many so well. However, nothing else will inspire the educational renewal of public schools more or guide the educational renewal of public schools better than a moral commitment to the enculturation of the young into a social and political democracy.

NOTES

1. See John I. Goodlad, *Educational Renewal: Better Teachers, Better Schools* (San Francisco: Jossey-Bass, 1994), chap. 1. For criticisms, see Tony W. Johnson, "Taking a First Step Toward Reform," *Phi Delta Kappan* 72 (November 1990): 202–203.

2. Dates for the major documents of America's political founding are: 1776, Declaration of Independence; 1781, ratification of the Articles of Confederation and Perpetual Union; 1789, ratification of the U.S. Constitution; and 1791, ratification of the first ten amendments to the Constitution (the Bill of Rights).

3. These two founding documents are effective representations of the two competing traditions of democratic concepts that have structured American political experiences.

4. Both the Declaration of Independence and the U.S. Constitution were modified in collective reviews, but each was given its primary shape by a principal author: Thomas Jefferson for the Declaration and James Madison for the Constitution.

5. Madison, Hamilton, and Jay wrote the essays that became known as the Federalist Papers to persuade the citizens of New York to support ratification of the Constitution of 1787.

6. Madison's Federalist No. 10 is an elegant and comprehensive exploration of the political concepts and strategies at the heart of his proposed constitutional system.

7. During the ratification debates, Federalist supporters of the Constitution insisted that these constitutional elements provided sufficient and reliable protections for individual rights and liberties.

8. I have discussed the hybrid democratic tradition in the United States and the value of that synthetic pattern. See Robert W. Hoffert, *A Politics of Tensions* (Niwot, Colo.: University Press of Colorado, 1992), especially chaps. 1 and 8.

9. See Alexis de Tocqueville, *Democracy in America* (New York: Vintage Books, 1990), especially vol. 2, bk. 2, chaps. 8 and 9.

3

DEMOCRACY EDUCATION
FOR MORE THAN THE FEW

Kathleen Staudt

ONE FREQUENTLY HEARS Winston Churchill's famous comment as people applaud and apologize for their governments: "It has been said that democracy is the worst form of Government except all those other forms that have been tried from time to time." The singular attention to a form rather than the plural forms of government makes it seem as though all democracies are alike or that all residents have a voice. Institutional arrangements vary markedly among democracies, from parliamentary to presidential, from single-member constituency to proportional representation electoral system, and especially from policy frameworks that aggravate inequality to those that redistribute economic wealth and opportunity. Institutions matter.

And what do people mean when they use the word *democracy?* One hears the sentiments of Abraham Lincoln—of, by, and for the people—a sufficiently vague claim that virtually all governments espouse. Among the nearly two hundred nation–states that currently exist, most claim to speak for their people, and approximately two-thirds are labeled democracies or partial democracies (as opposed to nondemocracies). Freedom House, a nonprofit democracy advocacy organization, issues annual rankings and maps, using procedural criteria such as regular elections, rule of law, and freedom of speech and the press.[1] These many democracies, full or partial, embrace a wide array of nation–states with institutions that set the stage for more or less democracy for their residents, from male to female, rich to poor, racially prized to despised. Comparisons matter.

Once we establish the comparative importance of institutions within that huge group of nation–states called democracies, we must also pursue internal comparisons within those places that are called democratic spaces. Who is authorized to speak? Whose voices count? How many participate? Who benefits and who loses? What we will invariably find are huge differences among people—based on the above criteria of gender, class, age, and race—in their experience with democracies. Internal democracy (whatever the label) matters.

In the democratically labeled United States, the focus of this chapter, slavery long coexisted with supposed democracy, women obtained the voting franchise long after men, and poverty has deterred and continues to deter public voice and accountability. Violence within the home was tolerated until two decades ago, when vigorous organizations blurred the long-held dividing line between public and private—a line that offered questionable public protection within the confines of private spaces. And children, to whom and for whom we promote civic education, experience a highly truncated form of democracy compared to that enjoyed by adults.[2]

Before we promote one kind of democracy, authorize or compel one sanitized view of history, or export U.S.-style democracy to other countries, we need to examine the importance of institutions, history, and the graded experiences of people living in hierarchical societies. We must also consider the place of nation–states in the global economy, wherein capital movement and trade agreements undermine the ability of "nationals" to make decisions about their destiny, however democratic their institutions and however well their democracy embraces people of all identities, genders, classes, and ages. National borders offer especially instructive locations and vantage points from which to make our considerations.

All democracies have flaws. The same can be said about schools in democracies. Public schooling in the United States does a good job of preparing some—but not nearly all—students to engage in democracy. For some, according to the many reports on public affairs in the United States, the results are grim. The 1998 Civics Report Card prepared by the National Assessment of Educational Progress reveals that approximately a quarter of students in grades 4, 8, and 12 scored at the "proficient" level on national civics standards (with a mere 2 to 4 percent at the "advanced" level), but around a third scored below the basic level. That same report shows great disparities in scores by ethnicity and income levels, disparities that persist at the adult level in terms of voter turnout and organizational participation.[3]

In the eligible voter turnout population, the eighteen- to twenty-one-year-old group has the lowest level of any other age group.[4] Few high school graduates know how to think critically, write persuasively, organize people, and work in teams—all necessary for democratic engagement—and standardized multiple-choice tests rarely tap the comprehensive learning necessary for such engagement. But citizens, residents, parents, students, faculty members, and other stakeholders can reflect and organize around these flaws in a process we might call democratic educational renewal.

Democratic educational renewal occurs as a result of a more comprehensive, critical, and engaged learning process that builds knowledge, skills, and civic dispositions. It is about solving problems, organizing ideas, writing clearly, and thinking critically. It addresses people's historical and contemporary experiences with U.S. democracy, noting the varying rates of participation, the significance of money for political influence, and the selective denial of democratic rights and freedoms because of race, class, age, and gender. But democratic educational renewal is also comparative—recognizing that not all democracies are alike and that institutions matter—and global: its educational boundaries do not stop at 5 percent of the world's population (the U.S.), but rather it situates the United States in the global political economy.

This chapter focuses on optimal educational approaches that bring about democratic educational renewal by educating the many for democracy and then offers several practices that offer promise for fostering democratic educational renewal in schooling.

Democratic Educational Renewal: Comparative and Global

As a set of governing institutions, the United States has much to celebrate. It is the oldest continuously existing constitutional democracy, though by no means the oldest democracy. It has survived revolutionary origins and a civil war without a military coup, so common in countries to the south. It became home to settlers, some of whom arrived voluntarily and others involuntarily, in a way that immigration historian Lawrence Fuchs analyzes as compatible with U.S. "founding myths": promising equal rights, including the "right to develop an ethnic-American identity." Fuchs acknowledges what he calls persistent xenophobia, racism, and ethnic prejudices, but he points to periodic legal commitments to the founding myth that the United States is "an asylum for those who seek freedom and opportunity."[5] A post-1960s myth, Fuchs notes, also celebrates ethnic diversity.[6]

What Fuchs calls myths are said to be national values, some of them legitimized and enshrined in constitutional documents and legal decisions. Individual freedom, opportunity, and diversity are celebrated in classrooms and passed on to children over generations through the political socialization process. They are worthy values, but political and economic institutions get in the way of realizing such values in practice. Institutions divide or consolidate authority, make responsiveness to popular will more or less difficult, and facilitate timely or delayed decision making. In democracy education, there would be value in comparing U.S. institutions with those of other strong democracies around the world, focusing on decision-making bodies, electoral systems, and consequent political party choices.[7] The most striking contrast between democracy in the United States and that found elsewhere is the United States's presidential rather than parliamentary form; the parliamentary form of democracy is the more common worldwide.

Presidential Versus Parliamentary

To balance power among institutions, presidential governance requires strong legislative and judicial branches. (Many countries to the south of the United States lack a strong judiciary, thus leading to overpowering presidential offices.) Presidents and legislators in the United States serve fixed terms of office and spend considerable time forging common ground to pass legislation. However, what presidential systems gain in stability from fixed terms of governance, they may lose in responsiveness to the popular will and in fragmented, delayed, and inefficient decision-making processes.

Parliamentary governance fuses legislative and executive action in the form of a prime minister, a cabinet, and a majority (or majority coalition) of the predominant political party's (or parties') seats in the parliament. In response to shifts in the popular will, members of parliament may be subject to new elections before their regular terms expire, should the majority face a vote of no confidence or itself call for new elections in the hope of gaining more seats. Decision making tends to be quick and efficient, for less competition exists between branches of government. However, what parliamentary governments gain in terms of responsiveness and efficiency, they lose in terms of stability. Moreover, parliamentary majorities can abuse their power without rule of law and other basic freedoms of speech, assembly, and press.

More than parliamentary and presidential contrasts are at work in institutional formulas. Comparative thinking digs deeper, to the type of electoral systems in place.

Electoral Systems: Single Member Versus Proportional Representation

Electoral system choices add complexity to the strengths and weaknesses of democratic institutions. In general, the United States relies on single-member as opposed to proportional representation electoral systems.[8]

That is, voters in the United States elect a single person to represent what is usually a geographic constituency. Systems like these generally offer voters two party choices, and candidates seek the largest number of votes in the presumably nonideological middle. Those parties rarely position minority groups or women at the center of their agendas in representation or outcome terms, and to gain reelection, the party in power attempts to represent specific geographic regions well enough for the powerful stakeholders therein. James Madison's concerns about factionalism (voiced in Federalist No. 10) are met very well.

Proportional representation systems distribute legislative seats to multiple members in proportion to the votes won in the districts. These systems generally offer multiple party choices with ideological agendas across the right-to-left spectrum. A voter's choice of party tends to be based on ideology or policy rather than on geographic region or personality. To the extent that internal party processes are democratic and inclusive, parties infuse their agendas with democratic and inclusive ideas, and their candidates reflect their relative diversity.

Beyond governance institutional formulas, however, is the larger civil society, which may or may not exercise sufficient leverage to move the representatives and the political parties during or between election times. Civic and party activists and representatives together produce policy agendas that shift the distribution of economic opportunities and resources. The demographic composition of those strategic players often has some bearing on the negotiations and compromises achieved through the democratic process.

Civil Society and Policy Outcomes

Civil society, consisting of networks and organizations outside government, may or may not be active in presidential or parliamentary, single-member or proportional representation systems. These networks and organizations can counter or reinforce the flaws in governance institutions to the extent that they gain visibility, legitimacy, and leverage in parties' and representatives' agendas.

What effect do parliamentary, presidential, and electoral institutions have on policy agendas and legislative bodies made up of members reflective of the larger populations? Over the past thirty years, Western European, parliamentary, proportional representation systems have achieved successes in demographic representative governance and in the pursuit of social justice agendas. Scandinavian countries (Norway, Sweden, Denmark, and Finland) regularly elect more than 30 percent women to their parliaments (with comparable numbers on their cabinets), as do the Netherlands and Germany. All of these countries have sizable labor or social democratic parties in multiparty systems that pursue policies that distribute income in somewhat more equitable ways than do countries like the United States, India, and Mexico. In addition to providing hospitable environments for redistributive policy agendas, these countries support programs that provide a bottom-line safety net in health and social services for their citizens. Canada is notable in that regard, which explains its emergence at the top of the United Nations Human Development Index over the past several years.[9]

Contrast the records of the Scandinavian countries or Canada with those of the United States. While elected representatives in the United States have become more diverse demographically, especially at the state and local levels, this is not so at the national level, where women compose just a tenth of both houses in Congress. This figure is well below that of other democracies, including North American Free Trade Agreement partners Canada and Mexico, which have nearly double the percentage of women in their national bodies. South Africa, a new democracy, seats a quarter women, and Argentina almost a third women owing to party *cupos* (the much-despised "Q"-word in English—quotas—with a broader meaning in Spanish that embraces "shares"). Even more compelling, however, is the absence of a social and economic justice agenda in the U.S. parties. Income inequalities in the United States are wide and growing. Democracies can either mute or soften the different practices of market economies or capitalism worldwide. Robert Bellah and his coauthors tell us that the French make reference to the "savage capitalism" of the United States.[10]

A mix of single-member and proportional representation may be optimal for enhancing choice among more than two political parties and fostering coherent policy agendas. Germany mixes both, as does Mexico. But U.S. resistance to institutional formulaic changes runs deep. Consider the experience of Lani Guinier, who was nominated for attorney general in President Clinton's first term. Critics treated her writings about reforming institutional and voting formulas to increase minority representation as near treasonous.[11]

Democratic Educational Renewal as Critical Thinking: History and "Standards"

Let us dig a bit deeper into the United States as a peculiar democracy in historical perspective. We expect students to gain historical and contemporary knowledge. These learning "outcomes" are reflected in standards, and some kinds of indicators (often multiple-choice questions) are used to measure achievement. The ways students are assessed drives the ways teachers teach to some extent. Critical thinking, writing, and problem-solving processes are less amenable to the typical multiple-choice formats deemed efficient for testing and comparing millions of students.

In this section, I use examples from three sources: the national civics standards, the National Assessment of Educational Progress (NAEP), and the Texas Assessment of Academic Skills (TAAS). The second most populous state, Texas has used high-stakes accountability testing since 1990, and in 1999 the legislature empowered the test makers even more by passing laws to end "social promotion" and using TAAS scores for grade-retention decisions. Neither approach grapples with the critical thinking and writing necessary for students to gain the skills and knowledge necessary for genuine democratic citizenship.

The Hierarchy Within

U.S. history is constructed in ways that allow instructors and students to study key themes in civic education. Textbooks and the faculty who use them frequently focus on the Founding Fathers (capitalized with reverence), the Constitution, and the institutions of governance. The ideals of freedom and democracy, about which students read, differ from the grounded experiences of the majority of people—women and slaves—living during the first half of the nation's history. Central here are the legal controls of men over women and the centrality of slavery to the U.S. experience. Consider slavery. Cornel West has written in "The Moral Obligations of Living in a Democratic Society" that "what is distinctive about this precious experiment in democracy called America is that it has always been inextricably interwoven with white supremacy and its legacy."[12] Introductory textbooks in political science do not treat slavery as central to the whole founding story of U.S. "democracy" and its slave-dependent form of capitalism, despite slaves' having composed nearly a fifth of the population in 1790.[13] The recent fascination with Washington and Jefferson in their roles as slave owners and the incongruities between their words and reported ideals is instructive. It is hardly news that these founders and others owned slaves, but scholars and the general populace of the United States were long willing to ignore this fact, as if it were some sort of aberration. Furthermore, political science textbooks rarely raise comparative questions. How, for example, do we explain the relative delay in abolition in the United States, which trailed both Britain and Mexico in taking that step? Similar questions could be raised about gender and the centrality of inequality to how our political economy evolved.

Reductionism? Content Standards, Assessment, and Accountability

On national standards in civic education, two important documents can be analyzed, neither of which encountered the contentious and fractious debates among historians that occurred in a similar standard-setting process. Yet much in civic standards documents is historical, so one point of inquiry would be to ask when, how, and where content appears on the complex process of evaluating conflicting principles and laws on liberty and slavery and gender inequality or of (surely less controversial) comparing democracies.

The Center for Civic Education published the *National Standards for Civics and Government* in 1994, a 179-page document that organizes content summaries and content standards by grade levels: K–4, 5–8, and 9–12. In sidebars, compelling quotations highlight content material. Most of these come from men, but there are a few comments from Abigail Adams, Eleanor Roosevelt, Helen Keller, two suffragists, Judith Shklar, and Lady Mary Wortley Montagu. Among scores of thousands of words, the word *slavery* comes up six times but never gains a full sentence. Rather, slavery is an example or part of a phrase in a sentence. For example, following a thesis about the absence of feudalism, inherited castes, or nobility in the United States, we find in several places (from standards in grades 5–12): "Notable exceptions that have worked against the attainment of social equality are the history of slavery, the treatment of Native Americans, and discrimination against various groups."

The 1998 Civic Achievement Levels in the NAEP are categorized at the fourth-, eighth-, and twelfth-grade levels, and within each, at the "basic," "proficient," and "advanced" levels in six to nine content standards per grade and proficiency level and in performance sample questions.[14] To their credit, philosophical conflicts, engagement, and problem-solving approaches merit rank as standards of achievement. And assessment examples range from knowledge to skills, multiple-choice and short-answer questions to the interpretation of data and maps. However, only in grade 8, at the advanced but not basic level, should students "be able to evaluate results of past efforts to address discrepancies between American ideas and national reality." This seems to be an extremely subtle, nearly muted way to open the door to content on a "discrepancy" (slavery) that is central to U.S. historical experience, as Cornel West and others have stated.

The 1998 NAEP standards include comparative content, but only at the twelfth-grade level. But even for graduating high school seniors, the "basic" standards focus on the United States alone. At higher expectations (proficiency and advanced levels), students are expected to understand parliamentary government and comparative constitutional democracies. With the United States making up only 5 percent of the global population, "basic" students seem expected to know little about either the other 95 percent or the global economy as it impinges on the nation. The Center for Civic Education contains a British parliamentary contrast in grades 5 through 8.

Millions of children in Texas learn and get tested about that learning under the nearly decade-old accountability measure: the TAAS. Eighth graders take social studies TAAS tests with questions on government and history (Texas and U.S.), economics, and geography. Past sample questions, available to teachers, offer a range of knowledge- and skills-oriented questions in multiple-choice format. The students must, under one objective, "evaluate the contributions of the Founding Fathers as models of civic virtue" and under others "explain . . . the spread of slavery," "the impact of slavery," and the "development of the abolition movement." They must also explain "why a *free enterprise* system of economics developed in the new nation" (my italics, for slavery hardly seems compatible with freedom despite the chronic use of this adjective before the word *enterprise* in most texts and standards).

These various objectives, including the word *evaluate,* open the door to discussions about the founders and the founding context on race and gender matters. Yet the kind of truth imposed on students in the multiple-choice format leaves little doubt about the width of that door. Evaluate the following sample question:

> In the Declaration of Independence the phrase "all men are created equal" means that—
> A. slavery should be abolished.
> B. men have more rights than women or children.
> C. all people have the same talents and abilities.
> D. everyone should be treated equally according to the law.

Query the informed, and their response may be "none of the above." Even the addition of the Fourteenth Amendment nearly a century later did not clarify this complex matter with the simplicity of a response of *D* (the right answer, according to the materials distributed to schools and teachers). If teachers do not teach to the test, their students, the campus, and the district will be penalized.

Schools do a disservice to students when truth is imposed on them in this fashion. Texas students take required courses in Texas history in which they learn much about the Republic of Texas and its proclaimed values of freedom and independence. Recent textbooks glorify the "multicultural" inhabitants of Mexican and African heritages but remain mute about the dramatic growth in the nineteenth century in the absolute and proportional numbers of slaves in Texas, which so valued freedom.[15] Isn't that part of the story?

Democratic Educational Renewal as Problem Solving, Action, and Organizational Struggle

Slavery existed in full force when Alexis de Tocqueville and his companion made their visit to the United States in the 1830s. His book, *Democracy in America*, left a comparative legacy that celebrated U.S. exceptionalism with respect to the importance of voluntary organizations. However ironic his words are as we reflect on the preemancipation, pre–female suffrage period, Tocqueville's analysis applauds the balance between individualism and community that existed among men of European heritage. Those lacking individual rights would struggle for them and eventually gain many of those rights, at least on paper.

The peculiar history of the United States is a reminder of how important it is that people struggled for constitutional rights and that gains became possible with that struggle. The rule of law alone could not accomplish gains in civil rights. After all, the supreme judges of the land deemed racial segregation at one historic moment to be compatible with the Fourteenth Amendment to the Constitution (1896, in the case of *Plessy v. Ferguson*), and a half-century later incompatible with that same document (1954, *Brown v. Board of Education*). Laws may institutionalize oppression as well as liberate people from that oppression.

The United States is most certainly a nation of plural groups, although active citizenship is unevenly spread among the population, as is indicated by the wide range of voter turnout rates by majority and minority groups, education, age, and income level. Studies of participation find that group membership does mute somewhat the general pattern whereby higher income, age, and education are associated with higher voter turnout. At the height of voter turnout, around 1960, political scientists Gabriel Almond and Sidney Verba concluded from a five-country study that the United States and Britain achieved a "civic culture" in contrast to the parochial cultures of Italy and Mexico or the subject culture of West Germany.[16] In a civic culture, they said, citizens view institutions and policies as legitimate, tolerate plural interests, and feel politically competent.

Since the heyday of such praise, things have changed. Voter turnout in the United States has diminished to approximately half the eligible population for presidential elections and less than two of five during off-year elections. Depending on local political cultures, turnout is often lower at election levels closer to the people. American government textbooks at the university level do a good job of contrasting low U.S. turnout with higher rates in a variety of democracies in Asia, Europe, and Latin America. Even the much-vaunted, group-oriented political culture of the United States has undergone revision, at a time of great cynicism and mistrust coupled with high-visibility connections between money interests and successful political campaigns.

Social commentators such as Robert Bellah and Robert Putnam have bemoaned the loss of community in the late twentieth century. As Putnam describes the decline of neighborhood, civic, and parent organizations like the parent-teacher organization or association, he highlights the importance of social capital, or networks and relationships of trust that enable people to accomplish goals together. Putnam's famous essay "Bowling Alone" drew inspiration from comparative work in Italy described in his book *Making Democracy Work*, which contrasted two regions: one with considerable social capital and one with much less. Implicitly, the Italy analysis became a foundation from which to launch the rally to renew social capital in the United States. Curiously, though, Putnam had nothing to say about school governance in Italy, centralized as it was and is amid contentious and unstable parliamentary politics in which representatives are selected through proportional representation.[17]

Teachers can build on (or undermine) social capital among students, a kind of capital that could sustain or renew democracy in education. To the extent that teachers build or renew social capital among their students, their actions have ripple effects on critical masses of adults, prepared or unprepared to live and work in democracies.[18]

Children learn about their national history (at least some versions of that history). They practice the civic rituals that sustain nationalism. New immigrants too learn these histories and rituals, although many are stuck at the very bottom of the hierarchy. Consider the following example of Mexican immigrant children and their struggle to recite the Pledge of Allegiance in English: "I pledge allegiance to the flag of the United States of America . . . one nation, under God, *invisible* with liberty and justice for all."[19] Students' replacement of the word *indivisible* with *invisible* is a reminder of the limbo within which non-English-speaking citizen minorities and immigrants are situated, living a precarious economic life and lying low, awaiting naturalization before any new legal shifts and surprises undermine their intentions.

But active citizenship can be learned in schools. Students can learn problem-solving, organizing, writing, and critical-thinking skills in schools. This is the essence of civic education for democratic renewal; it is not memorizing facts for multiple-choice tests or reciting words that have no meaning to the people saying them.

U.S. Democracy in a Global Economy: Border Vantage Points

Civic education occurs in an increasingly global economy, with growing gaps between rich and poor in the United States. The "free trade" regimes of this era offer less and less protection for job retention within U.S. borders. Even Robert Bellah, commentator on the U.S. decline in community, has gone global. He tracks inequality in vivid contrasts: "In 1960 American CEOs made forty times the average factory worker's income; in 1990 it was eighty times the average factory worker's income, and more recently it is estimated at one hundred or two hundred times the average factory worker's income."[20] Bellah says that we need to act on national and global levels "to counter the deeply divisive consequences of the reign of the global market" at the same time "we repair our civic culture."[21]

From what governance levels should people hold officials accountable: local, national, transnational, or global? For Robert Reich, our national and local governments are all we have left, for "corporate nationality" is increasingly irrelevant. Reich's "we" is composed of several classes of workers: routine production service workers, in-person service workers, and symbolic-analytic workers (his elite), who identify problems, solve problems, and engage in strategic brokering activities. The rest of the workers, Reich says, are mostly government employees, including public school teachers. Does civic education matter for the majority of workers? For myself and most readers, the answer is yes; democracy matters for more than the few. For Reich, the chief worry is how "to organize the market in ways that motivate symbolic analysts to discover means of helping mankind while inflicting the least amount of harm."[22] What does that mean for teachers in a democracy? Let us not give up on the majority, teachers and non-symbolic-analytic workers among them.

Following are several vignettes from an actual international borderland, the U.S.-Mexico gateway of the Americas, wherein critical masses of diverse residents (not all of them official citizens) live everyday lives below the poverty line. Consider these vignettes for how they might inform relevant civic education—or more profoundly, democratic educational renewal.

○

High school students compete in an annual civic competition modeled on spelling bees. In preparation, they memorize facts and details about U.S. current events, history, government, and economy. The multiple-choice questions in the actual event run the gamut from trivia ("What state produces the most cranberries?") to significant matters about the structure and founding of the nation.

In one particular competition, two questions are asked about African Americans and women, but none about people of Latino heritage, who make up most of these male contestants and a quarter of the state labor force. At the close of the meet, the coordinator differentiates this competition from others in a three-column story in the city's newspaper: "It's the only one that emphasizes the American heritage . . . of being proud of being an American and all that means." Five students take home monetary awards, but each participant takes a bag of mementos, including a "Be All That You Can Be" army cup stamped "Made in China."

In a frequently touted model of relevance, a school sponsors a Microsociety. Elementary-aged students consume and bank in this society with Microbucks and checks. If disagreements occur, they are resolved in the Microcourts, with fines levied. Microsociety consumers obey laws and pay their taxes. Five students serve in its fledgling legislature, approachable only by individuals and corporations, not intermediary groups (civic society?).

"Kids Voting" is in its third year, turning out forty thousand children to vote at real precincts accompanied by their parents, who are sometimes voting for the first time in their lives, egged on, no doubt, by the kids.

The curricular materials are nonpartisan, and the ballots contain candidates' names and their pictures. Teachers pay to attend all-day, newspaper-sponsored workshops, where they receive more curricular materials, free newspaper subscriptions for their schools, and fifty plastic U.S. flags, with wooden stems stamped "Made in China."

Across the Rio Grande, a few miles to the south, youngsters vote in a hastily organized campaign on children's rights sponsored by UNICEF and the Instituto Electoral Federal (the official national electoral institute), "La Elección es Tambien Nuestra" ("The Election Is Ours Too").

Students rate having a "right to an education" at the very top (a right guaranteed in the Mexican constitution). But the government directs a declining percentage of annual expenditures to education, around 5 percent, and teachers' salaries consume more than 80 percent of the education budgets. Most teachers are paid the equivalent of $60 to $90 (in U.S. dollars) per week, two to three times the minimum wage, but many work two jobs (the morning and afternoon school shifts) to make their livelihood.

The middle school son of a school board trustee plays his cards for all they are worth. His teachers treat him with kid gloves. He moves from bottom to top squad of the athletic team. He periodically puts a parent's name card ("School Board") on his classroom desk, just in case others do not remember. He failed the state standardized test but is classified "GT" (gifted and talented). He publicly refers to classmates of Mexican heritage as "wetbacks" and those of African heritage as "niggers."

---

o

These vignettes come from an aspiring global city, a twin-city metropolitan area of 2 million people, at least a quarter of whom are migrants from national heartlands and other nations.[23] El Paso–Juarez was Mexican territory until 1848, and after that a gateway for the official encouragement of labor migration (the Bracero Program through 1964) and the unofficial toleration of migration when demand for immigrant labor was high. Immigration law added employer sanctions only in 1986.

Currently, El Paso–Juarez is a hub in which NAFTA is both celebrated and cursed. Ostensibly, NAFTA opens commerce in trade—the movement of capital—but by 2000 (six years after the momentous birth of NAFTA in 1994), twelve thousand jobs had been lost in El Paso's largest industry, garment manufacturing. NAFTA does not permit free people movement, which the Immigration and Naturalization Service (INS in English, but SIN in Spanish) controls through Border Patrol guards and technological surveillance.

El Paso's 70 percent majority of Mexican-heritage people exists in a historically Anglo-dominant mainstream culture, making it a cultural borderland. This "minority" (Hispanic), immigration-rich area parallels the cultural complexity found in many large urban areas of the United States, where the global economy has begun to transform business, employment, and wage structures. The El Paso vignettes, therefore, may be relevant elsewhere.

These vignettes inform us about a complicated civic education occurring both inside and outside classrooms on this North American border. Borderlands, metaphoric and material, exist in many U.S. cities in the zones that separate and join people along lines of culture, language, gender, and class. Many issues are highlighted in the vignettes:

- Winners and losers in the policy distribution game, particularly the working poor in the context of global economic job loss

- Such educational master narratives as consuming in a market economy, about which Neil Postman so vividly writes[24]

- Civic master narratives that turn education toward fragmented details or nationalistic jingoism

- Daily reminders of social structures that both privilege white men and illustrate gaps between policy or principled rhetoric and realities

Children have absorbed and lived some of these contradictions already, leading to basic disjunctures between the official civic education they receive in classrooms and the realities of their particular form of democracy in peculiar institutions that make diverse representation and social justice agendas so difficult. To this, though, we must add the inability of our particular form of democracy to hold financial capital accountable to residents and citizens within national boundaries, a concern Reich continually raises in *The Work of Nations*. That "Made in China" appears on national symbols (flags) and institutional gimmicks (army recruitment mugs) makes a compelling statement about the global economy in which we all have a stake. China's per capita income, though it is more than a dollar a day—the World Bank's line that indicates global poverty for almost 1.3 billion inhabitants of the world—amounts to a mere $860 (U.S.) per year.[25] We are all implicated in the institutions that facilitate (or eliminate) global poverty.

Benjamin Barber has eloquently written about the need for civic literacy: "If education is to support school-to-work initiatives that adapt pedagogy to the needs of the workplace, it must also support school-to-citizen initiatives that adapt pedagogy to the needs of the public square."[26] But civic society is no longer just national. From the vantage point of borders, this public square is local, national, transnational (the NAFTA community), and global. We err if we fail to provide students (not only the symbolic analysts, not only the advanced) with analytical and problem-solving skills that relate to democratic action about policies from the global economy all the way down to their campuses and classrooms.

This education must occur in democratic contexts. Without people practicing and engaging in democratic politics, children see, experience, and learn little about public democratic affairs. Compare that to how much they see, experience, and learn about consumer choice and the marketplace. Amy Gutmann puts it so well: "Without an active democratic politics among its citizens, a nation may give all its children free public schools, but it cannot foster the spirit of democratic education."[27] Her remarks cause us to reflect on the first two sections of this chapter. How democratic is politics for different kinds of citizens and residents? Are there different kinds of democracies that engage more residents and citizens and represent their interests with coherent policy choices?

We all have a grand opportunity to engage in renewed civic education that embraces democracies in the classroom, uses comparative perspectives, and goes beyond the clerical scorekeeping mentalities of those who design the assessment tools for civic standards. This is a *civic* education, not just a national citizenship effort. It can build on the strengths and weaknesses of the three-way categorization that Harry Boyte and James Farr offer but move beyond their citizen terminology. "Citizens," they write,

> have been understood as . . . rights-bearing members of a political system who choose their leaders, preferably men of distinctive virtue and talent, through elections; caring members of a moral community who share certain values and feel common responsibilities toward one another; and practical agents of a civic world who work together in public ways and spaces to engage the tasks and try to solve the problems that they collectively face.[28]

Boyte and Farr critique the first conception, the liberal view with roots "in a classical republican tradition" along with the second view, which they label "service learning," to favor the third notion of "public work." Their citizenship terminology excludes noncitizen residents whose children are entitled to public education and suggests that public action stops at national borders, although capital and labor movements are the stuff of our global economy. Moreover, their distinction between service-learning and public work is slippery. Campus Compact colleges and universities, numbering 520 schools, offered 19 million hours of public service in 1994–1995. However, service programs struggle over motivations—

undoubtedly varying from class to class—from orientations toward serving or toward "metapolitical work" among "emerging citizens in a fragile democracy."[29] Adding to this is the AmeriCorps program, which, like VISTA, takes community service far above the depths within which it is lodged in some minds: that is, judge-imposed penalties on convicted criminals, with oversight from parole officers.

Nevertheless, the critique of the liberal view raises a major challenge to what we teach and how we teach; substance and approaches must be connected to high but broader standards of excellence in problem-solving activities and public engagement. We need to facilitate learning that engages students in the real world, national and transnational. We need to move beyond a teacher-centered, frontal lecturing method with an audience of individual competitors, isolated from the community, who memorize details for standardized tests. According to the Third International Mathematics and Science Study (TIMSS), students exposed to fragmented ideas (today we divide fractions, tomorrow we multiply them) do not learn in depth.[30] The same outcome is likely from the fragmented, fact-and-detail approach to teaching civics and government. But students do need substantive knowledge.

In Praise of Promising Civic Initiatives for Democratic Educational Renewal

Democratic educational renewal occurs in a social context wherein people practice what Lappé and DuBois call "living democracy" rather than just hear lectures about "formal democracy."[31] Short of that—for living democracies in our communities, homes, and workplaces are surely lacking—what promising approaches might lead toward democratic educational renewal? First we must start with caring, as Nel Noddings always reminds us, but caring looms larger than teaching and classrooms.[32] A characteristic of our "culturally decadent civilization," argues Cornel West, is "the relative erosion of systems of nurturing and caring, which affects each of us, but which has an especially devastating impact on young people."[33]

Schools themselves remain among our few public responsibilities, however loudly the privatization voices shout in the name of "choice." They are public places with the trappings of democratic governance in need of renewal. They recruit faculty members from teacher education programs and institutions of higher education that can be renewed. Schools, teacher education programs, colleges, and universities: all of these offer hope and space for democratic educational renewal. Following are some promising practices.

Parental Engagement

School campuses range from relatively open places that provide space for parental engagement to closed places that view parents as problems. Some respond to state mandates to appoint one or two parents to committees (in Texas the term is *Campus Improvement Team*). At school boards, participation ranges from merely casting an informed vote to engaging sustained, collective civic capacity at those meetings. Many residents are not engaged at all. Residents and parents are unorganized in many districts, and school board elections draw some of the lowest turnouts of all elections. In Mexico, such low turnout would be labeled *abstencionismo* (abstentionism). Using this linguistic insight, might we call paltry participation levels in the United States abstention? If so, why have parents and residents opted out of exercising voice?

Public attention requires collective action as parents and residents exercise more effective oversight over schools and serve as better advocates for children and future worker-citizens. One model is that offered in the Industrial Areas Foundation (IAF). In Texas, for example, the state IAF network organizes parents and educators in mostly low-income, minority neighborhoods, using notable success stories for inspiration. These stories relate small victories (getting traffic lights for school safety) as well as larger triumphs (systemic reform toward high academic standards in cities with once-intractable public school disaster zones).[34] Often organized with a faith base, these organizations also address the related policies that provide contexts for healthy households: better jobs with decent pay, health care for the uninsured, and potable water and sewers in *colonias* (unplanned settlements outside the city limits).

Teacher Engagement in Preparation and in Service

Teacher preparation programs undergo periodic redesign, and curricular revisions should prepare teachers to engage in democratic educational renewal, both with their students and as major stakeholders in school governance themselves. Most teacher preparation programs fail to grapple seriously with comparative institutions, democratic governance, or budgets in an already overloaded curricular agenda. Neither do they focus much on U.S. educational governance (a strange void in introductory political science textbooks) as they prepare teachers for lives in allegedly democratically managed public schools.

Suppose teacher preparation students are required to complete a political science course. This is better than no course work, but it is a requirement that might not take them far, given the ways those courses are typically taught. Introductory political science courses focus primarily on U.S. politics, and one is hard pressed to find textbooks that incorporate material on schools or illuminate comparative and global perspectives. This can and should change, and the responsibility rests in political scientists' hands.

If introductory texts focused on both comparative and educational governance, readers would find that most nations centralize educational governance. Whether governance is parliamentary or presidential, single member or proportional representation, educational stakeholders would need to work through parties and organizations as well as individually to exercise public voice in the wide landscape of national politics. In European countries, officials periodically aim to stimulate parents' participation at local levels, but efforts are often organized from the top down.[35]

The United States and Canada are rather remarkable in their emphasis on decentralized school governance at levels closer to people. This is a feature to highlight, celebrate, and develop organizational skills around within civic education. The U.S. federal system takes state and local control of education seriously, unlike that of many other democracies where education policy is centralized, including supposed federal systems like Mexico's. Voters in the United States elect trustees to serve on school boards without salaries in many districts.

Of course, for much of U.S. history, this local control over schools was used to sustain virulent racial segregation as well as gender and ability tracking. But selective federal intrusion and increasingly active state laws in the last quarter of the twentieth century opened school governance and accountability to all children, despite economic inequalities among them. And the U.S. commitment to public education is generous, despite constant challenges about the effectiveness of that spending. Most Central and South American countries spend a much smaller fraction of the public purse on education—about $100 per pupil—than does the United States, with its investment of $5,000 per pupil in the 1990s (including teacher salaries). This 1:50 ratio is unmatched in comparative per capita terms. In the non–North American nations of the Western Hemisphere, public education is a low budgetary priority.[36]

Once in the profession, teachers have collective stakes in substantive educational policies (surely more than salary policy) as well as collective responsibility for a great deal of students' understandings of democracies—from classrooms to campuses and from local communities to global ones.

Student Engagement

In our civic education agenda, we should expect all students (not just the elite—the proficient, advanced, or promising symbolic analysts) to acquire knowledge and to exercise that knowledge in individual, social, and comparative ways. Classrooms should provide opportunities for dialogue wherein students practice the arts of democracy and team-based problem solving on matters that extend beyond the school. Classrooms should also encourage critical thinking and writing. Faculty should choose books and readings with widely varied content ranging from procedural, formal democracy and the founders to social justice concerns.[37] Whether in service-learning or doing public work, students need connections to and relationships with reality, however contradictory those connections and relationships may be.[38]

Traditional civic education is not effective for preparing an engaged public involved in community and affairs. But even beyond civics and social studies courses, faculty in all content areas might ask themselves whether they are building or undermining social capital with the way they teach and the approaches they use.

Deepen Democracy Within Nations and the Global Economy

Above all else, societies must be more democratic places in which to live, for students learn what they live. Young people learn contradictions just as adults do; we cannot pretend those contradictions do not exist. And societies extend beyond traditional boundaries: public and private, local and global, and national dividing lines. Effective civic education instills knowledge about social capital and social accountability; more than the marketplace is operational. Robert Heilbroner's pronouncement of "the triumph of capitalism" need not be a triumph of savage capitalism.[39]

NOTES

1. Freedom House produces an annual list and map of what now totals 191 countries. See the organization's web site (www.freedomhouse.org) plus various publications. Procedural criteria are often associated with classic liberalism (not neoliberalism, or the active government of the twentieth century). Ironically, though, male monopolization of government might persist even with supposed democratic conditions. Many so-called democracies allow legal pluralism: the coexistence of secular law and religious or customary laws.

2. Mary Catherine Bateson made this insightful comment at the April 3–4, 1998, session of the Working Group on Developing Democratic Character, sponsored by the Institute for Educational Inquiry.

3. See the National Assessment of Educational Progress Web site at http://nces.ed.gov/nationsreportcard/ for the full Civics Report Card.

4. Sidney Verba, Kay Schlozman, and Henry Brady, *Voice and Equality: Civic Volunteerism in American Politics* (Cambridge, Mass.: Harvard University Press, 1995). American government textbooks routinely report the age-linked voter turnout rates.

5. Lawrence H. Fuchs, "The American Civic Culture and an Inclusivist Immigration Policy," in James Banks and Cherry A. McGee Banks (eds.), *Handbook of Research on Multicultural Education* (New York: Macmillan, 1995), p. 299. Note my use of *U.S.* rather than *American,* to avoid the wholesale appropriation of a hemispheric term for scores of countries to use for one country alone.

6. Fuchs, "American Civic Culture," p. 300.

7. The sections that follow come from a background paper I prepared for the United Nations Development Programme (UNDP) Human Development Report 1995 (New York: Oxford University Press, 1995), reprinted as Kathleen Staudt, "Political Representation: Engendering Democracy," in *Background Papers: Human Development Report 1995* (New York: UNDP, 1996), pp. 21–70. Comparisons like these are standard stuff in comparative politics, one of six major subfields of political science.

8. The single-member/proportional representation analysis was made famous in the classic work of Maurice Duverger; see, for example, *The Political Role of Women* (Paris: UNESCO, 1955). See also Wilma Rule and Joseph F. Zimmerman (eds.), *Electoral Systems in Comparative Perspective: Their Impact on Women and Minorities* (Westport, Conn.: Greenwood Press, 1994).

9. See the annual UNDP *Human Development Reports.*

10. Robert Bellah and others, *The Good Society* (New York: Vintage Books, 1992), p. 91. The Center for the American Women in Politics at the Eagleton Institute of Rutgers University keeps a current count of gender (im)balance. In recent years, women have held about a fifth of state and local elected positions. African American and Latino legislators moved from less than 5 percent representation a quarter-century ago to percentages more reflective of their populations at various levels of governance.

11. Lani Guinier, *The Tyranny of the Majority: Fundamental Fairness in Representative Democracy* (New York: Free Press, 1994), discusses cumulative and preferential voting to permit minorities a greater share. These procedures are practiced in some European democracies.

12. Cornel West, "The Moral Obligations of Living in a Democratic Society," in David Batstone and Eduardo Mendieta (eds.), *The Good Citizen* (New York: Routledge, 1999), p. 7.

13. In 1790, 17 percent of the population of the United States consisted of slaves; by 1860, slaves made up just 13 percent. Figures from Peter Kolchin, *American Slavery* (New York: Hill & Wang, 1993), p. 242. Thanks to University of Texas at El Paso historian Charles Martin for identifying the source.

14. These were posted in 1999 on the web at www.act.org/research/naep.

15. As the mother of two middle school Texas history course takers, I monitored state-selected, state-owned textbooks on this topic. To Charles Martin, thanks for information on the growing numbers of slaves as Texas moved from independence to statehood: only 5,000 slaves of 40,000 inhabitants (12 percent) in 1836, but 58,000 of 212,000 (27 percent) in 1850 (part of the Union by then), and 183,000 of 604,000 (30 percent) just prior to the Civil War.

16. Gabriel A. Almond and Sidney Verba, *The Civic Culture: Political Attitudes and Democracy in Five Nations* (Boston: Little, Brown, 1965).

17. Robert D. Putnam, "Bowling Alone: America's Declining Social Capital," *Journal of Democracy* 6 (January 1995): 65–78; and Robert D. Putnam with Robert Leonardi and Raffaella Y. Nanetti, *Making Democracy Work: Civic Traditions in Modern Italy* (Princeton, N.J.: Princeton University Press, 1993). See also Robert Bellah and others, *Habits of the Heart: Individualism and Commitment in American Life* (Berkeley: University of California Press, 1987); and *The Good Society*. See also the chapter on Italy in Nicholas Beattie, *Professional Parents: Parent Participation in Four Western European Countries* (Bristol, Pa.: Falmer, 1985).

18. See John I. Goodlad, Roger Soder, and Kenneth A. Sirotnik (eds.), *The Moral Dimensions of Teaching* (San Francisco: Jossey-Bass, 1990); Roger Soder (ed.), *Democracy, Education, and the Schools* (San Francisco: Jossey-Bass, 1996); and John I. Goodlad and Timothy J. McMannon (eds.), *The Public Purpose of Education and Schooling* (San Francisco: Jossey-Bass, 1997). The Goodlad-inspired Working Group on Developing Democratic Character that produced the chapters in this book continues this line of thinking.

The University of Texas at El Paso, a member of the National Network for Educational Renewal, reorganized its curriculum to require, among other revisions, a course called "Schools in Communities," in which students enroll after two state-mandated introductory political science courses.

19. Nearly a quarter of students in El Paso are enrolled in bilingual programs, and they recite the Pledge in English. I have heard this word switch and have conversed with various teachers who mention it as well. Some respond by breaking down phrases of the Pledge to discuss their meanings with primary-grade children.

20. Robert Bellah, "The Ethics of Polarization in the United States and the World," in Batstone and Mendieta (eds.), *The Good Citizen*, pp. 16–17.

21. Bellah, "Ethics of Polarization," p. 22.

22. Robert B. Reich, *The Work of Nations* (New York: Knopf, 1991), pp. 174–179, 186.

23. Kathleen Staudt, *Free Trade? Informal Economies at the U.S.-Mexico Border* (Philadelphia: Temple University Press, 1998), chap. 3. According to the 1990 U.S. Census, a quarter of El Paso residents are "foreign born," and the 1990 Mexico census reports that half of all residents of Juarez were not born there. The one-fourth foreign-born ratio for El Paso is shared by major cities like Los Angeles and New York.

24. Neil Postman, *The End of Education: Redefining the Value of School* (New York: Vintage Books, 1995).

25. See World Bank, *Human Development Report: Knowledge for Development* (New York: Oxford University Press, 1998–99), pp. 117–118, for this emerging way to define poverty. The per capita income figure for China is from *Human Development Report, 1997*.

26. Benjamin Barber, "Public Schooling: Education for Democracy," in Goodlad and McMannon (eds.), *Public Purpose of Education and Schooling*, p. 28.

27. Amy Gutmann, *Democratic Education* (Princeton, N.J.: Princeton University Press, 1987), p. 284.

28. Harry C. Boyte and James Farr, "The Work of Citizenship and the Problem of Service-Learning," in Richard M. Battistoni and William E. Hudson (eds.), *Experiencing Citizenship: Concepts and Models for Service-Learning in Political Science* (Washington, D.C.: American Association for Higher Education, 1997), p. 37.

29. Richard Guarasci, "Community Based Learning and Intercultural Citizenship," in Richard Guarasci, Grant H. Cornwell, and Associates, *Democratic Education in an Age of Difference: Redefining Citizenship in Higher Education* (San Francisco: Jossey-Bass, 1997), pp. 21, 30. As of June 2000, according to the National Campus Compact web page, the number of campuses involved was about 650. See www.compact.org.

30. See selections on math in Diane Ravitch (ed.), *Brookings Papers on Education Policy 1998* (Washington, D.C.: Brookings Institution, 1998).

31. Francis Moore Lappé and Paul Martin DuBois, *The Quickening of America: Rebuilding Our Nation, Remaking Our Lives* (San Francisco: Jossey-Bass, 1994).

32. See, for example, Nel Noddings, *Caring: A Feminine Approach to Ethics and Moral Education* (Berkeley: University of California Press, 1984), and *The Challenge to Care in Schools: An Alternative Approach to Education* (New York: Teachers College Press, 1992).

33. West, "Moral Obligations of Living in a Democratic Society," p. 10.

34. Dennis Shirley, *Community Organizing for Urban School Reform* (Austin: University of Texas Press, 1997). Thanks to the El Paso Inter-religious Sponsoring Organization, I have had the opportunity to participate in and observe various events in the city and Texas state capitol since 1998.

35. See the critique of the discipline in Kathleen A. Staudt and William G. Weaver, *Political Science & Feminisms: Integration or Transformation?* (New York: Twayne, 1997). See also Harry Boyte, *Building America: The Democratic Promise of Public Work* (Philadelphia: Temple University Press, 1996).

36. Kathleen Staudt, *Policy, Politics & Gender: Women Gaining Ground* (West Hartford, Conn.: Kumarian Press, 1998), chap. 4. For per capita figures in the Americas and elsewhere, see the *Human Development Reports* or the World Bank's annual *World Development Report* (New York: Oxford University Press).

37. For example, see William Ayers and others, *Teaching for Social Justice: A Democracy and Education Reader* (New York: Teachers College Press, 1998); and North Central Regional Education Laboratory, *New Leaders for Tomorrow's Schools* 4 (Spring 1997): special issue, "Educating for Democracy," available at http://www.ncrel.org/cscd/pubs/lead41/41intro.htm.

38. See Henry Giroux, *Border Crossings: Cultural Workers and the Politics of Education* (London: Routledge, 1992), which draws on the late Paulo Freire's ideas on critical or engaged pedagogy. Traditional civic education, including drills for standardized tests, resembles the "banking education" that Freire criticizes in *Pedagogy of the Oppressed* (New York: Seabury, 1970), chap. 2.

39. Robert L. Heilbroner, "The Triumph of Capitalism," *New Yorker,* 23 January 1989, pp. 98–109.

4

MAKING DEMOCRACY REAL BY EDUCATING FOR AN ECOCENTRIC WORLDVIEW

Stephen John Goodlad

FOR MOST OF US, as we go about our daily business, life presents few opportunities to engage in anything resembling a democratic process. The experience of growing up is not a democratic one. A family is not a democratic institution. Classrooms are not democracies. The workplace is not democratic. The neighborhoods most of us live in are not democratic. The public airwaves, on which most of us rely for news, information, and a diversity of thought and opinion, are not supportive of or conducive to democracy.[1] They are privately owned and operated and tend to reflect the concerns and worldviews of their corporate owners and sponsors. They are certainly not governed democratically.

Our political system is dominated by two powerful political parties with little to differentiate one from the other. Both essentially represent the views of their wealthy benefactors. In fact, the American political spectrum itself, when compared to its counterparts in Europe, appears exceedingly narrow, far more so, it seems, than it was at the beginning of this century. And when, as a nation, we have intervened militarily in the affairs of other nations, we have not generally done so on behalf of democracy (despite political rhetoric to the contrary—rhetoric that is dutifully reported and rarely questioned by the media), but rather to protect corporate America's economic objectives.[2] Nor have our political or business leaders shown much interest in promoting human rights: virtually every leading recipient of U.S. foreign aid is a major human rights violator.[3]

Arguments that things are the way they are because that is the way most Americans want them to be do not hold up under scrutiny. Although our political system is dominated by two well-funded political parties, it is not because most Americans feel that these two parties adequately represent their interests and views. For example, a September 1994 survey conducted by the *Los Angeles Times* reveals that "Americans increasingly say they are willing to support a new party." Two years earlier a Gordon Black poll indicated that 54 percent of those surveyed wanted "a new national reform party." A 1988 election survey found that fully "two-thirds of the voters wanted candidates other than the Republican Bush or the Democrat Dukakis."[4] Such a percentage is remarkable when we realize that these two candidates were being heralded in the national press as front-runners.

None of this should come as a surprise given that most Americans apparently support policies that neither party is willing to put forward. Public opinion polls conducted in the late 1980s and early 1990s indicate, for example, that 61 percent of Americans want a socialized health care system (similar to the Canadian model). Eighty-four percent want a sur-tax on millionaires. In 1994, when both political parties were busy criti-cizing the welfare system, a December New York Times/CBS News poll revealed that 65 percent of Americans agreed that "it is the responsibility of the government to take care of people who can't take care of them-selves."[5] If we understand democracy to mean, as it does in the classical sense, rule by the people, then these findings should be reflected in our laws and public policies. They are not. In fact, a gap of alarming proportions exists between the way most of us grow up thinking and wanting to believe democracy works and the blunt reality of our existing political system. "A society like the United States," Robert McChesney explains, "which has rampant inequality, minimal popular involvement in decision making, and widespread depoliticization can never be regarded as democratic in an honest sense of the term."[6] Andrew Rowell arrives at a similar conclusion: "If democracy is meant to signify a representative government for all the people, in which everyone has an equal chance of being heard, of being able to influence their local politician, then democracy is dead, killed by the monoliths of the modern age—transnational corporations."[7]

Each student who enters a classroom brings with him or her a certain set of beliefs and assumptions, based on experience and observation, about how the world works and what his or her place is in it. The expe-rience of schooling either tends to affirm these beliefs and assumptions, or it tends to examine them in ways that may lead to their being altered. Often the worldviews that students hold conflict to some degree with those they encounter in school—as they should. After all, why would anyone send a child to school simply to have what that child already "knows" be affirmed?

If schools are to be given the responsibility of preparing students to participate effectively in a democratic society—or a society that aspires to be democratic—then these worldviews can pose significant problems. While teachers may espouse the virtues of democracy, the responsibilities of citizenship, and the cherished ideals that we would like to believe unite us as a people, their efforts are often and all too easily met with skepticism, indifference, even outright incredulity on the part of those students, who view democracy as a vague concept existing only between the covers of textbooks and having no relevance or application to the real world as it exists outside the classroom door. Such barriers are not easily overcome and make educating for democratic character and democratic citizenship all but impossible.

This is a problem quite like that often encountered by teachers who want to instill in students an ecologically sustainable worldview, only to discover that students are well aware that the consumption-driven society in which they live is responsible for a disproportionately large amount of the world's pollution, ecological destruction, and antienvironmental policy and rhetoric. Is it possible that those committed to educating for democracy might benefit from the lessons learned by those who have struggled with the problems of what might be termed ecological citizenship? The recent work of Mitchell Thomashow in the development of what he calls an "ecological identity" suggests that such a possibility does exist.[8]

Thomashow's approach has been to try to "show how an ecological worldview can be used to interpret personal experience, and how that interpretation leads to new ways of understanding personal identity." Thomashow calls this process "ecological identity work."[9] By exploring the concept of ecological identity, it is possible to begin to formulate a useful, practical approach to developing democratic character in the young; moreover, as the concept of ecological identity itself is more fully understood, it becomes doubtful that democratic character can genuinely exist independent of it.

Just as the development of ecological identity must, at present, take place in a political and economic context that can be viewed as essentially hostile toward those who have been labeled "environmentalists,"[10] so too are teachers being asked to develop democratic character in a context that is not particularly hospitable to substantive, participatory democracy.[11] Given our current economic and political structures, it will seem to some disingenuous, even absurd, to propose that students be educated to participate in a democracy that exists almost exclusively on a theoretical level. This is in part why I want to emphasize educating for democratic character:

doing so does not absolutely depend on the existence of a functioning democratic political system. However, implicit in such an undertaking is the hope that the development of democratic character in the young today will result in a far more democratic society—socially, politically, economically, and otherwise—tomorrow.

Power, Dominance, and Human Relationships

Most—possibly all—human beings seek to dominate one another and their surroundings to some degree. Whether this tendency is the result of deep-seated fears and insecurities or simply a by-product of particular cultural contexts seems uncertain.[12] What is certain is that over the long term, this tendency has proven to be enormously destructive in many cases (and usually depending on what technologies are available). This tendency toward domination has led us, time and again, to go to war. It has caused us to do great, even catastrophic damage to the environment. The psychological fallout it has generated has tended to alienate us as individuals from one another and, as a species, from other life forms, from our natural heritage, and so from the very essence of what it is to be human. The cultivation and nurturance of both an ecological identity and democratic character must struggle with this tendency toward domination. As part of that struggle, we must learn to confront issues of social, psychological, economic, and political power. It is in these realms that our tendency toward dominance most commonly and overtly manifests itself.

In exploring the relationships between psychological experience and political life, James M. Glass notes that "the feel of power, the reality of power for psychotic selves, suggests a firsthand knowledge of tyranny. In this sense, the raw, primitive, archaic quality of the schizophrenic experience demonstrates how power works." Glass goes on to explain that "what the schizophrenic self suffers is a microcosmic representation of the *political* form of power as tyranny and domination. Power is exercised on the self; it defines the world of knowledge and meaning in rigid terms of absolute good and evil. This power derives not from social or consensual bases but from narcissism and solipsism. It seeks omnipotence. It is destructive, parasitic, and violent."[13] Glass does see an alternative to "power as tyrannical domination," suggesting that it "could be eclipsed by a developing experience of power as cooperation, mutuality, exchange—what might be called a democratic exercise of power."[14]

In keeping with this example, it is the developing of this alternative experience of power that would be one critical task for a teacher engaged in educating students for democratic character or ecological citizenship, or both. In the case of ecological citizenship, the individual might experience power in a positive sense by recognizing her or his affiliation with and embeddedness in the great and vibrant web of all living things. We can contrast this experience with what can be seen as a negative (in this case, tyrannical) sense of power, such as that experienced by those who kill, maim, or torture other animals for the thrill of it or by those who otherwise destroy or exploit the nonhuman world in an effort to affirm some misguided sense of superiority, even omnipotence. In fact, it would not be all that fallacious to characterize Western civilization's recent treatment of the rest of the living world as destructive, parasitic, and violent.

We must be careful, however, that we do not oversimplify the complexities of our tendency toward dominance. Not all of the destructiveness such a tendency can generate is intended. Daniel Quinn offers some insight into this issue:

> People with good intentions often tell me we have an obligation to be "good stewards" of the earth. I must ask, who gave us this stewardship? Those who believe Genesis contains actual words spoken by God will say He gave us this stewardship when the earth was created. . . . But people who know that the earth got along just fine without man for three billion years have no such excuse for believing in our stewardship, which is . . . nothing but arrogance and vanity and anthropocentric tomfoolery. We have as much business being stewards of the world as infants have being stewards of the nursery. It is we who are dependent on the world, not the other way round.[15]

Issues of this sort are complex and often controversial. Just as ecological identity work nevertheless requires that students delve into such issues, so too does education for democratic character require a similar kind of engagement. *"Political identity work,"* as Thomashow explains,

> is a series of reflective approaches that enable people to reconceptualize the role of power and controversy in their lives: how issues of authority, conflict, and consensus are intrinsic to their sense of self and define their participation in a social system. Just as ecological identity work is intended to broaden and expand the circles of ecosystem identification, political identity work is intended to broaden one's perception of the circles of *relational power*, enabling people to see how power permeates all aspects of everyday life—not as an instrument of control, but as a means to expand choices; not as something external to a situation, but as intrinsic to an inclusive decision-making process.[16]

From this we gain some understanding of the ways in which "environmentalism and democracy are intrinsically linked." Just as "environmentalism informs [democratic] citizenship by placing an ecological perspective on notions of property, money, community, land, and power," so too does democratic citizenship inform "environmentalism by placing a mutual, participatory, and public orientation on human-nature relationships."[17] This prompts one to ask: Is it possible to develop democratic character without also developing ecological identity? In other words, is democratic character a concept that has application only to interactions among human beings, or does it have implications for how we interact with the millions of other species that share our world as well?

The answer may lie in how we choose to define ourselves. If we do this by creating a narrative that separates us from the rest of the living world, as—for the most part and up until quite recently—it seems most of us have, then we need not acknowledge any moral responsibilities toward other living beings. In effect, we make ourselves over into miniature gods and create a "natural order" atop which we conveniently place ourselves. We are then free to redefine the world as a warehouse of resources that we may plunder at our leisure, confident in the knowledge that, as gods, we are immortal and therefore immune from the consequences of such actions. We ought to bear in mind, however, that this narrative may have a downside, as Gregory Bateson explains:

> If you put God outside and set him vis-à-vis his creation and if you have the idea that you are created in his image, you will logically and naturally see yourself as outside and against the things around you. And as you arrogate all mind to yourself, you will see the world around you as mindless and therefore not entitled to moral or ethical consideration. The environment will seem to be yours to exploit. Your survival unit will be you and your folks or conspecifics against the environment of other social units, other races and the brutes and vegetables.
>
> If this is your estimate of your relation to nature *and you have an advanced technology,* your likelihood of survival will be that of a snowball in hell. You will die either of the toxic by-products of your own hate, or, simply, of overpopulation and overgrazing. The raw materials of the world are finite.[18]

Implicit in Bateson's warning is the recognition that most of us do not see ourselves as integral to, or even dependent on, what we call the natural world, which helps explain why it may have been necessary for certain humans to create the concept of nature in the first place.[19] Once the psychological groundwork has been laid, exploitation becomes an incremental, almost invisible series of steps from the near-benign to the catastrophic. As a result, many of us see nothing wrong with exploiting other animals, often simply for our own amusement (as in circuses, rodeos, and bullfights). Many of us think little about the moral implications of locking other animals up in zoos or aquariums or of using them experimentally for any number of reasons (sometimes, perhaps, legitimately). Without understanding the intellectual context created by our anthropocentric mind-set, it would seem highly implausible that a species as intellectually sophisticated as we humans like to think we are would wreak such ecological havoc.

It is not my intention to argue that no nonhuman animal should ever be harmed by humans. I am not prepared to advocate that we all become vegetarians (although I will admit that there are some compelling reasons for doing so). I am not suggesting that we abandon all scientific research that requires the involvement of nonhuman species. These are complicated issues that deserve widespread, informed public discussion, which they do not currently receive. And what better place to begin such a discussion than in our nation's classrooms? Given the severity of our ecological crisis, addressing such issues as part of a nationally agreed-on curriculum would seem well-nigh mandatory.

Such a curriculum might begin by asking some simple, straightforward questions—for example, How did we get ourselves into this predicament in the first place? That question alone would force students to examine and compare the histories of different civilizations, belief systems, economic systems, political systems, philosophies, languages, technologies, traditions, and so on. This curriculum would not only meaningfully integrate aspects of almost every academic discipline historically deemed important to the development of educated persons, but it would do so in a way that is both timely and relevant. Carolyn Merchant offers this overview:

> [Our] psychological adaptation to altered environments helps to explain the rise of intellectual movements, conceptual structures, and new human behaviors. As European cities grew and forested areas became more remote, as fens were drained and geometric patterns of channels imposed on the landscape, as large powerful waterwheels, furnaces, forges, cranes, and treadmills began increasingly to dominate the work environment, more and more people began to experience nature as altered and manipulated by machine technology. A slow but unidirectional alienation from the immediate daily organic relationship that had formed the basis of human experience from earliest times

was occurring. Accompanying these changes were alterations in both the theories and experiential bases of social organization which had formed an integral part of the organic cosmos.[20]

It is difficult to believe that teaching students how to surf the Net deserves to be a greater priority than, say, studying the narratives that humans have created to try to understand themselves and their place in the world better. Yet if the distribution of resources is any indication, there appear to be few school districts that would agree. This is troubling in that were we to move in the direction of adopting a narrative that places us in the world instead of apart from it, we might then be well on our way toward addressing issues of power and dominance at the most fundamental level. If we were to do so, it would be virtually impossible to avoid articulating a moral framework. And without a moral framework there can be no such thing as democratic character or, indeed, democracy. Lawrence Kohlberg's research helps us understand why this is the case:

> Our studies show that reasoning and decision making about political decisions are directly derivative of broader patterns of moral reasoning and decision making. We have interviewed high school and college students about concrete political situations involving laws to govern open housing, civil disobedience for peace in Vietnam, free press rights to publish what might disturb national order, and distribution of income through taxation. We find that reasoning on these political decisions can be classified according to moral stage and that an individual's stage on political dilemmas is at the same level as on nonpolitical moral dilemmas (euthanasia, violating authority to maintain trust in a family, stealing a drug to save one's dying wife). Turning from reasoning to action (public protest, civil disobedience), similar findings are obtained.[21]

Kohlberg concludes: "From a psychological side, then, political development is part of moral development."[22]

An exploration of human-nature relationships can help lay the groundwork for precisely this kind of moral development. In a meticulously detailed philosophical assessment of environmental ethics, Paul Taylor concludes that

> in addition to and independently of whatever moral obligations we might have toward our fellow humans, we also have duties that are owed to wild living things in their own right. . . . Our duties toward

the Earth's non-human forms of life are grounded on their status as entities possessing inherent worth. They have a kind of value that belongs to them by their very nature, and it is this value that makes it wrong to treat them as if they existed as mere means to human ends. It is for *their* sake that their good should be promoted or protected. Just as humans should be treated with respect, so should they.[23]

I do not expect readers to accept Taylor's conclusion without having read the argument that supports it. I cite his work because it makes the moral component of ecological identity work explicit. Just as Kohlberg has observed the connection between political development and moral development, Taylor articulates the moral aspect of developing ecological relationships and, for that matter, one's own ecological identity.

In his definition of ecological identity, Thomashow points out the crucial importance of relationships (connections) in the development of the individual self. Just as one cannot develop democratic character without having democratic relationships with diverse others—relationships that public schools make possible in ways that other institutions generally cannot—it can also be said that one cannot develop an ecological identity if one does not see oneself as being part of (and ultimately dependent on) an ecosystem. As Thomashow explains,

> Ecological identity refers to all the different ways people construe themselves in relationship to the earth as manifested in personality, values, actions, and sense of self. Nature becomes an object of identification. For the individual, this has extraordinary conceptual ramifications. The interpretation of life experience transcends social and cultural interactions. It also includes a person's connection to the earth, perception of the ecosystem, and direct experience of nature.[24]

This statement suggests that ecological identity work could help us develop a positive alternative to our existing moral framework and the pernicious human-nature dichotomy as it now exists. As testimony to the viability of using such an approach in our schools, we need only recognize that the concept of ecological identity is grounded in our own biological and psychological evolution. To be "ecological beings" should not seem alien to us, as it certainly was not alien to our ancestors. On the other hand, the extreme forms of domestication that can result from living in modern, industrialized societies *is* biologically and psychologically alien and alienating and can result in strange, irrational patterns of behavior and downright bizarre value systems.[25] To pick one example, there is nothing sensible about destroying local communities, their economies, and their ecological surrounds for the purpose of promoting foreign trade. Similarly, there is nothing sensible or "natural" about a political system engineered largely to benefit the already inflated pocketbooks of a wealthy few, often at a staggering cost to everyone else. Conversely, Robert Dahl has speculated that "some form of primitive democracy may well have been the most 'natural' political system" for human beings to adopt.[26] Whether it was more "natural" or not, it certainly was a lot more sensible and a lot more fair.

Conceptually, then, the development of pedagogical and curricular approaches aimed at the reintroduction of ecological identity—as well as democratic character—would not be an endeavor lacking precedence.[27] The same cannot be said of schooling designed to orient human beings to a life in cyberspace (which is really just a form of conditioning, aimed at preparing at least some people for the drudgery of a life's work spent sitting in front of a computer terminal).[28] To put the matter somewhat differently, we ought to learn to think of an ecocentric approach to education as one that draws on our own ancestral past in a way that creates a new, more positive conception of the self and the communities—from the immediate to the global—in which we live. If such an education sounds as if it might be a recipe for facilitating the development of democratic character as well, that is because it is.

Alternatives and Consequences

Education that has as its goal the cultivation of ecological citizenship, rooted in an ecocentric (as opposed to an anthropocentric) worldview, coupled with and giving rise to the development of democratic character, is but one path we might take on our journey into the twenty-first century. There is another path, quite plausible, that might be regarded as the path of least resistance, and it is one along which many of us appear to be headed. Setting aside moral and ethical considerations, given the state of world affairs today, it can also be argued that this alternative is the most rational—indeed, the only rational—way to go if we are determined to maintain the status quo for as long as possible. To understand this alternative and its implications, we need to consider in greater detail the predicament in which we find ourselves.

We are faced with a rapidly escalating environmental crisis. Perhaps there was a time not too long ago when we could plead uncertainty or ignorance of the severity of the crisis. This is no longer the case. In October 1993, for example, following a summit on world population held in

New Delhi, India, a joint statement was issued by fifty-eight scientific academies from around the world warning of "severe environmental stress," indicators that "include the growing loss of environmental diversity, increasing greenhouse gas emissions, increasing deforestation worldwide, stratospheric ozone depletion, acid rain, loss of topsoil, and shortages of water, food, and fuelwood in many parts of the world."[29] That same year, 1,700 of the world's leading scientists, including 104 Nobel laureates, signed the *World Scientists' Warning to Humanity*, which was then presented to the United Nations. The introduction read:

> Human beings and the natural world are on a collision course. Human activities inflict harsh and often irreversible damage on the environment and on critical resources. If not checked, many of our current practices put at serious risk the future that we wish for human society and the plant and animal kingdoms, and may so alter the living world that it will be unable to sustain life in the manner that we know. Fundamental changes are urgent if we are to avoid the collision our present course will bring about.[30]

Considerable data have been collected to demonstrate the epochal proportions of this crisis. The Worldwatch Institute is one organization that does such collecting. Each year it publishes *State of the World Report*. The 1998 edition offers the following summary:

> While economic indicators such as investment, production, and trade are consistently positive, the key environmental indicators are consistently negative. Forests are shrinking, water tables are falling, soils are eroding, wetlands are disappearing, fisheries are collapsing, rangelands are deteriorating, rivers are running dry, temperatures are rising, coral reefs are dying, and plant and animal species are disappearing. The global economy as now structured cannot continue to expand much longer if the ecosystem on which it depends continues to deteriorate at the current rate.[31]

Destruction of our planet's ecology is only one facet of the problem. Those who acknowledge only the physical, biological aspects of the crisis are focusing on symptoms and ignoring the disease. To learn something of the disease, we can again turn to the available evidence. "Of the world's hundred largest economies," Robert Kaplan points out, "fifty-one are not countries but corporations. While the 200 largest corporations employ less than three fourths of one percent of the world's work force, they

account for 28 percent of world economic activity. The 500 largest corporations account for 70 percent of world trade."[32] Paul Ehrlich and his
colleagues add, "In 1960 the ratio of the income of the richest 20 percent
of humanity to that of the poorest 20 percent was 30:1; according to the
United Nations *Human Development Report 1997,* it was nearly 80:1 in
1994. . . . [In fact] 40 percent of humankind accounts for a mere 6.5 percent of the world's income."[33] This is not just a matter of grotesque economic inequality; it is also an enormous inequality of power and influence,
in light of which it seems inconceivable that democracy, in any substantive form, could possibly exist anywhere. Such extreme economic inequalities have ecological ramifications as well. Ehrlich and his colleagues go
on to explain:

> Since 1950 the richest fifth of humankind has doubled its per capita
> consumption of energy, meat, timber, steel, and copper, and quadru-
> pled its car ownership, greatly increasing global emissions of CFCs
> [chlorofluorocarbons] and greenhouse gases, accelerating tropical
> deforestation, and intensifying other environmental impacts. The poor-
> est fifth has increased its per capita consumption hardly at all.[34]

Many of our business and political leaders tell us that somehow more
of the same—that is, more economic growth, an ever-increasing consumption of goods and services, the opening of more and more markets
abroad, and the spread of consumptionism—will solve the very problems
(political, social, and ecological) for which they are responsible in the first
place. We are asked to believe, in other words, that those who have been
responsible for ruining numerous local economies while devastating their
ecological surrounds are somehow suitable candidates to run an immense
global economy; that somehow bigger is the same as better and that
increasing scale is a way to solve complex problems.

From this emerges yet another myth: that economic growth works to
save the environment and promote greater equality. The facts, rarely
reported and largely ignored, suggest otherwise. Indeed, we find that as
the wealthiest nation on earth, our own economic growth has been largely
at the expense of a healthy global environment. "With only 4.5 percent
of the world's population," Ehrlich and his colleagues state, "the United
States uses about 25 percent of the earth's resources and contributes more
than 20 percent of global emissions of carbon dioxide—the atmospheric
pollutant that accounts for about half of global warming. In 1996 the
United States contributed one fifth more carbon to everybody's atmosphere than did China, which is 4.5 times as populous."[35]

This places the United States in a very uncomfortable position. A succinct and remarkably candid summation of this position was provided by George Kennan in 1948 when he was the head of the Policy Planning Staff of the State Department. As an architect and commentator on U.S. foreign policy for almost fifty years, Kennan stated:

> We [the United States] have almost 50% of the world's wealth but only 6.3% of its population. In this situation, we cannot fail to be the object of envy and resentment. Our real test in the coming period is to devise a pattern of relationships which will permit us to maintain this position of disparity. We need not deceive ourselves that we can afford today the luxury of altruism and world benefaction—unreal objectives such as human rights, the raising of living standards, and democratization.[36]

Kennan's words may have even greater relevance today than they did in 1948. If 4.5 percent of the people on earth now live in the United States and that 4.5 percent uses about 25 percent of the planet's available resources, what will happen, to pick just one example, as China, with over 20 percent of the world's population, moves toward achieving a standard of living on a par with that of the United States? For this to happen would mean that China and the United States alone would require well over 100 percent of the planet's resources. Even if the United States were to cut its consumption of resources in half (just for the sake of argument) and China's goals were adjusted proportionately, we are still faced with the prospect of two countries whose combined populations total less than 25 percent of all humanity determined to use well over 50 percent of the planet's resources, leaving hundreds of other countries, some of them with nuclear arsenals, to battle over whatever has not already been gobbled up by the big two.

All of this, of course, ignores the fact that those so-called resources are finite and fast dwindling. It does not take into account the fact that India's population is expected to exceed that of China within the next two to three decades. In fact, it ignores projected population increases altogether. It was not until 1800 C.E. that the population of *Homo sapiens* reached its first billion. It took another 130 years to reach its second billion (in about 1930). The third billion arrived 30 years later (1960). The fourth billion took only another 15 years and arrived in 1975; the fifth arrived in 1987; and the sixth in the 1990s. Assuming that current trends (which suggest a gradual leveling off) continue, the most optimistic projections indicate that the human population might stabilize in about 2100 at roughly 10 billion (though it could easily be 15 billion). Our planet cannot support such numbers, as Peter Ward points out. To reach the level of organic productivity such a human population would require would mean that

> virtually the entire arable surface of the earth—every forest, every valley, every bit of land surface capable of sustaining plant life, as well as much of the plankton of the sea—will have to be turned over to crops if our species is to avert unprecedented global famine. In such a world, animals and plants not directly necessary for our existence will probably be a luxury not affordable. Those creatures that can survive in the vast fields and orchards will survive. Those that need virgin forest, or undisturbed habitat of any sort, will not.[37]

In short, even the most optimistic forecasts look pretty bleak. To "maintain" such a "position of disparity," as Kennan suggests we should, will require that the United States not only continue but escalate its economic and political dominance of other nations wherever and whenever possible, and increasingly at the expense of such "unreal objectives" as "human rights, the raising of living standards, and democratization."

Eventually we will need to adopt some form of totalitarian rule of a kind that will not only ensure our control of the planet's remaining resources but also somehow insulate us from the suffering of others. Those others in turn will, understandably, do whatever they can to destroy us (thus necessitating ever greater "security measures" while sacrificing ever more personal freedoms in a sort of debilitating, downward spiral).

There are no guarantees that by adopting such a course of action the United States would emerge victorious—whatever victory might look like given such a scenario. In this age of nuclear, chemical, and biological weapons—again setting aside for the moment whatever moral and ethical scruples we may have—it seems highly improbable that any nation could get away with such heavy-handed tactics for long. History teaches us that all such attempts have so far met with cataclysmic disaster. But perhaps we will prove to be the exception.

Our victory would come at a steep price. Among the sacrifices we would be called on to make would be those moral and ethical standards our ancestors have cherished and struggled to uphold for generation upon generation. Chief among such standards are those that have collectively come to be called human rights. As globalization gains momentum, trends become increasingly clear. The rights of people who live in places like the remote areas of Papua New Guinea, for example, are being routinely violated for the sake of national profits as multinational timber and mineral companies "develop" such areas. There are no local negotiations, and no compensation is paid when coastal fishing villages on Lake Malawi are bulldozed to make way for tourist resorts. When business interests convert the Honduran mangroves into shrimp farms, an area that local communities once relied on for sustenance is converted into a rich maricultural export sector, with profits going into the pockets of an emerging global elite that contributes little or nothing to local economies. As a matter of course, the rights of native peoples in the Siberian tundra are conveniently disregarded as transnational ventures and bilateral agreements are cobbled together to construct the roads, railways, and other infrastructure needed for the extraction and transport of oil, gas, minerals, and timber. Similarly, the plight of the people of Tibet has received some attention since their native lands were invaded by the Han Chinese "in the name of national economic development" and largely, it seems, for the sake of mineral extraction.[38] These trends are not newly emergent. As Walter LaFeber points out, "No area in the world is more tightly integrated into the United States political-economic system . . . than Central America," yet Honduras, "the closest ally of the United States in the region," remains "the poorest and most undeveloped state in the hemisphere other than Haiti." For purposes of comparison, "the economically most powerful nation in Central America" is Guatemala, where "half the population average only $81 income each year."[39]

The immense scale on which such human rights violations, economic oppression, and ecological devastation occur makes them extremely difficult to comprehend. That they are routinely ignored by much of the mainstream news media infuses them with a quality of the surreal when they do surface. They are seen as aberrations instead of commonplace recurrences. To try to put a human face on these issues, we might consider the fate of Ruiz Aranda and his hometown, Rincón-i-Ybycuí, a rural community of approximately three thousand people some seventy-five miles from the Paraguayan capital of Asunción. In November 1998, the Delta and Pine Land Company dumped 660 tons of expired cottonseed over a four-acre area on private land in the center of Rincón-i-Ybycuí. The cottonseed was then covered by a thin layer of soil. Health problems began to surface almost immediately; vertigo, nausea, headaches, neurological disorders, memory loss, insomnia, and skin rashes were among the symptoms treated. These problems were especially alarming given that the dumpsite was located only two hundred yards from an elementary school. The reason for the outbreak appears to have been that the cottonseed had been treated with high concentrations of toxic pesticides, including the organophosphates acephate and chlorpyrifos. Soon the poisons claimed their first victim, Ruiz Aranda. Ironically, Aranda had been active in the

Commission for the Defense of the Environment and Human Rights initially formed by the local community to call attention to the problem and demand government action. His death certificate declares that at the time of death he was being treated for "acute poisoning due to pollution caused by toxins of the Delta & Pine Land seed deposit on the property of Julio Chávez." Ruiz Aranda was thirty years old and the father of five.[40] (The Delta and Pine Land Company, incidentally, jointly holds the patent rights and exclusively the licensing rights to the notorious "Terminator" technology.) The company was purchased for $1.76 billion on May 11, 1998, by the agrochemical, seed, and biotechnology giant Monsanto, the company responsible for Agent Orange, PCBs, and bovine growth hormone. Monsanto also manufactures the world's biggest-selling herbicide, Roundup.[41]

Such evidence—and there is a great deal more—suggests that not only will we find ourselves faced with the proposition of having to sacrifice many, even all, of our most sacrosanct moral and ethical standards, but we may, in effect, also be called on to abandon what we have generally come to regard as our humanity: our ability to empathize with and care about others, show compassion, value and respect difference, and work together collectively to make the world a healthier, more peaceful place for all to live.

Making Democracy Real

Most Americans do not want to abandon their humanity or make the kinds of moral and ethical sacrifices this alternative requires. The preferences that the majority of Americans express are plainly on the side of humane treatment for all human beings and the preservation of a healthy, ecologically robust planet. In a democracy—or in a society that seeks to become a democracy—it seems reasonable to expect the educational system to reflect its citizens' highest ideals and aspirations. I cannot imagine how it would be possible to achieve or to sustain democracy otherwise.

To be sure, schools alone cannot change society. But schools can and must play a role in preparing citizens to do so wisely and compassionately. While this might persuade some that simply educating youngsters in the mechanics of democracy and the basic responsibilities of democratic citizenship is enough to fulfill the requirements of a democratic society, such a conclusion is erroneous in light of our predicament and given the more complete definition of democratic character that emerges as a result of that predicament. In other words, it is not enough to equip young people with only the means to participate in a democratic society. Hitler and Mussolini both came to power by democratic means without democratic ends. Democratic citizenship without democratic character cannot meet the requirements of a healthy democracy. Once this is understood, the purpose of education in a democratic society becomes clear: to prepare an informed, thoughtful, and creative citizenry for active and critical participation in a democracy, while simultaneously creating and sustaining a caring and just social environment, and ensuring that the very best educational offerings are available fully and equally to all members of that society.

Unfortunately, if the accounts provided by the popular media are any indication, there appears to exist a great deal of uncertainty about what ought to be the purpose of American education. Politicians, business leaders, and often educators themselves seem reluctant to admit that most young people can learn to read and write from others at home or in their community; that they can and (rest assured) will learn to use computers and all sorts of other technologies at home, on the job, and on their own;[42] that employers are in a much better position to train their workers than schools are or ever will be;[43] that when all is said and done, there are actually very few things that schools do, or can do, that are of critical importance—until, that is, we begin to think in terms of how we, as individuals and as citizens, will acquire and develop the kinds of skills and habits of mind necessary for us to participate responsibly in a democratic society. It seems clear that that kind of education can be made available, in a society such as ours, only through a system of public education committed to meeting such needs. Democracy is, after all, by definition a public—not a private—endeavor.

For democracy to become a meaningful, integral part of our daily lives, we must begin to think differently about what it means. Donna Kerr has given this subject considerable thought. As she points out, "A person can fact-find, vote, and obey the law, yet still live a life constituted not by democratic relationships, but rather by those of domination and subservience."[44] To move beyond a shallow, superficial conception of democracy—to make democracy a way of life as well as a political and economic reality—will require that our public schools embrace, first and foremost, the mission of educating for democratic character. The environmental crisis, and the occasion it presents for all of us to begin to develop a moral framework based on an ecocentric worldview, offers an unprecedented opportunity to advance humankind's most noble and cherished ideals.

Some Implications for Change

The preceding discussion has many implications for educational practice. I want to highlight several. One of the foremost is well summarized by David Orr:

> In democratic societies, wise public choices about environmental issues
> depend largely on the extent and breadth of public knowledge of ecol-
> ogy and concepts such as thermodynamics and energetics and their
> interrelationships with economic prosperity, unemployment, war and
> peace, and public health. If large numbers of people do not understand
> the environmental facts of energy, resources, land, water, and wildlife,
> there is little hope for building sustainability at any level.[45]

Clearly, teachers are going to need to be better prepared and better educated than ever before. Since the philosophical bases for both democracy
and the preservation of the natural world are rooted in ethics, the study
of ethics ought to be at the core of every curriculum at every age level.
Similarly, given that we cannot address the problems we face today if we
do not understand why they are problems and what caused them, a core
curriculum that encompasses anthropology, biology, ecology, history, economics, political science, and sociology (a list that is surely incomplete)
would seem essential for all students regardless of their chosen area of
specialization. Currently, our educational system (higher education, most
notably) is geared toward producing an elite class of specialists. We find
among such graduates, for example, engineers and technicians with little
or no understanding of the ethical implications of their work or what
might determine legitimate and illegitimate applications of their expertise,
save for the corporate bottom line. What we ought to be doing instead is
producing the twentieth-century equivalents of the Renaissance man (and
woman): people who are broadly and deeply educated, not simply technically proficient. Do this, and specialization will take care of itself.

Another implication to emerge is the need to reconstitute individual disciplines given this context of democracy and environment. Borrowing
from David Orr's work, for example, anthropology might stimulate a student's thinking about alternative models of sustainability. History might
focus on the consequences of resource mismanagement; on the social,
political, and economic consequences of technological change; and on the
ongoing struggle for freedom and dignity. Political science might help students understand politics as resource distribution; the need for and the
relationships between freedom and authority; the effects of centralization
and decentralization and what might be desirable when, where, and why.
Economics might present an opportunity to explore the strengths and
weaknesses of systems such as capitalism, socialism, and communism; it
could help students to think about more equitable and sustainable economic
arrangements (such as alternative pricing systems that more accurately
reflect the real-world costs of such activities as driving automobiles and eat-

ing hamburgers). Agriculture might shift its focus toward the reintroduction of natural (as opposed to genetically engineered) diversity in food crops, the elimination of nonorganic substances from our soil and food supply, and the decentralization and diversification of farming itself.

This is not a vision of education that many of our political and business leaders share. If schools are to make headway toward educating for democracy and ecological sustainability, they will need strong, broad public support, not corporate or partisan political sponsorship. This suggests that school-university partnerships, and coalitions of these partnerships, will be needed, both to bring about and maintain the process of change and to evaluate and, as need be, stand up to the political, economic, and ideological assaults brought to bear by groups whose agendas may not be in keeping with the needs of a democratic society or long-term environmental sustainability. The legitimacy of this proposition is evident if we keep in mind that democracy, like clean water and fresh air, serves everyone's best interests, not those of a special few.

The need for accountability, at least in matters educational, continues to receive a good deal of lip service, as it should. This suggests (among other things) that educators, regardless of their area of specialization, ought to be able to state clearly where their field of knowledge fits into the broader landscape of learning; why their particular expertise is important; for what and for whom it is important; what the ecological ramifications of their work are; how their work affects the long-term human prospect; the contribution their work makes to a democratic, ecologically sustainable society; and what the social, ethical, and political implications of their work are or are likely to be.[46] Such questions should become a routine part of the academic performance review process (an idea that could prove useful in the political arena as well).

All of these proposals will require that limited funds be cautiously and wisely spent. Before we contemplate using our schools as conduits to funnel money into the coffers of computer manufacturers and software companies,[47] we should first attend to the real and fundamental needs of teachers, students, and staffs. Among those, we ought to be certain that class sizes have been reduced to levels commensurate with our best understandings of what those levels ought to be if we are to maximize the effectiveness of the educational process. We ought to be certain that classrooms and school grounds are clean, safe, and well cared for. Efforts ought to be made to see to it that a significant proportion of a young person's educational experience takes place in the outdoors, not in the classroom or the computer lab. After all, we cannot care about or develop an affinity for something that we do not experience and know little or nothing about.

We need to be sure that instead of peddling junk food in exchange for football uniforms, our schools are providing nutritious food at a price that students, faculty, and staff can afford (which means it will have to be free in some cases). Finally, we need to make a determined effort to meet the emotional and psychological needs of students, faculty, and staff. The reason is simple: if these needs (and nutrition counts high among them) are not met, then the mission of schooling itself ceases to be viable.

There is a need as well to ensure that school libraries are, without exception, well stocked with a wealth of the world's great books (and, hence, great ideas). The Internet is not a reasonable or reliable substitute for credible ideas supported by substantive arguments—ideas of the kind that require the space and accessibility that only books can provide. One does not sit down at a computer terminal to read James Joyce's *Ulysses* or John Stuart Mill's "On Liberty" or Aldo Leopold's *A Sand County Almanac*. Information is not a substitute for knowledge or wisdom or patient, reflective thought, nor has a lack of information ever been a problem in our nation's schools.

It is testimony to how far we have yet to go in realizing our social, political, and ecological goals that many of these ideas will seem far-fetched, even absurd, to most readers. And as long as the majority of us, or at least those in positions of power, regard them as such, they will certainly remain so. It is this rigidity of mind, this narrowness of thought, and our perhaps innate tendency to focus undue attention on the trite, trivial, and inconsequential that may prove our greatest obstacle to meaningful educational and cultural change. As Francis Parker observed over a hundred years ago, "By far the greatest barrier to making the common school what it should and can be, by no means springs from active opposition to the system or from the patronage and pulls of pot-house politicians: *the greatest barrier is the profound indifference of the most intelligent people in regard to the possibilities of radical improvement.*"[48] To overcome this perhaps greatest of barriers, each of us must look first to ourselves.

NOTES

1. Robert W. McChesney, *Rich Media, Poor Democracy: Communication Politics in Dubious Times* (Urbana: University of Illinois Press, 1999); Edward S. Herman and Noam Chomsky, *Manufacturing Consent: The Political Economy of the Mass Media* (New York: Pantheon Books, 1988); Martin A. Lee and Norman Solomon, *Unreliable Sources: A Guide to Detecting Bias in News Media* (New York: Carol, 1991); Michael Parenti, *Dirty Truths: Reflections on Politics, Media, Ideology, Conspiracy, Ethnic Life and Class Power* (San Francisco: City Lights Books, 1996); Herbert I.

Schiller, *Culture, Inc.: The Corporate Takeover of American Expression* (New York: Oxford University Press, 1989); Cass R. Sunstein, *Democracy and the Problem of Free Speech* (New York: Free Press, 1993).

2. Walter LaFeber, *Inevitable Revolutions: The United States in Central America*, 2d ed. (New York: Norton, 1993); Noam Chomsky, *Deterring Democracy* (New York: Hill and Wang, 1991). As Noam Chomsky points out, corporate America's economic objectives are often euphemistically referred to as the "national interest," although the real interest of these groups "correlates only weakly with interests of the general population." See Noam Chomsky, *Profit over People: Neoliberalism and Global Order* (New York: Seven Stories Press, 1999), p. 96.

3. Noam Chomsky, in an interview by David Barsamian, *Progressive* 63 (September 1999): 34.

4. Howard Zinn, *A People's History of the United States: 1492–Present*, rev. ed. (New York: HarperPerennial, 1995), p. 634.

5. Zinn, *People's History*, p. 634.

6. McChesney, *Rich Media, Poor Democracy*, p. 5.

7. Andrew Rowell, *Green Backlash: Global Subversion of the Environmental Movement* (New York: Routledge, 1996), p. 69.

8. Mitchell Thomashow, *Ecological Identity: Becoming a Reflective Environmentalist* (Cambridge, Mass.: MIT Press, 1995).

9. Thomashow, *Ecological Identity*, p. 2.

10. Neil Evernden has pointed out that *environmentalist* is itself a pejorative term. As he explains, the "term 'environmentalist' was not chosen by the individuals so described. It was seized upon by members of the popular press as a means of labeling a newly prominent segment of society. But, of course, any term selected by the news media is likely to be drawn from common usage and to reflect common assumptions. It is difficult to imagine, therefore, that this agent would have great success in concisely describing something distinctly uncommon. In fact, the act of labeling a group may constitute an effective means of suppression, even if the label seems neutral or objective. For in giving this particular name, not only have the labelers forced an artificial association on a very diverse group of individuals, but they have also given a terse public statement of what 'those people' are presumed to want." From *The Natural Alien: Humankind and Environment* (Toronto: University of Toronto Press, 1993), p. 125.

11. On the problems faced by the environmental movement, see Rowell, *Green Backlash*; David Helvarg, *The War Against the Greens* (San Francisco:

Sierra Club Books, 1994); Christopher Manes, *Green Rage: Radical Environmentalism and the Unmaking of Civilization* (Boston: Little, Brown, 1990); on problems facing democracy, see William Greider, *Who Will Tell the People: The Betrayal of American Democracy* (New York: Simon & Schuster, 1992); Noam Chomsky, *Necessary Illusions: Thought Control in Democratic Societies* (Boston: South End Press, 1989); Christopher Lasch, *The Revolt of the Elites and the Betrayal of Democracy* (New York: Norton, 1995).

12. There is some evidence to suggest that the tendency toward at least social dominance is culturally based. In his study of human destructiveness, Erich Fromm introduces evidence to suggest, for example, that "social relations among the members of hunting-gathering society are characterized by the absence of what is called 'dominance' among [other] animals." See *The Anatomy of Human Destructiveness* (New York: Holt, 1973), p. 165.

13. James M. Glass, *Psychosis and Power: Threats to Democracy in the Self and the Group* (Ithaca, N.Y.: Cornell University Press, 1995), p. 5.

14. Glass, *Psychosis and Power,* p. 6.

15. Daniel Quinn, *Providence: The Story of a Fifty-Year Vision Quest* (New York: Bantam Books, 1994), pp. 143–144.

16. Thomashow, *Ecological Identity,* p. 105.

17. Thomashow, *Ecological Identity,* p. 94.

18. Gregory Bateson, *Steps to an Ecology of Mind* (New York: Ballantine, 1972), p. 462.

19. For more on how humans came to create "nature" and the implications of that creation, see Neil Evernden, *The Social Creation of Nature* (Baltimore, Md.: Johns Hopkins University Press, 1992).

20. Carolyn Merchant, *The Death of Nature: Women, Ecology, and the Scientific Revolution* (San Francisco: Harper & Row, 1980), p. 68.

21. Lawrence Kohlberg, "Moral Reasoning," in Walter C. Parker (ed.), *Educating the Democratic Mind* (Albany: State University of New York Press, 1996), p. 211.

22. Kohlberg, "Moral Reasoning," p. 212.

23. Paul Taylor, *Respect for Nature: A Theory of Environmental Ethics* (Princeton, N.J.: Princeton University Press, 1986), p. 13.

24. Thomashow, *Ecological Identity,* p. 3.

25. John A. Livingston, *Rogue Primate: An Exploration of Human Domestication* (Boulder, Colo.: Roberts Rinehart, 1994); Paul Shepard, *Nature and Madness* (Athens: University of Georgia Press, 1982).

26. Robert A. Dahl, *On Democracy* (New Haven, Conn.: Yale University Press, 1998), pp. 9–10.

27. On the history of Western civilization's relationship to nature, see Merchant, *The Death of Nature;* on the evolution in the West of ecological thinking and the history of what has become the modern environmental movement, see Donald Worster, *Nature's Economy: A History of Ecological Ideas,* 2nd ed. (Cambridge: Cambridge University Press, 1994).

28. For a detailed, well-documented discussion of the origins of our current scholastic obsession with all things technological, see Douglas D. Noble's *The Classroom Arsenal: Military Research, Information Technology and Public Education* (Bristol, Pa.: Falmer Press, 1991).

29. Reprinted in Paul R. Ehrlich and Anne H. Ehrlich, *The Betrayal of Science and Reason: How Anti-Environmental Rhetoric Threatens Our Future* (Washington, D.C.: Island Press, 1996), p. 236.

30. Ehrlich and Ehrlich, *Betrayal of Science,* p. 242.

31. Worldwatch Institute, *State of the World 1998: A Worldwatch Institute Report on Progress Toward a Sustainable Society* (New York: Norton, 1998), p. 4.

32. Robert D. Kaplan, "Was Democracy Just a Moment?" *Atlantic Monthly* 280 (December 1997): 71.

33. Paul R. Ehrlich, Gretchen C. Daily, Scott C. Daily, Norman Myers, and James Salzman, "No Middle Way on the Environment," *Atlantic Monthly* 280 (December 1997): 104.

34. Ehrlich and others, "No Middle Way," p. 104.

35. Ehrlich and others, "No Middle Way," p. 104.

36. George Kennan in a memorandum quoted in Sheila D. Collins, "From the Bottom Up and the Outside In," *CALC Report* 15 (March 1990): 9–10.

37. Peter Ward as quoted in Christopher Stringer and Robin McKie's *African Exodus: The Origins of Modern Humanity* (New York: Holt, 1996), p. 241.

38. Barbara Rose Johnston, "The Abuse of Human Environmental Rights: Experience and Response," in Barbara Rose Johnston (ed.), *Who Pays the Price? The Sociocultural Context of Environmental Crisis* (Washington, D.C.: Island Press, 1994), p. 221.

39. LaFeber, *Inevitable Revolutions,* pp. 5–9.

40. "Harvest of Shame," *Earth Island Journal* 14 (Fall 1999): 6.

41. "Terminator" technology is essentially a kind of genetically engineered suicide. It causes a next generation of plant seeds to self-destruct, thus requiring

that farmers purchase new seeds each season rather than using the seeds that would have been produced by their existing crops, as farmers have traditionally done. The entire issue of the *Ecologist* 28 (September–October 1998) focuses on Monsanto and the objectives and likely consequences of genetic engineering.

42. Joseph Weizenbaum, a professor emeritus of computer science at no less technologically prestigious an institution than MIT, states that MIT's new students can acquire all the computer skills they need "in a summer." See Todd Oppenheimer, "The Computer Delusion," *Atlantic Monthly* 280 (July 1997): 54.

43. Patrick MacLeamy, an executive vice president of Hellmuth Obata & Kassabaum, the largest architectural firm in the United States and one that is firmly committed to the use of computer technologies, has said that he finds the company's two-week computer training course to be adequate and that computer skills do not even enter his list of priorities in the hiring process. See Oppenheimer, "The Computer Delusion," pp. 54–55.

44. Donna H. Kerr, "Toward a Democratic Rhetoric of Schooling" in John I. Goodlad and Timothy J. McMannon (eds.), *The Public Purpose of Education and Schooling* (San Francisco: Jossey-Bass, 1997), pp. 75–76.

45. David W. Orr, *Ecological Literacy: Education and the Transition to a Postmodern World* (New York: State University of New York Press, 1992), p. 137.

46. These questions are based on a similar set of questions suggested by David Orr in *Earth in Mind: On Education, Environment, and the Human Prospect* (Washington, D.C.: Island Press, 1994), p. 102.

47. Given that this year's purchases will be obsolete next year, or soon after, this is a highly dubious proposition anyway.

48. Francis W. Parker, *Talks on Pedagogies: An Outline of the Theory of Concentration* (New York: A. S. Barnes & Company, 1894), p. 441.

5

DEMOCRACY
AND SUSTAINABLE
ECONOMIC ACTIVITY

Paul Theobald, Clif Tanabe

AS PARENTS AND TEACHER EDUCATORS, we both have spent many hours in public schools over the past several years, enough time to notice an unmistakable trend that we call the "rain forest phenomenon." Elementary, and sometimes middle school, teachers have received careful instruction on how to create a miniature rain forest in the classroom. Using large sheets of plastic, lighting techniques, water, and other props, teachers can, in a low-cost way, facilitate an active, hands-on learning unit that students from Maine to California, Alaska to Florida, seem to enjoy immensely.

The lesson is popular for many reasons, and among them, of course, is the current concern over clear-cutting going on in several developing countries, most notably Brazil. There are many good things to say about the rain forest learning unit, not the least of which is that it provides an opportunity to heighten environmental awareness among the young. Students also learn something about tropical flora and fauna. And they generally come away from the unit convinced that clear-cutting should cease. Some students even complete the lesson with deeper understandings and see the rain forest as an example of the tension between economic activity and environmental well-being.

The rain forest phenomenon, however, popular as it is, may present some difficulties for educators who seriously reflect on curricular issues. First is the question of why teachers will go to great lengths to create an artificial environment that has seemingly little connection to the day-to-day lives of most children in the United States. These students come to learn about tropical species when most cannot name more than one or two plants and animals native to the place in which they actually live. There is an intellectual discontinuity here that thoughtful educators readily acknowledge.

A second concern is that the unit tends to teach children that environmental degradation or, for the more sophisticated students, the tension between economic activity and environmental well-being is a concern that troubles people elsewhere in the world. Through perhaps an inadvertent omission, the popular rain forest units used in the nation's public schools teach children that *our* economic activity is unrelated to the fate of the rain forests in, say, Brazil. Nothing could be further from the truth. When developing countries get behind in debt repayment to United States–based world creditors such as the International Monetary Fund, "structural adjustment packages" are negotiated, forcing the debtor nations to orchestrate massive resource depletion operations, such as clear-cutting rain forests.[1]

Third, as these units unfold, children rarely ask questions for which we have no readily available answer. For instance, although we know that fully one-half of all the plant and animal species on earth today exists within the confines of the remaining Third World rain forests, we do not know what will happen to life on the planet once the rain forests are cleared and the high levels of biodiversity are gone. There is good reason for concern, however, for the elimination of biodiversity could easily wreak havoc close to home. A good example of the danger is our incredible dependence on corn. Paul Gruchow has nicely summarized the situation:

> A person born in our time will as an infant be clothed in a diaper made in part of corn and fed a formula based upon corn syrup. That person will grow into adult life sustained in thousands of ways by products made from, packaged in, or manufactured with derivatives of corn, from every kind of food except fresh fish to plastics, textiles, building materials, machine parts, soaps and cosmetics, even highways. And when that person dies, some laws require that the body should be embalmed—in a fluid made in part from corn.[2]

Our fetish for standardizing and maximizing corn production has left us in a precarious position. Because all of the corn we cultivate shares a common cytoplasm, we are only one persistent pathogen away from what could only be described as complete cultural devastation. This circumstance and many others, like the never-ending accumulation of carbon dioxide in our atmosphere, the slow but steadily increasing presence of atmospheric chlorofluorocarbons (CFCs), and the persistence of acid rain in different regions of the globe, leave many of the earth's residents with fairly deep-seated anxieties about the future.

A fourth concern is the extent to which the rain forest unit raises or fails to raise student understanding and appreciation for democratic arrangements. If preparing students to become citizens in a democracy remains a primary purpose of public education, what leverage over the concept do students acquire as a result of engaging the rain forest unit? This is an important question, for as environmental circumstances erode, our ability to meet the basic needs of citizens also erodes. This circumstance can only result in increasingly high levels of anxiety, and historically, anxiety has not been conducive to democratic arrangements. A quick example is our willingness to suspend during periods of war certain rights and privileges normally accorded citizens. The concept of democracy suffers too during periods of economic depression, as examples in California of the 1930s demonstrate. It was periods of extreme volatility that ushered in the careers of individuals such as Napoleon, Hitler, and Stalin.

In addition, to the extent that the tension between economic activity and environmental well-being represents a fundamental conflict of values, students ought to learn something about democracy from the rain forest unit. More specifically, they ought to learn something about deliberative democracy. The idea of deliberative democracy suggests a form of political arrangement that is specifically designed to encourage open, genuine, and rational debate about conflicting values.

The rain forest phenomenon is an active, hands-on unit clearly superior to passive, text-driven pedagogy. If the goal is making curricular decisions that will squarely address education's public purpose, however, teachers may wish to think through the creation of units grounded in the circumstances that surround students on a day-to-day basis, for reasons we will explore here. At this point, however, we explore some of the larger questions brought into relief by the rain forest unit and then return to the classroom at the chapter's conclusion.

A Perennial Dilemma

Stephen Goodlad argues in Chapter Four of this book that an ecological identity is a crucial component of democratic character. It is worth exploring just what he means by this. At its most basic, democracy means shared governance or shared decision making. In other words, if a decision will affect the lives of more than one individual, as most decisions do, that decision should be made by all of those affected, or by as many as possible. Since the health and well-being of a particular place on earth are shared by those who live there, decisions that affect the local environment are the prerogative of those who share the place. The fundamental truth at work here is that the earth is shared. Its health, its beauty, its vitality, its ability to sustain human, plant, and animal life are shared burdens. Given the "sharedness" of the environment, recognition of oneself as a contributor to its health (or ill health)—that is, recognition of an ecological identity—is a crucial component of democratic character.

The relationship between economic activity and environmental well-being is and always has been a central question surrounding the human condition. It is a question that is answered differently depending on the quality and extent of democratic arrangements in a given society. At various times and at various places around the world, vast deserts have been created by the widespread practice of unsustainable economic activity. At other times and in other places, human groups have exhibited remarkable ability to increase economic production while simultaneously improving the health of the local environment.[3] In short, we know that humanity can create sustainable circumstances, and we know that the opposite potential exists as well. Two questions, it seems to us, therefore emerge as pertinent:

1. Because for the first time in human history we have begun to see the orchestration of global affairs as a single economic unit, does this increase the likelihood that our economic activity will be of the sustainable or the unsustainable sort?

The best answer to this question that one could hope for, and this requires turning one's attention away from some dramatic counterexamples (such as the *Exxon Valdez,* Chernobyl, and Bhopal), is that currently regnant transnational corporations will turn to sustainable practices out of their own long-term self-interest. Compelling arguments have been made that suggest, however, that such movement is unlikely given the structures, metaphors, and mechanisms that govern transnational corporate operations. Holding back these arguments, however, one is still prompted to ask a second question:

2. Regardless of the answer to question 1, what might be done to increase the odds that economic activity in the future will be of the sustainable sort?

Reflections on Question 1

Scholarship predicting the decline of the nation-state has been around for quite some time, but only relatively recent developments, such as the General Agreement on Tariffs and Trade (GATT) and the North American Free Trade Agreement (NAFTA), have allowed us a glimpse of how such a world might look. Corporations can now move in and out of countries at will, unencumbered by the regulations and tariffs that historically have been used to protect native industry. In fact, native industry scarcely exists. By the current rules of the game, if General Electric builds a plant in Uruguay, General Electric becomes a Uruguayan corporation. What has happened as a result of these recent developments is that the power to make decisions about economic activity has shifted away from governments and the people who elected them, to the boardrooms and councils of the major transnational corporations.[4] Again, the question is, Does this increase or decrease the odds for a sustainable future? Framed another way, the question becomes, Do the best chances for a desirable future come with an ostensibly well-informed (perhaps even expert) but unelected and essentially unaccountable corporate global elite—or with ostensibly less well-informed but democratically determined and accountable decision makers?

Although culturally we seem to praise the idea of democracy, we have at the same time exhibited very little resistance to policy recommended by unelected experts. Throughout the century, scholars have argued that the best sort of citizen habitually defers to experts. One might count the likes of Charles Eliot, Walter Lippmann, and Joseph Schumpeter in this camp. And their arguments were persuasive. There is no natural law that says the desire of the majority of the people will yield the best set of circumstances. As an example, the majority of American citizens at one time were in favor of or indifferent to chattel slavery.

There is, however, some history that we might examine in the interest of obtaining more leverage over this question. This history allows us to identify some trends that seem to undergird the decisions of the transnational corporate elite and the decisions of "we the people" through democratic mechanisms. We begin with a look at transnational corporate propensities.

The first unmistakable proclivity governing the behavior of corporations is the pursuit of profit. Countless examples indicate that the profit motive almost always takes precedence over employee or community well-being. A quick drive on the south side of the Rio Grande quickly demonstrates this principle. The readily identifiable corporate logos proclaim the loss of jobs and community well-being in different locales across the United States. Corporations stand ready to diversify production efforts or to eliminate competition by acquiring other corporations. The economic reckoning is surprisingly simplistic: what is the ratio of income to expenses? The size of the profit margin determines whether a thing will happen.

Related to the constant drive for profits is the imperative that says that corporations must grow. Expanding the size and reach of the corporation signals to consumers and investors that it is healthy. As a consequence, corporations seek to grow as fast as possible. This trend complements the search for resources in distant parts of the globe. Even small, privately held corporations seem to operate according to the dictates of the growth imperative.

Corporate decision making starts from the premise that all economic activity is adversarial. In other words, growth and the pursuit of profit are competitive acts, and competition is deemed to be natural, healthy, and appropriate. Corporations compete for market share, and in the process, they imbue the organization with a competitive ethos, a competitive culture. Employees must work together, but at the same time they must compete with one another to gain a higher level of productivity in the interest of moving up the corporate ladder.

Although there are exceptions to these corporate propensities, they are rare.[5] One occasionally hears of corporations that put a premium on producing a kind of corporate version of social justice and use it as a screen for decision making. Such companies reject the tendency to maximize profits by minimizing employee wages and benefits. And while this might seem to indicate that corporations can operate by different rules, there are too few counterexamples to make a persuasive case. The vast majority of transnational corporations embrace the idea that economic activity must of necessity be competitive, that it must unfailingly pursue growth and profits.

It would be an extraordinarily difficult intellectual exercise to deny the existence and importance of these corporate propensities. Collectively, they define corporate culture. The clear, simple rules (and simplistic assumptions) that corporations follow seem to make matters in the economic policy arena simple as well. In other words, the best economic policies are those that remove obstacles to corporate expansion in the pursuit of profit. This is the wisdom that undergirds both GATT and NAFTA.

Returning to the question, does the ability of transnational corporations to treat the earth as a single economic entity increase the likelihood that future economic activity will be of the sustainable sort? Any amount of reasonable reflection on this question will end with the same conclusion: we will not see movement toward sustainable economic activity emanating from the boardrooms of the transnational corporate elite. An argument could be made that the primacy of profit should suggest sustainable practices, at least if one looks at the long term, but two things seem to deny this possibility. First, corporations rarely look at the long term, and second, when they do, they opt for growth as their vehicle for ensuring long-term profits. This is another reason that corporations expand and diversify. If the environment fails to continue to provide a particular resource, there are other corporate operations to fall back on. The specter of a general environmental failing, say severe global warming, is something that will be solved by a technological solution when the time comes, or so the corporate argument goes. To think otherwise would call into question the wisdom undergirding the rules of the corporate game.

This is the crux of the matter. The corporate system has set up rules that permit it to operate in almost machine-like fashion. Working within the machine, individuals become replaceable parts, as Warren M. Anderson discovered. Anderson was the chief executive officer of Union Carbide when its Bhopal, India, plant accidentally released a harmful gas, injuring 200,000 and killing 6,000. After the accident, grief stricken at the trauma and suffering his company had created, Anderson said publicly that he would spend the rest of his life trying to make things right. A year later, however, Anderson told *Business Week* that he had "overreacted" and that he was prepared to lead his company in the legal fight against paying reparations to the victims.[6]

Warren Anderson discovered that he could not act outside the rules of the game. Company profits must take precedence over the concerns of humanity. This is why we cannot look to transnational corporations to point the way to sustainable economic activity.

Reflections on Question 2

What can be done to increase the odds that economic activity in the future will be of the sustainable sort? The answer to question 1 suggests that the status quo—our current trajectory toward a single, integrated, global economic system orchestrated by an unelected corporate global elite—will not get the job done. To determine the answer to question 2, we will need to fall back on democratic arrangements, with all of their inherent shortcomings. People in large numbers have demonstrated that life can be lived well without making profit and expansion imperatives, and cooperation, rather than competition, can successfully serve as a guiding human principle.

In short, history tells us, fairly unequivocally, that there is something to work with, that we are not "prewired" to engage in economic activity that is ultimately destructive of our environment. This is good news, for if there are any natural laws that are immutable, certainly this is one: the species that destroys its habitat destroys itself. But how do we get there when there are those who claim that the transnational corporations of the world have become so powerful that not a government on earth can stop them? How do we muster all the power available in the idea of democracy to ensure a sustainable future?

There are many ideas, everything from "computer democracy," which would enable direct rather than representative voting at the state and even the federal level (thus eliminating the effectiveness of corporate lobbying efforts), to the creation and implementation of new state charters of incorporation. The U.S. Constitution says nothing about corporations. They are given permission to exist, along with rules of operation to follow, by state governments. Theoretically, if the collective will were there, we could change those charters to ensure more sustainable economic activity.

To accomplish either of these ideas or any of the myriad others that exist, our functioning as a democracy will need to improve. This suggests that we will have to increase the efficacy of our educational efforts, for as John Dewey pointed out long ago, the problem of democracy and the problem of education are one and the same.

Historical Antecedents to the Current Predicament

Before turning back to the contemporary educational scene, we need to explore the two questions in more depth. Why are we now at a point where economic arrangements are orchestrated at the global level? And with respect to question 2, what kind of democratic arrangements will increase the odds that future economic activity will be of the sustainable sort?

If we are going to acquire as much leverage as we can over the two questions, we have to go back to the theorists who launched the modern era. In this regard, John Locke looms rather large. Locke popularized the idea that humankind existed for ages in a prepolitical state of nature. Natural man gathered foods, leaving "enough and as good" for the next man.[7] Gradually, according to Locke, individuals began to specialize, introduce new technologies, and use money as an alternative to barter and exchange. It was only when competition for scarce resources increased and armies appeared on the scene that the desire for security was heightened and humankind at last turned to the creation of government. Or so John Locke theorized.

We should not underestimate the extent to which government was seen as a kind of necessary evil. This, of course, was a predictable sentiment given the fact that those who developed "enlightened" political theory were generally—though not always—descended from the emerging middle ranks of feudal society, a group not overly fond of the too-often despotic tendencies of monarchical rule.

During the eighteenth century, as the idea of the social contract matured, so too did the idea of politics as something to be minimized. The stuff of life was not political activity but economic activity. In fact, political affairs required careful orchestration. The process of building a government was deemed to be tricky business. There were many options to choose from and no guarantee that the right option would be selected. On the other hand, economic activity was deemed to have a life of its own. Here Adam Smith, and a bit later the utilitarians John Stuart Mill and Jeremy Bentham, had a pronounced impact. There were natural laws that governed economic activity, and these laws, according to Smith and others, like human society itself, were considered prepolitical. This idea has proved to have amazing staying power, for it still defines mainstream economic thought in most of the industrialized West.

It would be difficult to critique the idea that life is lived inside the economy and outside the realm of politics if it were not for the existence of opposing views. The Locke-Smith version of how life happens may be culturally dominant, but that does not disprove theory created by others with different perspectives. On this list one might include a number of agrarian thinkers starting with Gerrard Winstanley in England at the midpoint of the seventeenth century. But a trajectory of French thought from Montesquieu through Tocqueville serves equally well and is somewhat more accessible.

Like many other Enlightenment thinkers, Montesquieu fashioned elaborate arguments concerning optimal governmental arrangements. He was as persuasive as anyone else with regard to creating checks and balances within political structures. Indeed, James Madison referred to Montesquieu as "the oracle who is always consulted and cited upon this subject."[8] But Montesquieu was pushed aside because he insisted on a monarchical government, albeit, as he called it, a "free monarchy" wherein power was checked by intermediate bodies.

What is interesting about Montesquieu (and his nineteenth-century colleague Tocqueville) is his claim that monarchical rule sets up attention to one's rights as a kind of second nature. In other words, for Montesquieu, politics is very much the stuff of life. Every citizen has a political role to play, and it is played out in a large variety of agencies and associations "through which power flows."[9] Thomas Jefferson, in some ways, saw the world through Montesquieu's eyes. His repeated arguments for "ward republics" and the widespread participation of citizens in political life represent a rather sharp contrast to the political theory Madison derived from the Locke-Smith heritage. Political scientist Richard Matthews described the contrast this way: "Where Jefferson wanted citizens involved in politics as a matter of their daily affairs, Madison designed a system that asked them, once every two years, to pick men of superior ability. Then they were to return to their private lives."[10]

Although the United States embraced Madisonian theory, Tocqueville saw in the United States of the 1830s the embodiment of Montesquieu's argument and a portion of Thomas Jefferson's dream: "In every case, at the head of any new undertaking where in France you would find the government or in England some territorial magnate, in the United States you are sure to find an Association."[11] What made American democracy great—in Tocqueville's eyes—was citizen participation in all kinds of associations, religious and secular, that had the effect of holding at bay, for a time, Locke's conception of society as prepolitical. But the age of frontier democracy and log cabin presidents did not last. Darwinian theory gave added fuel to the conception of society as an economy, and at the same time it powerfully suggested that the business of government was something best left to only a segment of society—in particular, that segment that was the most "fit." The first decades of the twentieth century saw the arrival of societal engineers who claimed to have the expertise required to ameliorate the adverse side effects of the free play of market mechanisms.

Intellectuals and politicians alike called on citizens to defer to experts in all facets of life. Michael Sandel has argued that the end result of this call has been the creation of a society of "unencumbered selves."[12] We live in the economy, but we leave it to those who ascend to the political sphere to arbitrate clashes of self-interest while they adjust the flow of production and money. Montesquieu's notion of a fundamental political dimension to life is nowhere in evidence. Life is about material acquisition.

If this definition represents our cultural druthers, so to speak, then it is not surprising that we hear of books with titles like Jean Bethke Elshtain's *Democracy on Trial*. History tells us that there are other political systems, most notably fascism, that can more readily grease the skids of an economy. Clarence Karier has argued that this is the direction in which we are headed.[13] In any event, almost everyone would agree that facilitating economic arrangements is not a great strength of democracies. They hinge on a higher value. Democracies are premised on the idea that justice is the principal virtue of social life, and à la Montesquieu, social life cannot therefore be construed as prepolitical.

But the idea of democracy, at least in the United States, has gone through several iterations. Theorists have sought to amend classical conceptions to adjust for the circumstances of modernity, and in the process, for better or for worse, the concept has been weakened. Simultaneously, transnational corporations have dramatically increased their ability to set social and economic policy. Corporate lawyers, working closely with members of Congress, continue to write and propose legislation to their companies' advantage. There are signs, however, that seem to indicate that stronger democratic conceptions, such as deliberative democracy, are gaining in popularity.

The currently ascendant conceptions of democracy, however, hinge on the idea that people live their lives outside the political sphere. Montesquieu, and the classical democratic traditions that he admired, suggests that this is a mistake. Citizen participation in the political arena is more than a matter of addressing collective security needs; it is, according to these theorists, a sine qua non for the just society and a prerequisite for the fulfilled life.

Deliberative Democracy

Is there a conception of democracy that takes seriously the idea that people live their lives inside the political sphere? And, if so, is such a conception capable of rebalancing the drive of transnational corporations (and the consumption that accompanies this drive) and the need for a healthy earth? We argue that such a conception exists and that it may indeed be capable of addressing the tension between economic activity and environmental well-being. However, this conception is not found in either the procedural or the constitutional models of democracy. These two standard models, we argue, do not provide a way of overcoming the most basic obstacle to a sustainable future: open and reasonable deliberation about conflicting values.

Amy Gutmann and Dennis Thompson on Democracy

In their recent book titled *Democracy and Disagreement,* Amy Gutmann and Dennis Thompson argue for a conception of democracy built on the idea that rational moral discussion in political life is both possible and desirable.[14] They label this conception *deliberative democracy.* Gutmann and Thompson suggest that their conception of a deliberative democracy is grounded by a set of specific deliberative principles (each will be discussed later). To a limited extent, citizens and public officials already practice the kind of reasoning dictated by these principles. Deliberative democracy merely requires that this reasoning be a consistent and comprehensive aspect of political life. Because such reasoning is already a part of our common experience, albeit a limited part, Gutmann and Thompson argue that there is "hope that it can survive and even prosper if philosophers along with citizens and public officials better appreciate its value in politics."[15]

Deliberative democracy seems possible, but is it desirable? What does a democratic process based on rational moral deliberation offer that other arrangements do not? In response to this question, Gutmann and Thompson write:

> In the absence of robust deliberation in democracy, citizens cannot even provisionally justify many controversial procedures and constitutional rights to one another. Insofar as deliberation is missing in political life, citizens also lack a mutually justifiable way of living with their ongoing moral disagreements. When citizens deliberate in democratic politics, they express and respect their status as political equals even as they continue to disagree about important matters of public policy.[16]

Gutmann and Thompson compare and contrast deliberative democracy with two more standard theories of democracy: procedural democracy and constitutional democracy. Ultimately, they argue that the procedural and constitutional models of democracy neglect the idea that ongoing discussion about moral disagreements is a necessary aspect of political life.

Procedural democracy is based on the idea that popular or majority rule, to the extent that it respects individuals as political equals, is the most appropriate way of resolving moral conflicts. The idea of popular rule can be expressed in the following manner. If there is moral disagreement between two groups of equal individuals, then the group with the greater number should rule. Procedural democrats believe that systems that are not based on popular rule and allow the minority, instead of the majority, to rule violate the democratic principle of political equality among citizens. Such systems are based on the assumption that "some citizens' moral convictions count more than those of others."[17]

Gutmann and Thompson note that procedural democrats do not suggest that the process of popular rule always leads to morally correct decisions. What makes popular rule legitimate is that it is a fair process, not that it produces results that are right. With this in mind, they argue that the strongest defense for the process of popular rule is that it recognizes that citizens will not be able to agree on solutions to certain moral conflicts and that they should not be forced to do so. Citizens should vote rather than be expected to agree. From this perspective, the process of popular rule seems grounded on the principle of political equality in that it seems to assume that the conflicting moral convictions of all individuals deserve equal respect.

However, Gutmann and Thompson assert that there is a critical problem with the idea of popular rule. They argue that decisions that result from popular rule but violate the basic liberty or opportunity of citizens cannot be justified. Most procedural democrats recognize that popular rule must be constrained by some substantive values. However, the values that they accept as constraints tend to be only those that are necessary to sustain the democratic process itself.

In response, Gutmann and Thompson ask: "If majoritarianism must be qualified by values internal to the democratic process, then why should it not also be qualified by values external to this process, especially if those values include a basic liberty or opportunity of individuals?"[18] They go on to answer this question by arguing that in the same way that proceduralism recognizes limits on popular rule in order to respect individuals as equal citizens, it is required to recognize limits on popular rule in order to protect basic liberty and opportunity of individuals.

In addition to this problem, procedural democrats are faced with a further one. In order to determine, collectively, whether popular rule or some other procedure is justified, citizens must deliberate about the substantive value of various procedures. Gutmann and Thompson assert that this fact seems to "undermine an important aim of proceduralism, which is to avoid substantive moral disagreement in the political realm."[19]

In their examination of constitutional democracy, Gutmann and Thompson assert that both procedural democracy and constitutional democracy protect individual rights against popular rule. The difference between them is that the former gives priority over popular rule "only to rights whose primary purpose is to make the democratic process fair," while the latter gives priority to some rights whose primary purpose is to "produce justified outcomes by protecting the vital interests of some individuals."[20]

Gutmann and Thompson argue that constitutional democracy suffers from two difficulties. First, like procedural democracy, it holds that citizens require morally justified procedures in order to make legitimate political decisions. And in order for citizens to agree on a specific and just procedure, they must engage in moral deliberation. Gutmann and Thompson write, "Constitutionalism in this respect moves, just as proceduralism does, in the direction of deliberative democracy."[21]

The second difficulty that constitutional democracy faces is not shared with procedural democracy. Constitutional democracy goes further than procedural democracy in using substantive standards to constrain democratic procedures such as popular rule. As a result, argue Gutmann and

Thompson, the standards that constitutionalists rely on to resolve disagreements become increasingly "contestable." Abstract constitutional standards such as the idea that majorities should not violate the basic liberties of individuals seem compelling on the surface. But because they are abstract, they are open to various (and often conflicting) interpretations. The more abstract the standard is, the more open to conflicting interpretations it becomes. "For resolving moral conflict in politics, the interpretation matters just as much as the principle," write Gutmann and Thompson.[22] And ultimately, coming to collective agreement on "the interpretation" requires a move toward deliberative democracy.

The conception of deliberative democracy that Gutmann and Thompson articulate is based on a simple idea. Citizens and officials ought to "justify public policy by giving reasons that can be accepted by those who are bound by it."[23] Put differently, citizens and officials should focus on arriving at mutually justifiable reasons for public decisions. Gutmann and Thompson argue that three principles are implied by this idea: reciprocity, publicity, and accountability.

The principle of reciprocity requires that citizens and officials appeal to reasons or principles that can be accepted by fellow citizens and officials who are similarly motivated to find reasons that others can accept. The foundation of reciprocity is "the capacity to seek fair terms of social cooperation for their own sake."[24]

The principle of publicity is straightforward. It requires that "the reasons that officials and citizens give to justify political actions, and the information necessary to assess those reasons, should be public."[25] Publicity, argue Gutmann and Thompson, helps to maintain democratic accountability. It works, in an obvious manner, to motivate officials to do their duty. It also seems to encourage citizens to learn and talk about public policy. This, in turn, allows officials to learn about and from public opinion.

Finally, the principle of accountability holds that each citizen and official is accountable to all citizens and officials. That is to say that citizens and officials are required to provide reasons for their claims to every individual who will be bound by them.

Joshua Cohen on Deliberation

In his essay titled "Deliberation and Democratic Legitimacy," Joshua Cohen describes a view of deliberative democracy that is similar to the one sketched by Gutmann and Thompson.[26] Cohen writes,

The notion of a deliberative democracy is rooted in the intuitive ideal of a democratic association in which the justification of the terms and conditions of association proceeds through public argument and reasoning among equal citizens. Citizens in such an order share a commitment to the resolution of problems of collective choice through public reasoning and regard their basic institutions as legitimate insofar as they establish the framework for free public deliberation.[27]

Although he holds the same basic view of deliberative democracy as do Gutmann and Thompson, Cohen adds to what they have to say when he articulates several aspects of what he terms "the ideal deliberative procedure." First, according to Cohen, ideal deliberation is free. It is free in the sense that prior norms do not constrain the deliberative process and that "participants suppose they can act from the results" of deliberation.[28] Second, Cohen argues, ideal deliberation is reasoned. Participants are required to provide reasons for supporting their proposals and rejecting other proposals. Third, ideal deliberation is "formally and substantively" equal. It is formally equal in that the rules of deliberation hold that all participants are equally capable of making, supporting, and criticizing proposals. It is substantively equal in that the existing distribution of money or power is not allowed to alter this equality. Finally, ideal deliberation "aims to arrive at a rationally motivated consensus."[29] Ideal deliberation does not guarantee consensus, but it holds consensus as a primary aim. If consensus is not obtained, then deliberation ends and a vote takes place.

By describing the fundamental aspects of the ideal deliberative procedure, Cohen helps to show how deliberative democracy might be employed at the institutional level.

Deliberative Democracy and a Sustainable Future

Earlier we presented two questions. The first asked whether the recent trend toward the global orchestration of economic affairs would lead to economic activity that is sustainable or unsustainable. The second question asked what might be done to ensure that future economic activity would be of the sustainable sort. In response to the first question, we concluded that current transnational economic trends do not seem to be pointing the way to sustainable economic activity. With regard to the second question, there may be more reason to be hopeful.

In short, we hold that the ideal of deliberative democracy offers a plausible way to address the complex question of sustainability. The most obvious advantage that deliberative democracy has over other arrangements is that it is designed to deal with disagreements grounded on conflicting values. Deliberative democracy does not shy away from tackling controversial debates over fundamental values. In fact, such debates are the cornerstone of effective deliberation.

If the question of sustainability comes down to a struggle between those who value short-term economic gain and those who value long-term environmental well-being, then engaging in deliberative democracy and deliberative procedure may be the only way to grapple with and overcome this issue in a collective manner. The alternative seems hopeless: increasing environmental destruction for short-term economic gain coupled with sporadic (albeit often heroic) attempts by a brave few to fight for the environment.

We believe that the only viable solution to the dilemmas created at the intersection of the economy and the environment is to bring "we the people" back into the policy arena. To do this we must dismiss that part of our Locke-Smith heritage that separates the social and economic life from the political sphere. This is not easily done given that so much of Smith and Locke went into the constitution we embraced at the end of the eighteenth century. But they did not acquire complete ideological hegemony at that time, nor do they have it now, as scholars such as Charles Taylor, Bruce Ackerman, and others have pointed out. There is a vestige of the Montesquieu-Tocqueville tradition here as well. Their emphasis on the intentional proliferation of *corps intermédiaires*—places where deliberative democracy can happen—has gained more and more attention, partially due to the popularity of Robert Putnam's work in Italy, but partially too because of the work of Robert Bellah, Amitai Etzioni, William Galston, and others in the United States.[30]

Reinserting a political dimension into our cultural definition of the fulfilled life can have positive spin-offs. First among these is that through the proliferation of intermediate bodies—all manner of civic associations—people are put into face-to-face contact with one another. The deliberation that can occur as this happens generates a key ingredient in our constitutional formula for the good society—that is, public opinion. As numerous scholars have pointed out, Noam Chomsky most vociferously, public opinion is now thoroughly controlled and carefully constructed by corporate enterprise.[31] A resurgence of public-generated public opinion could result in more systematic attention to the dilemmas created by the interplay of the environment and the economy.

In the end, perhaps the most important way to shore up our understanding of and commitment to the deliberative democratic ideal is to incorporate the teaching of this ideal into our elementary and secondary classrooms. The rain forest unit may have some advantages in this regard, but other ways of thinking through the school curriculum might hit the target more squarely.

Conclusion: Back to the Classroom

The tension between economic activity and environmental well-being will only become more pressing during the twenty-first century.[32] The inability of corporate entities to engage in moral reckoning means that the burden of creating sustainable circumstances falls on the shoulders of "we the people." Accustomed to deferring to experts, however, the American public is little practiced at democratic deliberation. This is where the public purpose of schools comes clearly into focus. John Goodlad, perhaps more than any other American scholar since John Dewey, has pushed and cajoled the educational establishment to live up to the burden of reinventing democracy—as each generation must—by enculturating the nation's young into the habitual, civil use of what he calls the "democratic arts."[33]

What is the contribution of the rain forest unit to the cultivation of persuasion, civility, reflection, considered assessment of evidence, dialogue, compromise, and good argument? In other words, what does it contribute to student acquisition of the democratic arts?

Certainly the unit provides a convenient forum for student debate over rain forest clear-cutting. Students might do research, compile information, fashion an evidential base, and create arguments. They might arrive at opposing viewpoints and participate in a rousing debate. All of this is good as far as it goes, but it is much like learning to drive in a simulator. The chief drawback is that it is not real. As a result, the consequence of this debate is nil, and students know this. Their intellectual investment in the project will run no deeper than the desire for their letter grade.

Much of the public school curriculum has this artificiality to it. Paul Gruchow has written poignantly about this phenomenon:

> The schools in which I was educated were by most standards first-rate. But they were, as our schools generally are, largely indifferent to the place and to the culture in which they operated. Among my science courses I took two full years of biology, but I never learned that the beautiful meadow at the bottom of my family's pasture was remnant virgin prairie. We did not spend, so far as I can remember, a single hour on prairies—the landscape in which we were immersed—in two years of biological study.[34]

Like most students in this country, he likely learned more about the rain forest than he did about his own home. We view this fact as a kind of silent American tragedy, for in bypassing the local context, teachers have missed a convenient opportunity to ground traditional subjects and thereby produce greater student understanding. The more significant loss is the missed opportunity for real enculturation into democratic life and the chance for students to make a worthwhile contribution to their communities.[35] In short, what is lost is the opportunity to foster democratic character by cultivating what Stephen Goodlad calls an ecological identity.

Every community must make decisions related to economic activity and the subsequent health, beauty, and vitality of its place on earth. Students can participate in those decisions and in the process learn to wield the democratic arts. Through this process, they will more readily come to understandings related to traditional school subjects, and they receive the bonus of experiencing the sense of fulfillment that comes with being of service to others. Focusing pedagogically on one's place is not difficult, but it does require teachers to think about curriculum in the light of education's public purpose. If learning to live well on an earth with finite resources is not a part of that purpose, one cannot help but ask in exasperation, as Aldo Leopold did years ago: "What is education for?"[36]

Mary Catherine Bateson has noted the connection between the concept of democracy and ecological concern.[37] The more that civic associations proliferate and thereby encourage democratic deliberation over shared prospects, the more that environmental well-being becomes a key concern. She has also commented on how readily available the prerequisite curricular materials are for learning about life's interactions with the environment. Consider her discussion of something as simple as an aquarium:

> The aquarium was beautiful but frustrating. In a low-keyed way, it could be both demanding and recalcitrant. What is critical is that it could not educate me about ecology without also posing wider questions. Aquariums stand in the schoolrooms of thousands of children, alongside cages of gerbils and guinea pigs, which also require care and teach the lessons of living and dying. Unlike much of what is done in a classroom, mistakes made in caring for an aquarium have real costs.[38]

The key here is real costs, real consequences, real rewards, real life. Students do not need to wait until they are eighteen years old to make substantive contributions to their communities. Simulations like the rain forest unit are not bad, but they are likely to end merely in the accumulation of information, and then only if they are done well. In schools all across the country, creative teachers are taking students into the community in an attempt to produce enduring understandings, but also in an attempt to increase the health, beauty, and vitality of their communities. These students are far more likely to fashion life plans that structure in a political dimension marked by a democratic concern for social, economic, and environmental justice. These students, exhibiting democratic character at least partially cultivated pedagogically, increase the odds that we may all enjoy a sustainable future.

NOTES

1. Richard Barnet and Ronald E. Mueller, *Global Reach: The Power of the Multinational Corporations* (New York: Simon & Schuster, 1974). See also *Noam Chomsky, Profit over People: Neoliberalism and the Global Order* (New York: Seven Stories Press, 1999).

2. Paul Gruchow, *Grass Roots: The Universe of Home* (Minneapolis, Minn.: Milkweed Editions, 1997), p. 67.

3. The American Dust Bowl of the 1930s is a good example of environmental depletion. On the other hand, some indigenous groups practiced noninvasive agriculture for centuries with no environmental damage. Twelfth- and thirteenth-century peasants were able to use plow agriculture to increase productivity while improving their environmental circumstances. See Carolyn Merchant, *The Death of Nature: Women, Ecology, and the Scientific Revolution* (San Francisco: Harper & Row, 1980), pp. 46–47.

4. Lest anyone doubt the magnitude of this process, consider the fact that forty-seven of the top one hundred economies are not countries at all but rather transnational corporations and that 70 percent of all global trade is controlled by a mere five hundred corporations. See Tony Clarke's "Mechanisms of Corporate Rule," in Jerry Mander and Edward Goldsmith (eds.), *The Case Against the Global Economy* (San Francisco: Sierra Club Books, 1996), p. 298.

5. One well-known exception is Merck & Co.'s donation of the antiparasitic drug Mectizan to fight river blindness in Africa, the Middle East, and Central and South America. See John Walsh, "Merck Donates Drug for River Blindness," *Science*, 30 October 1987, p. 610.

6. Jerry Mander, "The Rules of Corporate Behavior" in Mander and Goldsmith (eds.), *Case Against the Global Economy*, p. 315.

7. John Locke, *Second Treatise of Government* (Indianapolis: Hackett, 1980), p. 19.

8. James Madison, "Federalist No. 47," in Clinton Rossiter (ed.), *The Federalist Papers; Alexander Hamilton, James Madison, John Jay* (New York: New American Library, 1961), p. 301.

9. Melvin Richter, *Montesquieu: Selected Political Writings* (Indianapolis: Hackett, 1990), p. 122.

10. Richard K. Matthews, *If Men Were Angels: James Madison and the Heartless Empire of Reason* (Lawrence: University of Kansas Press, 1995), p. 243. Rousseau too wrote of the connection between a fulfilled life and political participation, although his citizen legislators were a far cry from the more universal participation that Montesquieu, Jefferson, and Tocqueville advocated.

11. Alexis de Tocqueville, *Democracy in America,* ed. Richard D. Heffner (New York: Mentor, 1956), p. 198.

12. Michael J. Sandel, "The Procedural Republic and the Unencumbered Self," *Political Theory* 12 (February 1984): 81–96.

13. Jean Bethke Elshtain, *Democracy on Trial* (New York: Basic Books, 1995); Clarence J. Karier, "Some Reflections on the Coming of an American Fascism," *Educational Theory* 37 (Summer 1987): 251–264.

14. Amy Gutmann and Dennis Thompson, *Democracy and Disagreement* (Cambridge, Mass.: Belknap Press, 1996).

15. Gutmann and Thompson, *Democracy and Disagreement,* p. 4.

16. Gutmann and Thompson, *Democracy and Disagreement,* p. 18.

17. Gutmann and Thompson, *Democracy and Disagreement,* p. 27.

18. Gutmann and Thompson, *Democracy and Disagreement,* p. 31.

19. Gutmann and Thompson, *Democracy and Disagreement,* p. 32.

20. Gutmann and Thompson, *Democracy and Disagreement,* p. 34.

21. Gutmann and Thompson, *Democracy and Disagreement,* p. 34.

22. Gutmann and Thompson, *Democracy and Disagreement,* p. 35.

23. Gutmann and Thompson, *Democracy and Disagreement,* p. 52.

24. Gutmann and Thompson, *Democracy and Disagreement,* pp. 52–53.

25. Gutmann and Thompson, *Democracy and Disagreement,* p. 95.

26. Joshua Cohen, "Democracy and Democratic Legitimacy," in James Bohman and William Rehg (eds.), *Deliberative Democracy* (Cambridge, Mass.: MIT Press, 1997), chap. 3.

27. Cohen, "Democracy and Democratic Legitimacy," p. 72.

28. Cohen, "Democracy and Democratic Legitimacy," p. 74.

29. Cohen, "Democracy and Democratic Legitimacy," p. 75.

30. Robert D. Putnam with Robert Leonardi and Raffaella Y. Nanetti, *Making Democracy Work: Civic Traditions in Modern Italy* (Princeton, N.J.: Princeton University Press, 1993). Robert Bellah and colleagues have produced two influential books in this regard: *Habits of the Heart: Individualism and Commitment in American Life* (Berkeley: University of California Press, 1985) and *The Good Society* (New York: Knopf, 1991). Amitai Etzioni founded the Communitarian Network and, like Galston, has made significant scholarly contributions suggesting the reinsertion of community as a value into ascendant political, economic, and educational theory.

31. Edward S. Herman and Noam Chomsky, *Manufacturing Consent: The Political Economy of the Mass Media* (New York: Pantheon Books, 1988). With respect to the corporate creation of public opinion regarding education, see David C. Berliner and Bruce J. Biddle, *The Manufactured Crisis: Myths, Fraud, and the Attack on America's Public Schools* (Reading, Mass.: Addison-Wesley, 1995).

32. Paul Kennedy has done a marvelous job documenting the pressing concerns of the twenty-first century. High on his list are land degradation and the drawing down of water tables across the industrialized nations. See especially "The Dangers to Our Natural Environment" in his *Preparing for the Twenty-First Century* (New York: Random House, 1993), pp. 95–121.

33. See, for example, his "Democracy, Education, and Community," in Roger Soder (ed.), *Democracy, Education, and the Schools* (San Francisco: Jossey-Bass, 1996), p. 71.

34. Gruchow, *Grass Roots,* p. 133.

35. John Dewey argued that schools should not be preparation for life; they should be life itself. In an interesting way, Montesquieu's political theory builds on this notion. In *The Persian Letters,* he argued that maximizing social harmony was contingent on the ability of a people to feel its history. In contrast to this thinking, we have set up schools where students are asked to learn history in preparation for some future date with full citizenship. If we were to take Dewey's admonition and Montesquieu's theory seriously, we would allow students to encounter the history that affected their families, neighbors, and communities and let them use that encounter to inform their interpretation of regional, national, and international developments.

36. Aldo Leopold, *A Sand County Almanac* (New York: Ballantine, 1966), p. 210.

37. Mary Catherine Bateson, "Democracy, Ecology, and Participation" in Soder (ed.), *Democracy, Education, and the Schools,* p. 71.

38. Bateson, "Democracy, Ecology, and Participation," p. 76.

6

LEARNING IN LAYERS

Mary Catherine Bateson

MY EARLIEST MEMORY OF A lesson in how democracy works was in 1948. This was the year of the first post–World War II election; Harry Truman, who had become president through Franklin Roosevelt's death, was running against Thomas Dewey. Dewey was widely predicted to win, so as an eight-year-old, I assumed that my mother would be voting for him. No, she said, she would not be voting for Dewey, for she was a lifelong Democrat. However, she went on, it would not necessarily be a bad thing if Dewey won. I was puzzled, for I must have assumed that the campaign was about winning and that everyone would want to be on the winning side. You see, she said, the Democratic party has been in power for a very long time (because of FDR's multiple terms), and it is not healthy in a democracy when one party is out of power for so long that its elders forget how to behave in power and its younger members never learn.

The preceding paragraph begins with a deliberately ambiguous phrase: "how democracy works." By the age of eight, from school and the radio and overheard conversation, I clearly knew something about the office of president, about the process of voting, about parties and campaigns, or the conversation with my mother would have been impossible. What I lacked, and what apparently many citizens as well as politicians and journalists lack, was a more abstract knowledge about how democracy works: systemic understanding of the contexts in which these different elements fit together. Indeed, I had already acquired unconscious assumptions about the zero-sum characteristics of rightness, a win-lose approach that is arguably inimical to democracy. I suppose the conversation has stayed with me because it was so disconcerting, challenging abstract assumptions I could not have put into words. On the other hand, one could argue that the self-observation involved in knowing that I had heard something startling—and not immediately exiling it from memory and attention—was itself a valuable framework for questioning future assumptions, a foundation for future learning.

I doubt that I had ever considered the need in a democracy for both minority and majority positions. Unanimity and the search for complete consensus are not necessarily healthy, as demonstrated by the use of referenda in totalitarian regimes. The American system of democracy depends not only on the mechanics of voting and party politics but on a curious mental attitude that functions at two logical levels. On the one level, it is important to be committed to particular policies and directions, to have preferences and alliances, and to express them. On the next, and more inclusive, logical level, it is important to be committed to a process that may well defeat those preferences: to be able to say, when one's own candidate is defeated, that at least this is a victory for democracy. As a Democrat my mother supported Truman; as the citizen of a democracy she supported the process that might lead to Dewey's election, and she would have supported Dewey if that occurred. Her comments on the need to learn how to behave in office suggest empathy with both parties. Interestingly enough, she also recognized that particular decisions belong at particular systemic levels: it is probably not appropriate to decide whom to vote for as a way of tuning the party system, as in casting a protest vote for a candidate one would not want to see in office (there were four candidates in the 1948 election). Thinking about the election turns out to be layered, like an onion.

There is a significant but imperfect formal similarity between the layered quality of logical structures, which Russell and Whitehead described as "logical types,"[1] the hierarchical structure of many organizations, and the levels of inclusivity and embeddedness involved in systemic thinking. Thus, a given party exists at one level of the democratic process, while the party system is more inclusive and functions at the next level up (the party system is not a party). Voting for a candidate as a way of criticizing the process is somewhat like chewing on the menu instead of using it to order, although voting in the election at all does support the system and the menu is a useful start in ordering something edible. Only a little reflection is needed to realize that no more than a fraction of the electorate thinks this way about voting decisions and that the educational system does not often encourage this kind of thinking, being all too committed to the notion of right answers: if Dewey is the right answer, Truman is the wrong answer, and vice versa.

The focus of this chapter is the need to teach citizens to entertain multiple points of view and even to hold two apparently conflicting points of view at different logical levels. This is increasingly necessary for living in a world of high diversity and rapid change, which presses us all toward either confusion or insight.[2] A range of skills is involved, some of them emphasized in several kinds of social science methodology and areas of training, but there are also "homely" skills underlying marriage and family life, where individual interests also have to be seen in the context of the larger whole. Our concern also includes the questions about the assumptions supporting such skills, which are not easy to change, for the institutions of society are in every case classrooms—contexts of learning in the broadest sense—imparting or reinforcing assumptions, above and beyond the goals of any specific lesson plan or the function of a given institution. What are the assumptions taught by a hospital, a jail, or the network news, above and beyond the performance of a specific task? How about schools themselves?

Entertaining multiple points of view is relatively familiar in Western pedagogy. We are often encouraged to try to imagine what we would feel or do in someone else's shoes. How would you feel if you were Bobby and someone spilled your juice? How would you feel if you were a factory worker and your factory were closed? What must it have felt like to be captured and carried across the ocean to a life of slavery? What would you do about Iraq if you were president? Why do you think the fairy godmother in the storybook did what she did? How did the ogre feel when he faced the hero?

The ability to imagine oneself into totally changed circumstances is a powerful adaptive and creative force, especially when the imagination goes on to devise a way to get there. Yet this ability to imagine oneself in the shoes of someone whose life situation is totally different is not universal, as researchers on the process of modernization have discovered.[3] When Turkish peasants were asked what they would do if they were the head of the government, they answered, "My God! How can you say such a thing?" They could not know because they had not had the experience.

Empathy is not an altogether comfortable skill. A slave owner is better off unable to empathize with a slave, and a soldier is happier if he does not reflect on the fear and homesickness of another frightened boy like himself across the border. In situations of conflict or differential power, it is often the weaker party who understands how the stronger thinks and feels and is likely to behave: the conquered observe their conquerors acutely, while oppressors are careful not to identify with their victims or to observe their own behavior. True believers in any tradition prefer that alternatives be strictly unthinkable to them. Years ago I taught a course titled "The Peoples and Cultures of the Middle East," and after a section on Islam, a student from a Christian fundamentalist background came to me and said, in distress, "It never occurred to me that Muslims actually believe their religion." Similarly, I was disconcerted when a white student said to me in the 1980s, after reading the autobiography of a black author, "Why, he's really angry at white people." "Wouldn't you be?" was a question she did not know how to deal with. Training in conflict resolution, including the ability to phrase an opponent's point of view in terms acceptable to that opponent, has begun to spread through the public school system. But when that skill is applied to areas of profound conflict, as in the attempt to understand and empathize with the convictions of an opponent in the abortion debate, it can be profoundly disturbing.[4]

We do teach children to put themselves in the shoes of others, but only some others and only in limited ways. After all, the idea underlies a great number of religious traditions in the various forms of the Golden Rule, "Do unto others as you would have others do unto you," or, more pointedly in the Jewish version, "That which you hate, do not do to others." Taken too literally (that is, at the wrong logical level), the advice is bad, for others have different tastes and desires: don't give your daddy a teddy bear, but give him something that cheers his heart as a teddy bear does yours.

Participation in a democracy, however, requires not only an ability to acknowledge the beliefs and preferences of others but also the capacity to recognize that divergence is essential to the health of the larger system that includes both the self and the other. Here, moving up the logical ladder involves the resolution of a sort of paradox, which recalls the use of paradox in such traditions as Zen Buddhism as a possible pathway to enlightenment. Teaching at George Mason University, I often wonder about George Mason, a Virginia gentleman who was one of the framers at the Constitutional Convention but who declined to sign the draft Constitution. He understood that the Constitution was deeply flawed because it lacked a bill of rights and because it accepted slavery. He participated by refusing to participate; his critique and adamant withdrawal no doubt hastened the passage of the Bill of Rights in the form of amendments (although the abolition of slavery took another century, and Mason, like other framers, was caught in the paradox of owning slaves himself). Historically, it was essential that most of those present should compromise and provide a majority, but the minority position did eventually prevail. Was George Mason grateful that his was a minority position—so he could feel free to cleave to it, knowing that the work of the Convention would not be lost? Or did he simply go home with a sense of failure? Often enough in discussions, someone takes a position that is unlikely to prevail—at first—but is important to include in the debate.

Democracy requires the ability to say, in the words attributed to Voltaire, "I disapprove of what you say, but I will defend to the death your right to say it." Put differently, it requires the affirmation that there is more than one way of thinking and acting in a given situation, and that these alternatives can be embraced by individuals who are both reason-able and moral and therefore worthy of debating, so that individuals can make choices among the alternatives—and maybe formulate new ones, thereby increasing the freedom of choice for others. We are not speaking of relativism, however; relativism requires suspending judgment, appropriate in some contexts but not to the role of citizen, because there the willingness to make and defend choices and to commit to particular courses of action remains essential. The contrast here is with the habit of demonizing opponents (as opposed to saying their views represent plausible, though perhaps less desirable, alternatives), which tends to subvert democracy and leads to using the structures of democracy for tactical purposes only. Democracy requires that the victory of the other party, even if its members are sadly mistaken in their policies, not be unthinkable; that an affirmation of and loyalty to the overarching system give recognition and respect to those who disagree. In the United Kingdom, it is common to speak of Her Majesty's loyal opposition, a constant reminder that opposition is intrinsic to the system rather than alien and invasive.

Living in a society structured as a democracy and maintaining continuity and stability through a period of rapid change depends on these attitudes also, for what seems right today may seem wrong tomorrow, but is not thereby culpable. Revolutions, by contrast, require the rejection of a whole set of ideas and, usually, of people, declaring them totally wrong and even perhaps deserving of execution. More gradual change, including educational renewal, involves a steady flow of linked interventions while participants continue to function in an imperfect system. This requires a compassionate awareness of change and diversity as systemic characteristics and at least the partial acceptance of their necessity, recognizing and affirming what exists in the process of building something new. We are all dealing with systems whose survival through time has depended on their capacity to resist environmental pressures or, when forced to change, to limit that change in space and time. For the advocates of change, this entails thinking about themselves and their opponents in the context of loyalty to a system that includes them all. In effect, it goes beyond understanding the viewpoint of the other to thinking at a higher and more complex logical level. It also entails valuing the resistance to change, for purposive cultural change involves modifying self-correcting systems while maintaining their viability. For conservatives, it means accepting the inevitability of change, which is a characteristic of any living system, and struggling to make sure that change is genuinely adaptive.

The capacity to maintain potentially contradictory commitments at different levels of systemic organization, then, is valuable in a democracy, even if it is not realized in every individual. But what is especially relevant here is the fact that, although lesson plans (and their testing) are often conceptualized at a single logical level (characterized by lists), learning in general occurs at several levels simultaneously, whether programs are designed to create commitment and sensitivity at multiple levels or not. Thus, in the example of the Truman-Dewey election, although I had learned many specific details about the democratic form of government, I had also formed unstated assumptions in a variety of contexts about such issues as winning and losing or being right versus being wrong. The way in which learning is linked to context affects the transferability of learning—for instance, the application of a given school lesson outside of school.

Gregory Bateson used the term *deutero-learning* to refer to learning of this kind, where learning at one level, specified in a teacher's explicit goals, carries with it potential learning at the next logical level. Deutero-learning is often paraphrased as "learning to learn." The paraphrase is both accurate and inaccurate and should at least be expanded as "learning to learn in a given context," because the real issue is the development of unarticulated assumptions based on the characteristics of a given context, sometimes so broad and so deeply rooted that these assumptions can be regarded as intrinsic to character and are almost impossible to change. Children who do well in school are children who have adapted to the school context. They have "learned to learn" particular kinds of lessons in spelling or history or arithmetic because they have absorbed the contextual assumptions within which these lessons are taught, all too often assumptions inappropriate to democratic society, like "might makes right" or "there is only one acceptable answer" (two alternative versions of "teacher knows best"), or destructive of other kinds of learning, such as learning from experience.

Gregory Bateson puts it this way, using the context of experimental psychology:

> In any learning experiment—e.g., of the Pavlovian or the Instrumental Reward type—there occurs not only the learning in which the experimenter is usually interested, namely the increased frequency of the conditioned response in the experimental context, but also a more

abstract or higher level of learning, in which the experimental subject improves his ability to deal with contexts of a given type. For example, the deutero-learning of the animal subjected to a sequence of Pavlovian experiences will presumably be a process of character formation whereby he comes to live as if in a universe where premonitory signs of later reinforcements (or unconditioned stimuli) can be detected but nothing can be done to precipitate or prevent the occurrence of the reinforcements. In a word, the animal will acquire a species of "fatalism." In contrast, we may expect the subject of repeated Instrumental Reward experiments to deutero-learn a character structure that will enable him to live as if in a universe in which he can control the occurrence of reinforcements.[5]

This suggests that our problem is with what schools teach without knowing it rather than with what they fail to teach.

Behavior can be changed by a variety of external pressures, rewards, or sanctions but may snap back if the underlying cultural system remains unchanged, and this is most visible in the perseveration of old values after revolutions. A program for sustainable change must be based on a broad, abstract recognition of the interconnected systems involved, and even so may take several generations to become fully embedded.

All of these issues are relevant to educational renewal and illuminate some of the reasons for failure in the past. Effective change must be pervasive and systemic, becoming part of a new equilibrium but also subject to new processes of adaptation. Even as we explore possible ways of modifying educational programs in order to promote democratic character in the young, it is important to recognize that such a change is subject to all the vicissitudes of the larger system, as well as the logical limitations of most schooling. But the conclusion that leaps off the page is the strategy of introducing change at several systemic levels simultaneously. The Institute for Educational Inquiry (IEI) recognizes this fact by asserting that real changes in education can be achieved through simultaneous renewal in teacher training and in the schools themselves, for change in the one without change in the other is likely to be reversed. This recognition is only a partial solution to the "you can't get there from here" quality of culture change, for it leaves untouched a number of other interconnecting systems: the families and households from which pupils come (with the history of enculturation of all members thereof); the faculties, administrations, and students of schools of education; and the general public and the political systems that fund, accredit, and otherwise support schools and schools of education when these are recognizable to them as fitting previously learned standards. There is no limit to the complexity, but this dual process and the partnerships it engenders promise to create contexts for genuinely adaptive change and learning.

This is especially true of change in the patterns of cross-generational transmission, which is, after all, what schooling is all about. We are the "time-binding" species, not only in the sense that we can remember the past and plan for the future, but also in the sense that cultural patterns and their transmission from generation to generation are designed to sustain continuity, constraining change over time. "Education for change" is sometimes seen as a necessity, but sometimes the words come too glibly: from the perspective of human history, education for change is an oxymoron, a contradiction in terms.

The commonest strategy for change is to introduce it at the top, but we all know from experience how often this fails. It is clear that new policy that comes down in command form from the top of a hierarchical system will not automatically be expressed through all levels. This works only in highly authoritarian organizations, and even there, policy initiatives coming from the top are subverted and distorted as they work their way down, phenomena familiar from such contexts as the Roman Catholic Church and the U.S. Army. School systems contain both authoritarian and democratic elements, but these seem to combine to make any effective change even more difficult. The approach that the IEI offers suggests change not from the top down but at several points and at different logical levels. Simultaneous renewal proposes addressing several nodes so that the resonance between these nodes becomes a systemic characteristic at the next level up, particularly by training individuals to function at several points of the system and to give each other mutual support. This may not be enough to overcome the necessary conservatism of institutions, for it remains necessary to contend with entire tenured faculties who do not accept the new direction. Still, the impact of two professors teaching a new approach in a school of education is far more than double the impact of one. Two courses in a curriculum, two teachers in a school, even two books in a library can create an effective resonance for the learner by suggesting a metapattern. When the situation offers a contrast between two courses or two teachers, it also suggests moving up to a higher level.

One of the most interesting features of the program of the IEI is that it focuses on the question of education for democratic character in the context of asking how to promote systemic change. Character, in Gregory Bateson's sense, is precisely what is learned from the contexts in which lower-level learning takes place. We want our schools to be the kinds of places where young people develop pervasive assumptions about the world that are compatible with a democratic society. We suspect that teachers must develop such a character in order to transmit it and in order to foster the gradual renewal of the system. And we know that any change that is achieved will be the result of the imperfect processes of a society that is only partly democratic in its functioning. Whether we are discussing K–12 classrooms or the lecture halls and seminar rooms of schools of education, we are faced with the need to look at multiple logical levels in order to make sense of a fluid, confusing, and frequently contradictory world.

Increasingly, learners need to make choices even as they receive incongruent and conflicting messages, and they need to be able to affirm a postmodern world in which such incongruities are part of the basic pattern. The necessary learning is unlikely to occur by precept, for teaching by precept notably ignores logical type differences, presenting "Love your neighbor" and "Sit up straight" as if these were parallel injunctions. We cannot simply specify "the right thing to do," for contexts shift and improvisation is critical.

Just as citizenship, conflict resolution, and psychotherapy pose the need for empathy, other areas of research or study also involve attending to more than one point of view and searching for resolution. The traditional methodology of anthropology (and sometimes of sociology) is participant observation, which involves just such a double awareness of self and the larger system and the possible dissonance between them, and this double focus has been enhanced and deepened by recent emphases on reflexive methodologies. I believe that in her comment on the 1948 elections, my mother, the anthropologist Margaret Mead, revealed the stance of a lifelong participant observer. It should be possible to teach children to be participant observers, able to think about dissonance between their position and the characteristics of the larger system, in order to prepare them to be citizens, just as it should be possible to teach beginning teachers to be loyal critics of the school systems in which they are immersed.

My interest in discussing participant observation in this context came from asking myself the question, "What would you do if you had the possibility of designing only one course out of, say, sixteen that a given future teacher will take?" If a course directly counters the prevailing doctrine, most students will compensate by keeping it separate and forgetting it when they move to other settings; a few will become disciples of the maverick professor and probably be unemployable, for if they reject everything else, they will be converted but uneducated. If the goal is to use that one course both to introduce new ideas and ensure that those ideas are integrated with other available ideas, it becomes necessary to introduce a process of thought that will be deutero-learned and follow the student into other contexts. My answer has been to propose teaching the skills of participant observation, including self-observation.

Participant observation involves two levels: I am present in the situation as a participant, and at the next level up I am outside the situation as an observer, so I am potentially aware of my double role and the ongoing situation that involves me in that double role.

A small example could apply to either a graduate student or a ten-year-old. Jan is invited to a meal at a neighboring house where one member of the household is known from school or from the workplace. Jan participates in the family meal, eating, joining the conversation, improvising some way of expressing appreciation. In the United States today, such an invitation may involve exposure to unfamiliar foods, table customs, and patterns of relationship.

At the same time, Jan is an observer, noticing and puzzling through the patterns in the behavior of others. The adaptive value of that observation may be effective conformity, learning to fit in, but Jan may be able to articulate the patterns observed in addition to simply imitating and may be able to make explicit comparisons. Part of our contemporary emphasis is on preparing the child not to reject whatever is new or unfamiliar, but tolerance is not enough without curiosity and respect.

Jan is more likely to be aware of being an observer if he or she comes from elsewhere, say another country or region, and has experienced alternative patterns, or if the neighbors belong to a different class or cultural group. Someone habituated to and trained in participant observation may become aware of several possibilities: discussing those observations with the hosts, making them also participant observers of the familiar pattern; reporting back on returning to familiar territory—perhaps influencing the alternative set of mores; beginning to tamper purposely with the pattern, whether through suggestions or initiatives; or making choices—resolving to practice some consciously chosen pattern in the future. Let us say that Jan is used to a sit-down meal, while the neighbor's household depends on catch-up meals, "grazing," and take-out. Or vice versa. Either pattern may be fascinating to someone accustomed to the other. In either case, the meanings of "home" and "self" may be changed. The differences are not trivial.

We can now explore the meaning of this experience. Let us first assume that Jan is enrolled in a graduate school of education. Participation in class is not usually reflexive—learning what you are told to learn is like eating what is set before you, except that the mores of the classroom require regurgitation. Graduate students do, however, all come from elsewhere in the sense that they have experienced other somewhat different kinds of classrooms and must acquire a slightly differing set of mores in order to conform, but the differences are not as great as forks to chopsticks. Teaching styles may vary also within the program, which can either strengthen it or weaken it.

Imagine now that Jan has been exposed to some experience (and this is the course we might choose to design) that makes him or her enter every classroom as a participant observer in the sense in which I am using the term. Jan notices patterns in the way each professor teaches and in the organization of the material, and questions these, pressing the professor to be increasingly self-observant, making comparisons, and challenging the others as well to consider alternative approaches. An awareness of variability becomes part of his or her work—exams and essays—and subsequent teaching style. Aware of making choices and influencing patterns, Jan begins to discuss this also, with colleagues, pupils, and mentors. Jan knows how to conform—how to play the game and meet a professor's or administrator's expectations—but also how to move up the systemic levels, to play a metagame. Without ever fully articulating what he or she is doing, Jan is able to model it for peers and colleagues and in responding to diverse learning styles as a teacher.

Jan has learned several lessons essential to living in a democracy and to teaching in a way that supports democracy: that there is more than one way of behaving in a given situation, ways of behavior that have their own order and elegance, patterns that can be described; that there are choices among these alternatives—and maybe new ones to invent; and that suggesting alternatives opens the freedom of making choices to others. With luck, Jan will go into practice teaching not as the apostle of a new dogma but as the practitioner of a new way of looking at dogma. Democracy requires all of these understandings.

The experience is no doubt different for a ten-year-old, and I believe it is even more important. Children encounter many profound contradictions: between households, between home and school and religious services, and as consumers of the media. To the extent that these experiences are simply juxtaposed, they may undermine the capacity to make sense of the world or support reactions of rejection or envy or confusion. Similarly, it is not sufficient to expose children to multicultural lists of differing customs, offering new and unresolved contradictions. In these confusing times, children need to learn to observe themselves observing even as they participate (even in the classroom, which in its own way is a foreign country from year to year) and simultaneously to move up logical levels when faced with contradictions.

A very small intervention in teacher training, involving training in participant observation and reflection on that experience, might change the way other parts of the system function. What Jan learns from each class may meet requirements and yet be different in logical structure from what the professor teaches; put simply, the professor may assert absolutes, and Jan may listen with respect but hear them as relative. As a teacher, Jan will also continue to learn, drawing lessons by reflecting on classroom experiences, relishing surprises, empowered by failures as well as successes. If we can design a model for teaching participant observation to both graduate students and ten-year-olds, we may also enable them to make the processes of teaching and learning mutual. Not a bad start in creating a school system that is itself able to learn and supporting in the next generation a necessary aspect of the democratic character.

NOTES

1. Alfred North Whitehead and Bertrand Russell, *Principia Mathematica,* 2nd ed. (Cambridge: Cambridge University Press, 1925).

2. Robert Kegan, *In Over Our Heads: The Mental Demands of Modern Life* (Cambridge, Mass.: Harvard University Press, 1994).

3. Daniel Lerner, *The Passing of Traditional Society: Modernizing the Middle East* (Glencoe, Ill.: Free Press, 1958).

4. Adrienne Kaufmann, "The Pro-choice/Pro-life Conflict: An Exploratory Study to Understand the Nature of the Conflict and to Develop Constructive Conflict Intervention Designs" (unpublished doctoral dissertation, George Mason University, 1999).

5. Gregory Bateson, "Naven: Epilogue 1958," in Gregory Bateson, *A Sacred Unity: Further Steps to an Ecology of Mind,* edited by Rodney E. Donaldson (New York: HarperCollins, 1991), pp. 53-54.

7

COGNITIVE ASPECTS OF
DEMOCRATIC THINKING

Benő Csapó

THE DEVELOPMENT OF DEMOCRATIC character can be studied from several different perspectives, among them cognitive psychology and the broader, more general, and interdisciplinary cognitive science. Cognitive psychology studies human reasoning and cognition as information processing. This processing involves not only such basic mechanisms as how we perceive, decode, represent, store, and retrieve information but more complex mental phenomena as well, including how we use knowledge in a familiar context, how we apply our existing knowledge to novel situations, how we draw inferences, and how we make decisions.

In the past few years, spectacular development has taken place in the field of learning and instruction, especially in areas influenced by cognitive science. Developing democratic character, one of the main aims of schooling, cannot be isolated from other processes of teaching. However, research into learning and instruction shows little overlapping with the research into democracy and education. Therefore, in this chapter I relate these two areas of research to show how methods of the cognitive approach can be extended and how its results can be applied to the field of democratic education.

Since *democracy* is, in common usage, a political term that is discussed in an educational context as mostly related to values and virtues, it is not obvious that cognitive science has a relevant message for those who aim at developing democratic character. Therefore, I first outline the historical background of the differentiation of the affective and cognitive

126

domains and trace the roots of their integration into unified frameworks. Then I discuss some of those cognitive processes that are involved in democratic thinking.

Research into social cognition has already identified a number of mental processes that play important roles when we think and make decisions in social contexts. However, cognitive research, especially the application of its results to education, has continuously been changing our view of the values and qualities of knowledge and has been reshaping the methods that are used in the schools to fulfill their basic missions. Beyond transmitting knowledge, other objectives receive growing attention in schooling: teaching thinking, improving cognitive abilities, and developing problem-solving skills, for example. New research provides us with theoretical frameworks and empirical evidence to satisfy these aims. These new resources also allow us to rethink the consequences of recent changes in the study of cognition for developing democratic character. Contemporary research suggests a new view of how we form mental representations of our social environment, accumulate our experiences, build a knowledge base about social phenomena that we face in everyday life, solve complex problems that involve social relationships, and make decisions in social situations.

The Relationship of the Cognitive and the Affective

Can we help our students to be more democratic thinkers by cultivating their cognitive capacities? Everyday wisdom suggests that being smart does not necessarily imply being moral; history has shown us that human intelligence can be used for good and bad purposes alike. On the other hand, it seems obvious that in order to make good and morally right decisions in situations that we face in a complex society, not only do we have to possess knowledge, we also need a number of highly developed social and cognitive skills that function smoothly and efficiently together.

This question of the relationship between cognitive and affective characteristics is not new at all. Philosophers and educators attempt to answer it from time to time. One of the earliest conceptualizations of this relationship was put forward by Greek philosophers around two and a half millennia ago. Socrates, who represented a firm view of moral intellectualism, nevertheless considered moral and intellectual virtues one and the same. He thought that all virtues were merely forms of scientific knowledge. According to Socrates, no one acts wrongly on purpose; the only cause of an immoral action is the lack of proper knowledge and intellectual capacity to find the right action. In short, the one who knows is good.

Not much later, Aristotle clearly differentiated two classes of virtues that we today would categorize as the cognitive and affective domains. He also distinguished the ways these virtues are acquired: "Virtue, then, being of two kinds, intellectual and moral, intellectual virtue in the main owes both its birth and its growth to teaching (for which it requires experience and time), while moral virtue comes about as a result of habit, whence also its name *(ethike)* is one that is formed by a slight variation from the word *ethos* (habit)."[1]

Aristotle not only identified these types of virtues, but he analyzed the relationship between them as well. After further differentiating the types of virtues and examining their connections, he concluded that moral and intellectual virtues mutually suppose each other's existence. As for the moral prerequisites of the cognitive side, he wrote: "Therefore it is evident that it is impossible to be practically wise without being good."[2] On the other side, moral virtues require intellectual foundations: "It is clear, then, from what has been said, that it is not possible to be good in the strict sense without practical wisdom, nor practically wise without moral virtue. But in this way we may also refute the dialectical argument whereby it might be contended that the virtues exist in separation from each other."[3]

It is often said that the history of science is mostly an elaboration of what Aristotle outlined in his philosophical works. Of course, scientific research has accomplished much more than Aristotle could ever have envisioned, but there is at least a morsel of truth in this statement. As for the relationship of the affective and cognitive attributes of the personality, his instructions may undoubtedly be followed.

After the birth of modern psychology and the educational sciences, several theorists working in different paradigms examined the relationships between cognitive and affective attributes. Jean Piaget, who devised one of the most complex and sophisticated cognitive developmental theories, extended his methodology to the study of moral development. He pointed out that children's moral judgment involves a number of cognitive components that are characteristic of specific ages.[4] Lawrence Kohlberg elaborated on this idea, basing his theory of the development of moral reasoning on children's cognitive development.[5] William Damon, employing a slightly different approach, also examined the relationships of reasoning and morality.[6] These studies and many others have shown that cognitive and affective—or moral and intellectual—attributes are closely interrelated, and their developmental processes are interdependent.

In schooling, on the other hand, the cognitive and the affective have often been separated. Instruction, that is, transmitting knowledge or cultivating the intellect, historically took place apart from improving morals: at different times, in different places, often in different institutions. Such frameworks as Bloom's cognitive taxonomies of educational objectives have appeared only recently on the educational scene. Although still separating the cognitive and affective domains, they treated the goals of both in an equal manner, or at least they handled them within the same comprehensive system. By offering methods for determining educational objectives more precisely, these taxonomies, despite their shortcomings, opened the way for a great deal of improvement in identifying the goals of education. And by providing patterns for the operationalization of affective goals, they also pointed the way to strengthening the moral side of schooling. One of the obstacles to encouraging the development of value systems in education is that although there is agreement on the importance of moral goals, these goals fade away as they are translated into a curriculum and as the curriculum is implemented in educational practice. Bloom's work made it possible to identify the affective goals at the level of observable behavior, and thus to monitor the curriculum's implementation. Unfortunately, however, the taxonomy of the affective domain was completed much later than that of the cognitive domain and has remained in the shadows, receiving much less attention and exerting much less influence than the cognitive taxonomy.[7]

In general, at the level of theoretical analysis we have to distinguish between these two notions under discussion. The cognitive and affective domains (or the intellectual and moral) are different enough to be analyzed and described separately. Furthermore, in the course of empirical research, attention may be focused on one or the other. Thus, there is no problem with the separation and differentiation if they take place at the level of scientific analysis. But results of recent cognitive research also suggest that the different components of democratic character are so closely interrelated that their developmental processes cannot be separated.

Democratic Thinking as a Cognitive System

If there exist areas in the study of cognition that are complex and do not lend themselves easily to a rational conceptual analysis, democratic thinking must be counted among them. However, the framework of today's cognitive psychology offers a variety of approaches, methods, and models to study human cognition; the continuous shift that is taking place in cognitive science, particularly within the cognitive psychology of school learning, makes these approaches more and more relevant for the study of the development of democratic thinking. These changes, although not independent of each other, take place in a number of different directions. The emphasis of research is moving from simple to complex, from content free to content bound, from context independent to context dependent, from individualistic to socially determined, from receptive to constructive, from active to interactive attributes of thinking, from direct instruction to applying indirect effects, and from teaching to organizing influential learning environments.

Earlier paradigms emphasized the universal attributes of thinking, with research focusing on its structure and form. These paradigms, ranging from the psychometric approach to Piagetian theory, paid little attention to the particular attributes of cognition, to its specific content, or to the environment in which it takes place. The first models of cognitive psychology considered the computer as the best metaphor of human cognition. Recent comparative studies, however, have revealed that thinking is much less computation-like and much less rational than early frameworks suggested. General thinking operations or formal thinking schemes play a much less significant role in everyday, real-life problem solving than previously supposed. Therefore, not only the structure but also the content of thinking is significant in determining its efficacy. Furthermore, domain- and context-specific thinking patterns are the mental tools that make human cognition really efficient.[8] These new focuses of cognitive research have their consequences for developing democratic thinking as well.

If the content of thinking is more crucial than its structure, then the possibility of transferring knowledge from one situation into another is limited. A more general aspect of this issue is the relationship of situation and social context. Early cognitive theories focused on the mechanisms of knowledge acquisition in pure, laboratory-like situations. Since knowledge mastered in such situations—including many school settings—is hardly applicable in other, especially real-life, ones, a number of theoretical frameworks have been proposed to conceptualize this feature of human learning and cognition. Technically, the theory of situated cognition, as Clancey formulates it, "claims that every human thought and action is adapted to the environment, that is, situated, because what people *perceive,* how they *conceive of their activity,* and what they *physically do* develop together."[9]

In a slightly different way, almost the same can be said about the role that contexts play in the application of knowledge. A number of studies in several domains (many of them dealing with problems in the fields of mathematics and science education) indicated that even when problems or tasks are well defined and their structures are identical (or isomorphic, to use the usual term of cognitive psychology) there may be great differences in solving these problems, depending very much on how familiar the contexts of the problems are. Ceci and Roazzi describe this phenomenon as follows:

> Transfer of learning across contexts appears to be quite limited. In fact, outside the case of those rare individuals who are recognized as brilliant, the norm is for subjects not to transfer. Depending on how much knowledge one possesses about the theme in question, and the social implications of various aspects of the physical context, cognitive processes will be deployed with differential efficiency.
>
> The failure to transfer learning from one context to another is pervasive, including both the young and old, educated and uneducated, and high and low IQ. . . . Based on the available research, it appears that even those students at good universities who take ample science, statistics, and math courses do not transfer the principles they learn in these courses to novel contexts.[10]

If this pessimistic account is true for mathematics and the sciences, where the structure of knowledge is more transparent and students spend hundreds of hours of concentrated effort to master the subjects, what can we say about the social studies? In the social sciences and the humanities, knowledge is much less well structured, and general principles are often hidden or overshadowed by incidental elements. There are more subjective components involved, and facts can be interpreted from many different points of view.

In our everyday lives, we learn patterns that differ from situation to situation. Politeness, for example, and the customs of good manners are context and situation specific to a great extent. We are socialized to behave in very different ways even in basically similar situations. Our decisions are influenced by particular rather than general attributes of interpersonal relationships. Academic school settings, peer groups, families, and workplaces offer different social environments in which to interact with others or to solve problems that involve other persons. In these environments, we even use different languages to negotiate and discuss issues or just to describe and communicate our experiences. We may well ask again whether these different settings facilitate the development of the same thinking schemes. Can the skills acquired in one of these situations be easily applied in another? To answer this question, let us consider what research says about the process of gathering experiences, representing and storing knowledge in memory, and retrieving and using that knowledge.

There is always a temptation to describe the acquisition of personal knowledge by using the model of how the sciences accumulate scientific knowledge. However, in spite of inevitable parallels in these processes, the components of the fine mechanisms are rather different. Scientific investigations are collective efforts; use a number of different resources, tools, and equipment; may aim at discovering the deeper structures of the examined phenomena; and construct general, formal models. In contrast, in our personal processes of accumulating experiences, what we first perceive are the surfaces of phenomena, and since we lack the resources and instruments of digging deeper, we usually represent and store in our minds what we have found at the surface.

This is especially apparent in social cognition, the process by which we gather experiences about our social environment. Cognitive psychology has suggested a number of conceptions, such as schemes and frames, to name and describe those larger units of meaning that can be identified in our organized body of knowledge. In the field of social cognition, stories are among such larger units or building blocks of our knowledge. Roger C. Shank has advanced one of the most well-known and most radical (and therefore most disputed) views of the role of stories in organizing knowledge. He claims that almost all of our social knowledge is represented in the form of stories.[11] Others, taking broader and less radical perspectives, argue for the relevance of a number of personalized storylike constructions that have been identified in several fields of research. Such constructions as narratives, accounts, autobiographies, and scripts indicate a convergence of research in social, cognitive, personality, and developmental psychology. As Harvey and Martin explain, "Storylike constructions that we call accounts . . . represent the *principal* grounds for understanding and conveying meaning, generally in social discourse. There would be no discourse nor meaning in social acts without the drive and ability to construct and report stories."[12]

Since stories are deeply personal constructs, different persons may form different stories about the same situation, and since stories for the most part capture the surface attributions of a phenomenon, an individual may compose different stories about situations that a more thorough analysis would describe as identical. For example, a child may construct a story about a phenomenon that a researcher may term "accepting others' point of view," but it may be a story about authority, friendship, or love, depending on whether it takes place at school, in a group of peers, or in the family. Since there are few coincidences between school experiences and those gathered within peer groups or the family, these experiences are usually represented as different stories.

In this framework, understanding other people means mapping their stories into ours. The impact of broader culture can be taken into account by the concept of *story skeletons*. In every culture there exist a number of story skeletons—basic common frames or structures (for example, "The teacher does not like my child.")—and when we are composing our personal stories, we may tap this common base. This common base offers good opportunity for education to influence students' construction of personalized stories about, for example, democratic practices. The other side of the coin is, again, the impact of diverse incidental peculiarities: there are no two identical understandings of the same phenomenon, and personalized versions of story skeletons may also be very diverse.

A similar construction, the script, can be considered as a common outline or generalized essence of stories that take place in identical or similar situations and therefore is also a relevant concept from an educational point of view. "A script is a set of expectations about what will happen next in a well-understood situation," observe Schank and Abelson.[13] It is a kind of structure of sequential events in which we may know our role or how we are supposed to act to make a story happen. Those teaching democratic practices might do well to focus on encouraging students to acquire the proper scripts.

Taking all this into account, we cannot expect that the principles students learn concerning society, social relationships, and democracy or the thinking skills they acquire in certain contexts will easily transfer to others. Thus, it is obviously not enough for us to teach broad democratic ideas in the schools. Children cannot be expected to apply these ideas to every specific situation of life; they have to learn these again and again in each new case. Or, at least, transfer does not come automatically; it requires further learning and practice if the same reasoning operations or structures are applied to new contents. For example, students who have just mastered a certain form of equality in one context—perhaps a set of rules for distributing among themselves some money that they have earned together—cannot necessarily apply the same conceptions of equality or rules of distribution when another type of reward is to be shared, such as the possibility of visiting an amusement park. Children may understand rules at a concrete level—for example, as thinking about money in the first case—and not at a deeper level that involves comprehending underlying principles.

If recent research suggests that human cognition is so much less rational than we have believed before and if the transfer of knowledge is so limited, how can we manage our lives at all? How can we use our knowledge to solve complex problems? One of the keys to understanding this paradox is that in most real-life situations, we base our decisions on experiences resulting from the same or very similar situations. We use particular information and rely on our tacit knowledge. Instead of transferring general skills mastered elsewhere or using "global" knowledge, we use specific skills mastered, as it were, at the site of the use.

Knowledge Base for Democratic Thinking

Discussing the content of thinking, John Dewey wrote over eight decades ago: "The material of thinking is not thoughts, but actions, facts, events, and the relations of things. In other words, to think effectively one must have had, or now have, experiences which will furnish him resources for coping with the difficulty at hand."[14] As Dewey noted, we obviously cannot think about nothing. Thinking needs a subject. The computer analogy may help to explain what this may mean in an information-processing model. Computer programs process certain types of information: word-processing programs deal with text, spreadsheets manage data, other programs process pictures, music, and so on. If it is functionally the analogue of software, thinking also requires information to handle. However, human information processing does differ from that of computers, especially when development is also taken into account. Processing mechanisms are attached to the information they process. A bond is formed between thinking and the content (domain, situation, context) on which it has been executed. In other words, cognitive competencies are domain specific and context linked to a great extent. Therefore, if the development of democratic thinking aims at expanding its functioning into broad areas of the social environment, it needs an adequate knowledge base for practice. In short, democratic thinking has to be contextualized properly. Its supporting knowledge has to be taken from domains that form natural subjects of thinking in school and in real-life contexts alike. But what kind of knowledge base would best serve democratic thinking? Nothing less than the knowledge we need to live in a democratic society.

In complex situations, democratic behavior (that is, democratic acting and decision making) requires a broad knowledge that can be obtained from several different sources. If the concept of democracy is not limited to political processes, and the purpose of education goes beyond reproducing the labor force, practically every relevant area of culture has its place in the knowledge base that democratic thinking requires.[15] However, different areas of culture play different roles in such an educational process: some may have direct effects, and others may be more indirect. From this analysis, two main domains of knowledge can be distinguished: general knowledge about information from a number of areas required for leading a successful life in today's democratic societies and knowledge required for acting in a democratic way in decision-making situations that a person faces at both the individual and the social levels.

In traditional school curricula, instruction is organized mostly according to the disciplines of the arts and sciences, and the coherence of knowledge is derived from each discipline. This setup may be satisfactory if the school intends to train future scientists or disciplinary experts, but it does not always fit the purpose of educating citizens. Cultivating students' minds and preparing them to be democratic thinkers requires a different logic of organization in education than that required by the teaching of the disciplines. In recent decades, researchers have continuously analyzed how school instruction should be changed and how it could be better adapted to the cognitive-developmental processes of children.[16] Instructional innovations aimed at improving the quality of students' knowledge have been organized around topics such as "teaching for understanding."[17]

How instruction should be better adapted to the needs of a democratic society has also been a continuous topic in the discourse on renewing education. Especially since the publication of Dewey's influential *Democracy and Education* in 1916, such questions as what democracy precisely means, how its attributes can be characterized in an educational context, and how educational processes can be tuned to its needs have become major issues. In this discourse, several new kinds of curricula have been proposed that draw from a wide spectrum of different traditional disciplines and new areas of research.[18] These curricula that focus on teaching for democracy—if we use this paraphrase of "teaching for understanding"—ensure coherence through the organization of teaching and learning around the aims of educating democratic citizens.

One of the most interesting aspects of Dewey's works is that he connected cognitive and democratic aspects of education very early.[19] Recently, exciting research has been published that combines these two aspects within the latest theoretical frameworks and provides cognitive analyses of teaching in several content areas that may significantly contribute to developing democratic character. Particularly noteworthy results have been reported in research on science education and social studies. For a long time—from Piaget's experiments until the latest research—conceptual development was characteristically studied through concepts from the natural sciences. Science education, especially in some of its current approaches, has a prominent place in "teaching for democracy," but social studies offers even broader possibilities. Recent research has proven that even the most classical area of social studies, history, can offer a wide range of new possibilities to shape students' society-related conceptual frameworks.[20] At the same time, researchers have developed and studied several concepts related to society and social organization that inevitably belong to that core of knowledge required for democratic thinking. In contrast to most previous studies that focused on the problems of particular disciplines, these recent ones approach teaching from a consideration of the needs of children's cognitive development. The development of students' conception, the process of conceptual change, and the interaction between development and instruction are among the most promising but so far not exhaustively studied topics. As Torney-Purta remarks:

> Even with the recent explosion of research on reasoning, two important questions concerning adolescents' thinking about political and social issues remain: How do we define conceptual change in the social and political domain of knowledge dealing with contemporary political events and with historical events? and What is important about developmental processes as they intersect with instructional processes to influence conceptual change in this domain?[21]

If the school introduces certain society-related concepts too late or if the curricula introduce concepts in a highly abstract, formal, and sterile manner, we face a danger. Children's conceptual development begins earlier and may take a different path than would be desirable; consequently, later they remain uninfluenced by school education. Research on science misconceptions provides a massive body of evidence on how children's simple generalizations and naive models may differ from the scientific knowledge that the school intends to transmit to them. Society, one of the most complex subjects of scientific research, seems to be difficult to describe in models that fit students' early developmental levels. Therefore, in traditional schools, social studies in the primary grades present simple historic stories—if such a field of study exists there at all. Themes that demonstrate concepts related to social processes and the structure of society are introduced later, and sometimes too late. On the other hand, our daily experiences as well as developmental research show that children's understanding of some crucial social concepts emerges very early.

The development of ideas related to society and social organization, which are inevitably parts of a knowledge base that democratic thinking requires, has recently become part of mainstream cognitive research. And instead of exploring how canonized scientific knowledge can be taught, research moves closer to children's real-life learning and developmental processes. Delval characterizes this shift as he experienced the change of focus in his own research: "For many years we have been studying children's ideas about different aspects of social institutions. More recently we started to look at the ideas they have about how society is structured and how they understand social differences and social strata change."[22]

Concepts such as possession and ownership are among the first things children learn in modern societies, and they gain hands-on experiences with money and prices at a very young age. Children may also have experiences that build their understanding of poverty, wealth, profit, and the sources of wealth.[23] If schools do not deal with these concepts early enough and do not help students to elaborate them by encouraging children to think about such concepts in a proper context, they may become fossilized in a simple or primitive form. Other concepts that extend thinking in the moral and democratic dimensions, such as equity and equality, which seem abstract but are nevertheless vital for democratic thinking, should also be involved very early in money- or economy-related thinking and should be associated inseparably with the other more materialistic and easily accessible conceptions.

Developmental research has also shown that children's conceptual framework of the organization of society emerges early. Some basic concepts—for example, social contract—are rooted in children's everyday experiences or originate from the family or peer groups. Others are shaped mostly by formal education: for example, the state, state formation, government, and law. But studies also point out that in school instruction, even such crucial concepts are not always properly treated. High school students may face difficulties when asked to interpret sociopolitical concepts such as reform, civil rights, or social class. At best, most of them can mention some examples.[24]

The changes taking place in science education in these years also drive learning closer to the aims of democratic education. The new way of thinking is indicated in the discourse about the mission of schooling by the replacement of the phrase "teaching of physics, chemistry, and biology" with "science education." The aim to provide future citizens with a broad scientific literacy is demonstrated by projects that are organized around the concepts of "science for all students," "everyday science," and "home science." All of these highlight the intention that general and compulsory schooling should concentrate on relevant, socially valid knowledge, while the transmittal of disciplinary knowledge may be left to the special training of future experts.[25]

There seems to be international agreement about this orientation of science education. Documents of international organizations, as well as theoretical frameworks of large-scale international assessment endeavors, emphasize the role of scientific literacy in the democratic operation of the society as a facilitator of decision making. For example, in the Programs for International Student Assessment (PISA) project that aims to assess students' knowledge every three years in Organization for Economic Cooperation and Development countries, scientific literacy is defined as "the capacity to use scientific knowledge, to identify questions and to draw evidence-based conclusions in order to understand and help make decisions about the natural world and the changes made to it through human activity."[26] And later, when the decision-making element is elaborated, the document highlights the importance of contexts and values:

> The phrase *understand and help make decisions* indicates first, that an understanding of the natural world is valued as a goal in itself as well as being necessary for decision making and, second, that scientific understanding can contribute to, but rarely determines, decision making. Practical decisions are always set in situations having social, political or economic dimensions and scientific knowledge is used in the context of human values related to these dimensions. Where there is agreement about the values in a situation, the use of scientific evidence can be non-controversial. Where values differ, the selection and use of scientific evidence in decision making will be more controversial.[27]

Thus, as exemplified in the PISA framework, a knowledge base is a necessary but not sufficient contribution to decision making. Decisions are always made in specific contexts. Since it is not always ensured that students can transfer their knowledge from one context to another, a number of new, integrated areas of research and fields of study have been emerging to help students study science in a social decision-making context. For example, science-technology-society (STS) courses integrate scientific knowledge, its transfer to technology, and the impact of both on society. Citizenship science organizes science knowledge to correspond more directly to the need to make decisions in simple, personal, everyday situations (for example, choosing recyclable materials or using renewable sources of energy) and to take a stand and vote on large-scale economic and political issues (building highways or airports, protecting nature, preserving biodiversity, taxing the tobacco industry, subsidizing research on alternative energy sources or less-polluting technologies, and so forth). Other educational programs bring in even broader problems like sustainable development or the global consequences of air pollution. (See also Chapter Five.)

Skills for Democratic Thinking

Regarding the operational or procedural aspects of democratic thinking, it must be stressed again that thinking itself, without the adequate content, does not necessarily help one to make democratic decisions. Thinking has to be contextualized; it has to operate in the appropriate situations. Continuing in this vein, for democratic thinking to be practiced, the social context requires the use of certain skills. Although every thinking process may be relevant in a way, some skills are more directly related to democratic thinking than are others.

Critical thinking may be the form of thinking that has received the most scholarly attention in the past half century, and it is quite closely associated with citizenship education. Some cognitive scientists have considered it the thinking process most vital to citizenship because it helps one to evaluate every piece of information and, especially, to resist political manipulation and ideological indoctrination.[28] For a long time, and for the lay public in particular, critical thinking meant little more than a healthy skeptical attitude, a generally critical disposition toward everything. Those who aim at a more precise technical definition still sketch a very broad set of thinking skills that include a number of inductive and deductive processes. For example, Halpern contends:

> Critical thinking is the use of those cognitive skills or strategies that increase the probability of a desirable outcome. It is used to describe thinking that is purposeful, reasoned, and goal directed—the kind of thinking involved in solving problems, formulating inferences, calculating likelihoods, and making decisions when the thinker is using skills that are thoughtful and effective for the particular context and type of thinking task. Other definitions include the notions that critical thinking is the formation of logical inferences . . . , the development of cohesive and logical reasoning patterns . . . , and careful and deliberate determination of whether to accept, reject, or suspend judgment.[29]

Perhaps the concepts connoted by "to accept, reject, or suspend judgment" are the most specific attributes of critical thinking, but these are still too general to make it easily identifiable. Recent research on cognition is more precise when identifying thinking skills relevant to processing information in social contexts. For example, categorization, generalization, probabilistic and correlational reasoning, logical operations (processing and comprehending the deep logical structures of verbal expressions), and causal inferences are among the skills that play an important role in social cognition. Many of these have been studied by social psychologists for a long time. As Wilkes notes about thinking processes described as relevant in other areas,

> We can expect the same basic processes that were involved there to be equally central in social cognition. However, they are labeled differently. Categorization comes under the heading of social stereotyping; reasoning comes in the form of social attribution; and knowledge updating appears in various guises including impression formation, attitude change, and persuasion. The research parallels are real and substantial and they reflect large-scale borrowings by social psychologists from methods and explanations that were first developed in the cognitive laboratory.[30]

Nevertheless, the parallels between cognition in different domains need more and careful clarification. The role of situation and context also must be taken into account here, as Wilkes continues:

> The extent of this borrowing would seem to corroborate the widely held view that individually derived cognitive models can be adapted (with some local changes) to cover the full range of social cognitive phenomena. Perhaps so, but there are other, more radical opinions that have set out to unsettle or, indeed, sever this dependent relationship.[31]

Indeed, it is hard to suppose that stereotyping or forming prejudices can be considered simple cognitive problems or that negative social phenomena can be attributed to a lack of elaborated cognitive skills. If a child's bicycle is stolen and the thief turns out to belong to a minority or to another ethnic group, the negative judgment about the thief can easily be generalized to his or her entire group, and in this way to every other individual with the same particular characteristic, especially if there are more such cases in that particular group. Although it is easy to point out where the child in this example errs, where the logical mistake is in the inference, this is obviously not a pure reasoning mistake. We do not make such generalizations with green-eyed or brown-haired people—partly because green-eyed or brown-haired people usually are not perceived as groups, and partly because other information received from other sources also influences the thinking process. Hints received from the social environment suggesting how people may be categorized and how events may be interpreted affect or, in most cases, even substitute for our inferences. We rely on the simple explanations we receive from others rather than on complicated logical inferences.[32] Therefore, it is clear that prejudices, chauvinism, and other antidemocratic behaviors cannot universally be overcome by shaping reasoning.

Still, a higher level of social understanding cannot be reached without the development of the underlying thinking mechanisms. For example, the control of variables plays an important role in cognition, as Piaget demonstrated in experiments involving simple mechanical tasks. Children learn to identify and separate variables and then determine their roles in a phenomenon. A naive thinker, for example, considers a pendulum to be a single entity. A step toward understanding why different pendulums swing with different tempos (the dependent variable) is to identify that the length of the string and the weight of the ball that hangs on it are two variables. Then, after guessing (hypothesis formation) and trying different settings (experimenting, hypothesis testing, and verification), the child learns that the length of the string in fact determines the pendulum's period of swinging. Social phenomena are much more complex than this, but understanding them requires basically similar mechanisms and insights. When thinking about a social phenomenon, such as law-breaking frequencies, one must separate variables such as ethnic group membership and socioeconomic status in order to identify their roles. Hands-on experiments in this case are excluded; the nature of this phenomenon is probabilistic rather than deterministic, and even if a child has already learned to control the variables in other contexts, this scheme cannot automatically be transferred to such a situation.

Poor reasoning skills block the development of democratic thinking and may hinder school education in its efforts to develop democratic character, especially in those cases when educational techniques assume, and their success requires, highly developed cognition. Someone who does not have the cognitive apparatus to process the presented information also lacks the alternative to form a cognitively understood model about the given phenomenon. If it does not provide children with the appropriate skills, education loses its means to shape or even influence children's moral development.

In teaching thinking, there are two main paradigms. One includes the stand-alone programs that attempt to teach thinking skills in separate courses. Although a plethora of such programs have been developed and implemented,[33] little evidence exists that they have long-term effects on intellectual development. As for teaching democratic thinking, separate courses may be useful, since there is a relevant knowledge base to think about (the content of social studies, civic education, citizenship education, philosophical and theoretical issues of democracy, and others). A good example of this approach with significant implications for developing democratic character is Lipman's work, both his "Philosophy for Children" approach and his more general works on the possibilities of developing thinking.[34]

The other approach to teaching thinking, which marks a shift from direct instruction to more indirect ways of fostering development, is labeled in a number of ways, from the more technical terms *(integration, synthesis)* to the more visual ones that move the imagination, like *embedding, infusion,* or even *infiltration.* These approaches take into account that most of our thinking skills are context bound and do not transfer easily to new domains. Therefore, multiple access of skills and thinking processes can be ensured only if they are mastered in multiple contexts, that is, if the same or similar skills are practiced in several different situations. Recent publications propose that if we expect long-term effects, thinking should be taught in a number of different school subjects across the curriculum. This has led to the concept of the thinking curriculum, which suggests that relevant thinking skills should be taught in as many subjects as possible.[35]

The embedding technique, or teaching thinking within subject-matter areas, has already been implemented in several domains and for the improvement of several thinking skills and processes.[36] However, since designing such educational programs demands competencies from many different domains, and implementing them at school requires coordinated efforts, its full potential in school is still to be seen. So far, improvement efforts have been concentrated mostly on simple, easily identifiable thinking operations (for example, integrated science courses offer a good area for practicing such skills),[37] but there are promising attempts to expand the focus on thinking to cover the whole spectrum of school subjects.[38]

On asking them for the first time, the questions "How can democratic thinking be taught across the curriculum?" and "How can thinking operations relevant for democratic thinking be embedded in a number of school subjects?" sound a bit startling. Yet the opportunities to integrate democratic thinking and subject matter can be found in abundance. Although it may sound absurd, even mathematics lessons can be used for this purpose. For example, when proportion is taught, students may calculate the proportion of people with different ethnic backgrounds on the city council, in the state legislature, or in Congress and compare the results to their respective proportions in the local, state, or national population. Another example of proportional reasoning might be to compute the distribution of income in a country over several social groups.

The concept of probability and correlation can also be taught and contextualized with social examples. Through comparing proportions in delinquency and income, students will understand not only mathematics but also something of the nature of correlational relationships in a social context. When students learn how to read multidimensional data tables, these tables may contain relevant social statistics; when they learn how to depict data on charts, they may depict, for example, the changes in the proportion of women attending college over a span of years, and so forth. With some comments and interpretation of the processed information, there is an authentic context to shape students' democratic thinking.

The sciences too offer a number of possibilities. For example, when students study carbon dioxide, they may learn about its impact on the environment and its contribution to the greenhouse effect and climate change. Although in many chemistry programs students already do this, they could go still further and study the figures of the carbon dioxide production of some countries, then compute per capita figures and compare them. In this way, they would also learn why studying chemistry is relevant, practice their proportional reasoning, and receive a moral message from the sphere of global environmental issues. Of course, exercises of this kind may take away some time from learning the core disciplinary knowledge, but what is learned in this way is learned better and for a longer and broader use.

Broader Contexts of Developing Democratic Thinking

The "learning for schools or for life?" dilemma is still alive. Since schools provide students with artificial environments, it is not obvious that school knowledge can be applied to real-life activities. Dewey described this problem as follows:

> As a consequence of the absence of the materials and occupations which generate real problems, the pupil's problems are not his; or, rather, they are his *only as* a pupil, not as a human being. Hence the lamentable waste in carrying over such expertness as is achieved in dealing with them to the affairs of life beyond the schoolroom. A pupil has a problem, but it is the problem of meeting the peculiar requirements set by the teacher. His problem becomes that of finding out what the teacher wants, what will satisfy the teacher in recitation and examination and outward deportment. Relationship to subject matter is no longer direct. The occasions and material of thought are not found in the arithmetic or the history or geography itself, but in skillfully adapting that material to the teacher's requirements. The pupil studies, but unconsciously to himself the objects of his study are the conventions and standards of the school system and school authority, not the nominal "studies." The

thinking thus evoked is artificially one-sided at the best. At its worst, the problem of the pupil is not how to meet the requirements of school life, but how to *seem* to meet them—or, how to come near enough to meeting them to slide along without an undue amount of friction. The type of judgment formed by these devices is not a desirable addition to character.[39]

If school processes are so distant from the needs of students' optimal development in the more neutral teaching materials, they are even more so when a sensitive issue that shapes students' democratic thinking is considered. Taking another perspective, a developmental one, Torney-Purta writes when comparing experiences inside and outside school:

> Instructional experience in the classroom can be contrasted with developmental experience. Developmental experience is rich in levels of meaning and social context, in redundancy as the same topics are visited and revisited, in opportunities to respond to others' ideas and to get their feedback, and in chances to construct a group identity and to experience loyalty. Instructional experience in the social studies classroom is more likely to be narrowly focused on facts, lean on context and connection, moving rapidly among topics, lacking opportunities to voice opinions without risking potential censure, and to be generalized to reach all students rather than responsive to a group identity or set of interests. Developmental experience is situated for child and adolescent in a meaningful context, often within the peer group or family or neighborhood. Instructional experience usually lacks such a context.[40]

Because of the differences between schools and "real life," it is clear that schools alone will never be able to do a perfect job of providing students with socially relevant and usable knowledge. This problem is not new, but recently a number of radical and unrealistic alternatives—from deschooling society to home teaching—have been proposed to solve it. Nevertheless, in modern societies, there are hardly any other viable alternatives to mass education than public schooling. Public schooling can be made more "lifelike" in two major ways: by bringing as many real-life processes into school as possible and by extending educational processes beyond the walls of school by encompassing more outside experiences.

If we consider what kinds of social practices relevant to social activity and related to democratic thinking should be transferred into the school, collaborative processes will most definitely be among them. In today's societies, the number of workplaces in which members of a group collaborate in ways that involve the extensive exchange of information is significantly growing. Since democratic thinking is practiced in social situations, implementing educational processes that foster democratic thinking is not only socially relevant but also reflective of real life. For a number of reasons, in the early 1990s collaborative processes became among the most extensively studied areas in learning and instruction.[41]

Several instructional processes that foster democratic thinking have already become part of mainstream education. For example, cooperative learning, group projects, modeling, and role playing offer more possibilities for practicing democratic thinking skills than teacher-dominated, frontal classroom work.[42] Recently, a number of new and refreshing ideas have appeared that may reshape these educational practices. One of them is the concept of distributed cognition, which reconfirms social and collaborative aspects of accumulating knowledge.[43] When implemented in the classroom appropriately, it constitutes a realistic model of students' future life situations, as Brown and colleagues write:

> We argue that schools should be communities where students learn to learn. In this setting teachers should be models of intentional learning and self-motivated scholarship, both individual and collaborative. . . . If successful, graduates of such communities would be prepared as lifelong learners who have learned how to learn in many domains. We aim to produce a breed of "intelligent novices". . . , students who, although they may not possess the background knowledge needed in a new field, know how to go about gaining that knowledge. . . . Ideally, in a community of learners, teachers and students serve as role models not only as "owners" of some aspects of domain knowledge, but also as acquirers, users, and extenders of knowledge in the sustained, ongoing process of understanding.[44]

The search for authentic content and activities for school learning may never end because society—the "real life" outside school—is continuously changing. Conventional wisdom notwithstanding, research and school practice alike quickly reflect these rapid changes—sometimes too rapidly. For example, recent developments in computer and information technology find their place in the school in connecting collaborating students and make it possible, without any exaggeration, to distribute components of cognition over the globe.

Turning to the other possibility of bringing education closer to real life—that is, extending formal learning beyond the school walls—the roles of families, peer groups, and other communities must be taken into account. The parts that communities play in education have recently been examined from a number of different perspectives.[45] Families and other communities outside school are often proposed as fertile fields for children's educational experiences, but they are not always the best examples for democratic practice. Therefore, studies that examine empirically how and under what circumstances family and community shape students' democratic thinking become particularly important.

In a series of both theoretically and methodologically sophisticated studies, Jacqueline Goodnow examined how people experience, interpret, and form expectations about household activities. The household work setting is the one that, for many children, offers the first context for thinking about some basic rules of a democratic community—for example, what each person should do in the home, what fairness means, how unpleasant chores should be shared, what incentives should be applied, how the work should be controlled and monitored, and how and when sanctions should be used. From these studies Goodnow created a general theoretical framework that, along with the methods devised in this context, can be applied to other work settings as well.[46]

Another study examined the developmental roots of the social contract in a cross-cultural comparative project in seven countries. As Flanagan and colleagues outlined the aims of the project, "Becoming a citizen, assuming the rights and responsibilities of membership in a social group, is a marker of attaining adult status in many societies. But what prepares people to assume those responsibilities? How do they come to understand and exercise their civic rights? What motivates them to become engaged in civil society?"[47]

Data collection took place in both industrialized countries with established democracies and countries from Eastern and Central Europe with political and economic systems still in transition. These settings offered insights into the differences in the development of civic identity that can be attributed to differences in the social environment as well as the consistent features that could be observed across countries. This survey also investigated how adolescents think about certain civic issues—for example, what importance they attribute to contributing to their communities, contributing to their society or country, helping the less fortunate, protecting the environment, and being active in politics. Interestingly, adolescents assigned the highest priority to environmental issues and then to their intentions to do something for their society or country. They attached low importance to political activism.

These studies in general also show the significance of family and immediate community in shaping students' democratic thinking. Nevertheless, for successful democratic thinking, all of the factors discussed in this chapter have to work together smoothly: affective and cognitive attributes, processes and content of thinking, individual and collaborative processes, and within-school and outside-school experiences alike. Schools provide a unique opportunity to educate commonly, but to assume that they are sufficient for the challenge of developing democratic character in the young is to ignore the complexities of the task portrayed in this book.

NOTES

1. Aristotle, *Nicomachean Ethics,* 1103a, trans. W. D. Ross, in Richard McKeon (ed.), *The Basic Works of Aristotle* (New York: Random House, 1941), p. 952.

2. Aristotle, *Nicomachean Ethics,* 1144b, p. 1035.

3. Aristotle, *Nicomachean Ethics,* 1144b, p. 1036.

4. Jean Piaget, *The Moral Judgment of the Child* (1932; New York: Free Press, 1965).

5. See, for example, Lawrence Kohlberg, "Moral Stages and Moralization: The Cognitive-Developmental Approach," in Lawrence Kohlberg (ed.), *Essays on Moral Development,* vol. 2, *The Psychology of Moral Development* (San Francisco: Harper & Row, 1984), pp. 170–205.

6. William Damon, "Early Conceptions of Positive Justice as Related to the Development of Logical Operations," *Child Development* 46 (June 1975): 301–312.

7. The influential book that is often referred to as "Bloom's Taxonomy" discussed the cognitive domain. It was first published in the mid-1950s and remained a major resource for developing curricula and designing tests until the late 1970s. See Benjamin S. Bloom, Max D. Englehart, Edward J. Furst, Walker H. Hill, and David R. Krathwohl (eds.), *Taxonomy of Educational Objectives: The Classification of Educational Goals,* Handbook 1: *Cognitive Domain* (New York: McKay, 1956). The taxonomy of the affective domain was not published until eight years later and had much less impact on educational practice. David R. Krathwohl, Benjamin S. Bloom, and Bertram B. Masia, *Taxonomy of Educational Objectives: The Classification of Educational Goals,* Handbook 2: *Affective Domain* (New York: McKay, 1964).

8. For a discussion of this issue, see, for example, David N. Perkins and Gavriel Salomon, "Are Cognitive Skills Context Bound?" *Educational Researcher* 18 (January–February 1989): 16–25.

9. William J. Clancey, *Situated Cognition: On Human Knowledge and Computer Representations* (Cambridge: Cambridge University Press, 1997), p. 1.

10. Stephen J. Ceci and Antonio Roazzi, "The Effects of Context on Cognition: Postcards from Brazil," in Robert J. Sternberg and Richard K. Wagner (eds.), *Mind in Context: Interactionist Perspectives on Human Intelligence* (Cambridge: Cambridge University Press, 1994), p. 82.

11. See Roger C. Schank and Robert P. Abelson, "Knowledge and Memory: The Real Story," in Robert S. Wyer (ed.), *Knowledge and Memory: The Real Story* (Hillsdale, N.J.: Erlbaum, 1995), pp. 1–85.

12. John H. Harvey and René Martin, "Celebrating the Story in Social Perception, Communication, and Behavior," in Wyer (ed.), *Knowledge and Memory,* p. 89.

13. Schank and Abelson, "Knowledge and Memory," p. 5.

14. John Dewey, *Democracy and Education: An Introduction to the Philosophy of Education* (1916; New York: Free Press, 1966), pp. 156–157.

15. This broader conception of democracy is elaborated in several of Goodlad and his coauthors' works. See, for example, John I. Goodlad, *In Praise of Education* (New York: Teachers College Press, 1997); and John I. Goodlad and Timothy J. McMannon (eds.), *The Public Purpose of Education and Schooling* (San Francisco: Jossey-Bass, 1997).

16. For an impressive account of the possibilities cognitive psychology offers to improve education, see Howard Gardner, *The Unschooled Mind: How Children Think and How Schools Should Teach* (New York: Basic Books, 1991). A more technical and systematic account is offered by Adrian F. Ashman and Robert N. Conway, *An Introduction to Cognitive Education: Theory and Applications* (New York: Routledge, 1997).

17. See, for example, Martha Stone Wiske (ed.), *Teaching for Understanding: Linking Research with Practice* (San Francisco: Jossey-Bass, 1997); and Tina Blythe and Associates, *The Teaching for Understanding Guide* (San Francisco: Jossey-Bass, 1997).

18. Walter C. Parker, "Curriculum for Democracy," in Roger Soder (ed.), *Democracy, Education, and the Schools* (San Francisco: Jossey-Bass, 1996), pp. 182–210.

19. Two of John Dewey's major works address cognition and democracy: *How We Think* (Boston: Heath, 1910), and "Thinking in Education," in *Democracy and Education* (New York: Macmillan, 1916).

20. For a review of current research in and new approaches to learning and teaching history, see Peter Seixas, "Conceptualizing the Growth of Historical Understanding," in David R. Olson, and Nancy Torrance (eds.), *The Handbook of Education and Human Development* (Cambridge, Mass.: Blackwell, 1996), pp. 765–783.

21. Judith Torney-Purta, "Dimensions of Adolescents' Reasoning About Political and Historical Issues: Ontological Switches, Developmental Processes,
and Situated Learning," in Mario Carretero and James F. Voss (eds.), *Cognitive and Instructional Processes in History and the Social Sciences* (Hillsdale, N.J.: Erlbaum, 1994), p. 103.

22. Juan Delval, "Stages in the Child's Construction of Social Knowledge," in
Carretero and Voss (eds.), *Cognitive and Instructional Processes*, p. 79.

23. See Adrian Furnham, "Young People's Understanding of Politics and Economics," in Carretero and Voss (eds.), *Cognitive and Instructional
Processes*, pp. 17–47.

24. See Anna Emilia Berti, "Children's Understanding of the Concept of the
State," in Carretero and Voss (eds.), *Cognitive and Instructional Processes*,
pp. 49–75.

25. For an overview of this new orientation of science education, see Wolff-
Michael Roth, *Authentic School Science* (Dordrecht, The Netherlands:
Kluwer, 1995).

26. Programs for International Student Assessment, *Measuring Student Knowledge and Skills: A New Framework for Assessment* (Paris: Organization for
Economic Cooperation and Development, 1999), p. 62. This document
elaborates the conceptual foundations of the first assessment cycle.

27. Programs for International Student Assessment, *Measuring Student Knowledge and Skills*, pp. 62–63.

28. For a review of the history of critical thinking in American education, see
Barbara Z. Presseisen, "Critical Thinking and Thinking Skills: State of the
Art Definitions and Practice in Public Schools" (paper presented at the
annual meeting of the American Educational Research Association, New
Orleans, April 1994).

29. Diane F. Halpern, *Thought and Knowledge: An Introduction to Critical
Thinking*, 3rd ed. (Mahwah, N.J.: Erlbaum, 1996), p. 5.

30. A. L. Wilkes, *Knowledge in Minds: Individual and Collective Processes in
Cognition* (Hove, United Kingdom: Psychology Press, 1997), p. 299.

31. Wilkes, *Knowledge in Minds*, p. 299.

32. For a systematic discussion of cognition in social context, see Wilkes,
Knowledge in Minds.

33. Costa published several volumes about American projects for teaching
thinking. See Arthur L. Costa (ed.), *Developing Minds: A Resource Book
for Teaching Thinking*, rev. ed., vol. 1 (Alexandria, Va.: Association for
Supervision and Curriculum Development, 1991); Arthur L. Costa (ed.),

Developing Minds: Programs for Teaching Thinking, rev. ed., vol. 2 (Alexandria, Va.: Association for Supervision and Curriculum Development, 1991). For a similar collection of European programs, see J.H.M. Hamers and M. T. Overtoom (eds.), *Teaching Thinking in Europe: Inventory of European Programs* (Utrecht, The Netherlands: Sardes, 1997).

34. Matthew Lipman, *Thinking in Education* (Cambridge: Cambridge University Press, 1991).

35. See Lauren B. Resnick and Leopold E. Klopfer (eds.), *Toward the Thinking Curriculum: Current Cognitive Research* (Alexandria, Va.: Association for Supervision and Curriculum Development, 1989).

36. For a more elaborated overview and description of one of the techniques, see Benő Csapó, "Improving Thinking Through the Content of Teaching," in Johann H. M. Hamers, Johannes E. H. van Luit, and Benő Csapó (eds.), *Teaching and Learning Thinking Skills* (Lisse: Swets & Zeitlinger, 1999), pp. 37–62.

37. In this category, Cognitive Acceleration Through Science Education is one of the most impressive programs. See Philip Adey and Michael Shayer, *Really Raising Standards: Cognitive Intervention and Academic Achievement* (New York: Routledge, 1994).

38. See John T. Bruer, *Schools for Thought: A Science of Learning in the Classroom* (Cambridge, Mass.: MIT Press, 1993).

39. Dewey, *Democracy and Education,* p. 156.

40. Torney-Purta, "Dimensions of Adolescents' Reasoning," p. 118.

41. This change of emphasis, sometimes dubbed the sociocultural revolution, was partly a backlash against early cognitivism, which, according to some critics, was too mechanistic, reductionist, and individualistic. This new trend drew from the cultural-historical approach, social constructivism, and other Vigotskyan and neo-Vigotskyan theories. See, for example, Denis Newman, Peg Griffin, and Michael Cole, *The Construction Zone: Working for Cognitive Change in School* (Cambridge: Cambridge University Press, 1989).

42. A systematic discussion of using collaborative methods in a broad range of school subjects can be found in Mary Hamm and Dennis Adams, *The Collaborative Dimensions of Learning* (Norwood, N.J.: Ablex, 1992).

43. Cole and Engestrom outline the development of the notion of distributed cognition from the birth of psychology in Wundt's laboratory through the theories of Russian psychologists to the most recent computer applications. See Michael Cole and Yrjö Engeström, "A Cultural-Historical Approach to Distributed Cognition," in Gavriel Solomon (ed.), *Distributed Cognitions:*

Psychological and Educational Considerations (Cambridge: Cambridge University Press, 1993), pp. 1–46.

44. Ann L. Brown, Doris Ash, Martha Rutherford, Kathryn Nakagawa, Ann Gordon, and Joseph C. Campione, "Distributed Expertise in the Classroom," in Solomon (ed.), *Distributed Cognitions*, p. 190.

45. See, for example, Goodlad, *In Praise of Education;* Sudia Paloma McCaleb, *Building Communities of Learners: A Collaboration of Students, Families and Community* (Mahwah, N.J.: Erlbaum, 1997); and Paul Theobald, *Teaching the Commons: Place, Pride, and the Renewal of Community* (Boulder, Colo.: Westview, 1997).

46. Jacqueline J. Goodnow, "Collaborative Rules: How Are People Supposed to Work with One Another?" in Paul B. Baltes and Ursula M. Staudinger (eds.), *Interactive Minds: Life-Span Perspectives on the Social Foundation of Cognition* (Cambridge: Cambridge University Press, 1996), pp. 163–197.

47. Connie Flanagan, Britta Jonsson, Luba Botcheva, Benő Csapó, Jennifer Bowes, Peter Macek, Irina Averina, and Elena Sheblanova, "Adolescents and the 'Social Contract': Developmental Roots of Citizenship in Seven Countries," in Miranda Yates and James Youniss (eds.), *Roots of Civic Identity: International Perspectives on Community Service and Activism in Youth* (Cambridge: Cambridge University Press, 1999), p. 113.

8

PUBLIC SCHOOLING, DEMOCRACY, AND RELIGIOUS DISSENT

Nel Noddings

PUBLIC SCHOOLING IN THE United States today faces one of the most daunting challenges since its inception. Significant numbers of people are now repeating the charges that were initially thrown at Horace Mann's proposals: public schools are not really "public" at all. They serve the interests of some and work against the interests of others. Among those disaffected today are members of the Christian right and various Protestant sects who were once staunch supporters of public schools. I shall examine their argument here, starting with a discussion of instances that raise grave concerns about the wisdom of allowing a separation of state and school, following this with an examination of the case made by advocates of separation, and then suggesting how defenders of public schooling might respond. In particular, I will argue that education (at least at the precollege level) is a public good, not a private, consumer good. That means not only that everyone should support education through taxes but that all citizens should rightly be concerned with the quality of the education (as preparation for life in a democracy) of every child, not just their own. Throughout the discussion, I will be concerned with the possible effects of adopting a view of education as a consumer good and, especially, with what is learned about democratic life.

I thank Milton Fisk, Chris Higgins, Nancy Holstrum, and Charlene Haddock Seigfried for helpful comments on an earlier draft.

Compulsory education has always posed a peculiar problem for liberal states. *Liberal,* as I am using it here, does not refer to a contemporary political position that stands in opposition to *conservative.* Rather, it points to a political philosophy that emphasizes individual rights and liberties. Both "liberals" and "conservatives" today share in that tradition. How does compulsory education pose a problem for liberalism? On the one hand, from a Millian perspective, it is absolutely essential (although John Stuart Mill expressed reservations about government-run schools and preferred that parents find suitable schools for their children). Education spells the difference, Mill said, between happiness defined in Socratic terms and the purely sensual wallowing pleasure of the pig. It should ensure the intellectual virtues required of a liberal citizenry. On the other hand, it requires coercion, and although Mill was willing to use coercion on children, the dependent young, and "barbarians," later liberals expressed deep concern about this.[1] I want to be clear also that what follows is not meant as a defense of liberalism. When I speak of life in liberal democracies, this is an acknowledgment of the widespread belief that we do in fact live in such a society and that the dilemmas we encounter can be resolved within a liberal framework. I am not at all sure this is true. It may well be that the state we should strive for is better described in Deweyan terms as a social democracy.

A second point to be made by way of preliminaries is that the matter under discussion is especially important for women. Some of the groups desiring separation have very conservative traditional views about the role of women. Girls educated by these groups might well be deprived of the knowledge and opportunities they need to make genuine choices. Second, although I will not be able to discuss it here, the increasingly vigorous campaign of the dissenters makes it difficult for feminist theorists to advance the project of valorizing women's traditional tasks and virtues, to talk seriously about the importance of home and home life. Whereas we may want to educate both boys and girls for a universal caregiver model,[2] valorizing the virtues associated with caregiving seems to give support to the separatists. Thus we must exercise great sensitivity in promoting the care orientation.

What Should Worry Public School Defenders

In his introduction to Sheldon Richman's *Separating School and State,* Jacob G. Hornberger writes: "It is time for the American people to rediscover and move toward the principles of individual liberty and free markets of their ancestors—and to lead the world out of the socialist darkness of the twentieth century. The best place to begin is to liberate America's families through the separation of school and state."[3] The attack on public schools is broad based and contains strange bedfellows: members of the Christian right who condemn the secularism of public education, entrepreneurs who see economic possibilities in the big business of education, libertarians who put their faith in free markets for everything, inner-city parents who despair of obtaining a decent education for their children, parents who are appalled and frightened by increasing violence in the schools, and citizens who have been persuaded (often by badly slanted news stories) that the schools are doing a poor job in academic studies. All of the reasons for challenging public education should be given attention, but here I will confine the discussion to what should worry us in the religious attack.

More than a few Christian schools advocate traditional patriarchal gender roles. Alan Peshkin reports the following comments made by a twelfth-grade teacher in a Christian school, after reading Ephesians 5 aloud to his class: "Relationship of man to wife—I'm the head of my wife and my kids come under her. That's God's order. If a wife doesn't submit, the doors are wide open to Satan. Wives learn to submit, husbands learn to love. If there's a problem, we talk it out. I allow her her say. If I make a wrong decision, then she's not responsible."[4] If these comments were unusual, it would be unfair to point to them as a source of worry for educators in a liberal democracy. But they are not unusual. In the school Peshkin studied, girls are advised: "Make sure the guy you're interested in is on a higher spiritual plain [sic] than you are, that he's someone you can look up to as a spiritual leader." And boys are advised to lead. They are told that girls respect men as leaders: "They need leaders; they need to be led. God didn't put them in a position to lead. He put them in a position to follow."[5]

Peshkin admits that he fears "those who know they have the Truth and are convinced that everyone else would do best to hold this same Truth," but he also strongly defends their right to exist without harassment.[6] Indeed, a liberal democracy must, by its own principles, allow illiberal groups to survive so long as they do not threaten the state itself. But their existence does create a paradox. What threats must the state take seriously, and how can it protect citizens who may fall under the control of such groups without consciously deciding to do so? In particular, a liberal-democratic state must be concerned with the education of its young for life in a pluralistic society.

From a feminist perspective, the worry is not so much that all women will be affected by a revival of patriarchal religion, but that girls who are trained from an early age in schools espousing such views will not gain either the knowledge or the opportunity to make the free choices a liberal democracy tries to ensure for its citizens. In agreement with Peshkin, most of us would still prefer to keep hands off the Christian (and other illiberal) schools. Providing public monies for them, however, may cross the line of constitutionality, and so we have to look carefully at arguments for vouchers that contend that voucher money would support parents, not institutions. But the worry goes well beyond the issue of using public money for religious schools.

Parents in the United States are already free to choose (at their own expense) nonpublic schools for their children, but how much control should they have over what is taught in the public schools? Consider the case of *Mozert* v. *Hawkins* (1987), in which a group of Christian fundamentalists brought suit against a school board for denigrating their religious views in a required reading program.[7] I discuss here just one component of the complaint. One of the stories in the required reader depicts a boy cooking, while his sister reads to him. The parents complained that this reversal of gender roles contradicts biblical teaching and that exposing their children to such views threatens the group's free exercise of religion. They did not insist that the reading program be eliminated, only that their own children be excused from it. Now, putting aside the possible nightmare of control that a multiplicity of such cases might induce, how should a liberal state respond? I will consider an answer to this question a bit later, but for now it should be noted that the decision of the appeals court did not put aside issues of control. On the contrary, the court majority noted that accommodating the parents' request "will leave public education in shreds."[8]

This conclusion, that responding positively to parents' requests would leave public education in shreds, is at least debatable. Critics regularly complain that the American school system has become both an unwieldy bureaucracy and an arrogant monopoly. There is some foundation for such a complaint. At the early stages of the *Mozert* conflict, some administrators and teachers were willing to respond positively to the parents' request. Older reading texts were available, and parents volunteered to come in and teach their children at the designated time. The pervasive notion that professionals know best and that everything "educational" must be handled by certified personnel gets in the way of a caring response. The American tendency to settle all things great and small by litigation does not help either. One might argue that some things should not be settled once and for all but should be left open for continuing discussion. At least law should not make it impossible for schools to respond positively to parents if such a response is not inordinately expensive. The alternative to increased responsiveness is a closing off that deepens distrust and separation. At its worst, growing distrust and dissatisfaction may destroy the public schools entirely.

The *Mozert* decision stands in some contrast to the earlier *Yoder* decision in which the Court decided that the Amish could remove their children from high schools entirely on the grounds that attending such schools would expose their children to lifestyles likely to undermine the Amish religious community.[9] The Court recognized that high school attendance put a special burden on the Amish's "free exercise" of religion. Allowing the Amish to opt out of secondary schooling did not, however, put any burden on the schools, and the Amish made no moves to influence public education. The *Mozert* complaint, in contrast, was much more modest, but it opened the door for further requests that might have involved significant accommodation on the part of schools. It is an open question, however, whether a positive response will lead to further demands or, instead, to an increase of trust and cooperation. If we approach these issues with a "give them an inch and they'll take a mile" attitude, we violate the precepts of associated living that John Dewey described as the essence of democracy.[10] In education especially, we should reject processes that work against the free interaction of differing groups.

Missing from most of the legal discussion is any consideration of children's rights.[11] Should parents control the education of their children as suggested by the separatists? Should government, through public schools, control that education? Here, whichever decision is made, we run into a liberal paradox. If parents control the education of their children, many children will be deprived of the legitimate choices offered in a liberal society. If government controls education, the perceived rights of parents are put into question. The only answer seems to be a parent-school partnership that until recent years has been largely taken for granted. That partnership, which in effect has operated as a check on the power of both groups and thus as a protection for children, is now at serious risk. Why do powerful groups want to dissolve it?

The Religious Case Against the Schools

A great variety of critics have made a general case against the public schools—their bureaucratic sluggishness, monopolistic power, and lack of responsiveness. The more specialized case brought by the religious right against the public schools is usually expressed in two phases. In the first, schools are criticized from a religious perspective; in the second, a recommendation is made for public funding of religious schools. It may be that the criticisms raised in phase one could be answered in a way that would make the recommendation of phase two unnecessary. That should be the first line of response. If no reasonable and caring reconciliation can be reached, defenders of public schooling should still resist the separation called for in phase two on the grounds that public schools play a vital role in developing democratic character.

Phase one arguments typically take one of two forms. One deplores the loss of God in schools and cites an antireligious school environment that tends to undermine the free exercise of religion; the other, less frequently heard but powerfully articulated by Christian intellectuals, charges that the schools are already soaked in religion—the religion of secular humanism. In a sense, this second form of critique charges violation of the establishment clause of the First Amendment, whereas the first depends for its force on the free exercise clause. Both draw heavily on evidence of changes in school structure, classroom behavior, and curriculum that they regard as the pernicious effects of secular humanism.

In 1963, the Supreme Court ruled in *Schempp* that required Bible reading and school prayer are unconstitutional.[12] Since then, many court cases have addressed religious practice in public schools and the relations between public and parochial schools. One might indeed argue that God has been dismissed from the public schools, and while this seems right and proper to many Americans, it represents a genuine loss to many others. One might also point out, however, that after some of the initial fear and attendant extreme decisions, there has been something of a rapprochement between those who would keep the wall of separation tall and solid and those who would open gates and windows for the sake of better educating children and allowing them freedom of speech.[13]

Some of the most interesting and worrisome arguments go well beyond technical claims to free exercise. Extremism on both sides has made it hard for citizens to assess the situation in public schools fairly. In the late 1970s and again in 1988, for example, Mel and Norma Gabler led a blistering attack on the public school curriculum. They identified humanism as the villain and accused it of promoting "situational ethics; evolution; sexual freedom, including public school sex education courses; and internationalism." Their later publication went further and said that humanism promotes "a Darwinian, anti-biblical, individualistic, relativistic, sexually permissive, statist, materialistic, and morally dissolute mindset."[14] On the other side, as Gilbert Sewall fairly points out, "evangelicals and fundamentalists have suffered great disrespect in the educational and popular press."[15] Called "'paleolithic spear throwers'" and many other unpleasant names,"[16] they have also been accused of complicity with various racist groups and racist agendas, and these accusations are often (although not always) unfair.

Fair or not, none of this name calling is helpful. Fundamentalists are not alone in noting and deploring what seems to be a general moral deterioration or at least malaise in our schools. The sticking point is identification of the cause. Fundamentalists are too quick to blame humanism. The truth is that many humanists also deplore the schools' reluctance to discuss moral issues and make a commitment to moral education. But when educators in public schools try to do something in the line of moral education, they are often opposed by the very people who complain most loudly about moral bankruptcy. Complaints against programs such as Values Clarification have been around for a long time and come from every sector including humanist philosophers, but fundamentalist opposition to newer character education programs has been vociferous as well. Why do people object to the inculcation of virtues that they themselves advocate? The reasons vary but usually fall along the following lines: the principles or rules are not made absolute; the teaching of tolerance may include tolerance of that which should not be tolerated (for example, homosexuality); character formation is not properly a function of government; and the recommended virtues are not traced to their authority in God.

Opposition of this sort places the schools in a classic "damned if you do—damned if you don't" situation. They are called on to encourage traditional virtues such as honesty, courage, loyalty, compassion, and the like, but when they do so without crediting God (which they cannot do constitutionally), they are attacked. This dilemma hit me forcefully in an exchange with Richard Baer, a professor of natural resources at Cornell University, at an annual meeting of the American Educational Research Association. Baer spoke eloquently of the values he and other evangelicals espoused, and as he named them, I objected that these values were not "theirs" but were in fact widely shared. After considerable debate, I understood his point. For him and others who share his religious perspective, the values we share are secondary. What counts most is the worldview that sustains and justifies the values. My heart sank at this disclosure. How would we ever succeed at moral education if we had first to agree on a worldview? Worse, if we are allowed only one worldview on which "to agree"—no compromise—how could further discussion be conducted?

John Goodlad too points out that the best moral values of secular and religious thinkers have much in common. He quotes W. Warren Wagar:

> This much, at least, is clear: if we descend from the mountain peaks
> of theology to the plateau of ethics, all the formulas for the spiritual

unification of man converge in perfect harmony. . . . About these four final values—life, personality, transcendence, and love—there is no disagreement whatever in nearly the whole range of contemporary prophetic literature.[17]

I think Wagar exaggerates the agreement, but he is close to what I was feeling as I listened to Baer's talk of values and virtues. One difficulty is that those who value the mountain peak over the plateau will not settle on the plateau. Another difficulty is that those of us who see this as narrow absolutism will not listen without prejudice to those who cling to the mountaintop.

The case that Baer and others brought is not easily dismissed. There is no constitutional proscription against discussing worldviews in public schools so long as students are not required to accept or affirm them. Would it satisfy the dissenters if curricula were amended to include discussion of the sources of virtue and moral law? Such a move would be in keeping with a recommendation that many of us have made to "teach the conflicts."[18] Schools would be far more interesting and educative places if we shared with our students the underlying beliefs and conflicts that have shaped the curriculum. At no point in these discussions need any teacher say, "Here is the truth," but rather, "This is a position espoused by X." It is not outlandish to suggest that high school students hear the words of great religious leaders and of secular thinkers on religion. With the inclusion of religious worldviews in the curriculum, dissenters could not claim that only a secular worldview is presented in the schools.

My guess is that this solution will satisfy neither the dissenters whose case I am considering nor the people who adamantly oppose them. A dissenter will likely object to having his or her view presented as one among many when he or she believes it is the only true view. The charge will be relativism. Opponents, who often want to avoid even the mention of religion in public schools, will object (and have objected) that teachers are not adequately prepared to teach this subject matter. Of course, if we were to take this objection seriously, we would have to abandon most of the subjects we now teach in schools. However, I want to leave open the possibility that further discussion might produce a viable compromise. The dissenters are right in complaining that the schools give short shrift to the great existential questions and almost no attention to what might be called metaphysical longing.[19]

The second prong of the attack addresses not the lack of religion in schools but what is seen as a religious monopoly. Baer and James Carper, for example, write that "it is fair to say that public schools today are saturated with religion, but of a secular and humanistic variety."[20] Using a functional definition of religion—one that defines religion in terms of "how ultimate commitments and worldview convictions actually operate in the lives of individuals and communities"—they claim that secular humanism is a religion.[21] To give this claim credibility, they note that sociologists and anthropologists frequently use a functional definition, but in fact this is a matter of some dispute. Sociologists Rodney Stark and William Bainbridge give a powerful argument against using such a definition. They caution that the inclusion of nonsupernatural, political creeds in religion "makes it needlessly difficult to explore conflicts between these contrary systems of thought or to identify the rather different capacities present in each. . . . We are prepared to assert that there can be no wholly naturalistic religion; that a religion lacking supernatural assumptions is no religion at all."[22]

Stark and Bainbridge have a powerful argument, but Baer points to the words of John Dewey to further his claim. It is true that Dewey wanted to retain use of the adjective *religious* to describe a secular faith and commitment—faith in the capacity to better human life through inquiry and commitment to this betterment. I think Dewey was wrong—and wrong in at least two ways—to do this, but it is crystal clear that he did not regard secular humanism as a *religion:*

> I should be sorry if any were misled by the frequency with which I have emphasized the adjective "religious" to conceive of what I have said as a disguised apology for what have passed as religions. The opposition between religious values as I conceive them and religions is not to be bridged. Just because the release of these values is so important, their identification with the creeds and cults of religion must be dissolved.[23]

Dewey himself recognized the risk he was taking when he tentatively defined God as "this *active* relation between ideal and actual." He immediately noted that he had been warned by sympathetic critics that "the associations of the term with the supernatural are so numerous and close that any use of the word 'God' is sure to give rise to misconception and be taken as a concession to traditional ideas."[24]

It would have been better, for reasons that Stark and Bainbridge cited, if Dewey had not used the language of religion to refer to his humanism. Furthermore, and this is the second way in which he was wrong, there is something insensitive about appropriating the language of believers to launch a scathing attack on their central beliefs. Now we in education are faced with the task of clarifying and modifying the words of one of our most powerful thinkers.

The strategy of Baer and others in classifying secular humanism as a religion is to argue for the protection of the establishment clause. But the strategy does not work well for them. It puts them in the embarrassing position of demeaning a worldview they themselves have called a religion. They would not denigrate the religion of Catholics, Jews, or Muslims. Yet Baer writes:

> Under the banner of secular neutrality, sex education curricula and home economics texts simply assume and implicitly teach that rational behavior is self-interested behavior. Public schools routinely indoctrinate school children with humanistic beliefs like those found in values clarification; . . . these "secular" courses teach (implicitly if not always explicitly) that self-fulfillment and satisfying one's personal needs are the goals of human existence. They insist that all value judgments are subjective and matters of personal opinion. They view tradition and traditional wisdom as a hindrance to achieving the good life.[25]

Much of this is simply untrue. Most schools today are trying hard to develop ideas of cooperation, caring, and civility, although the current demand for unprecedented levels of academic achievement is getting in the way of such humanistic purposes, and this worries many secular humanists quite as much as it does fundamentalists. Where the schools are promoting the values Baer accuses them of, they are not following the ideas of "secular humanism," certainly not the humanism of Dewey. There simply is no real philosophy—religious or secular—guiding the public schools. Many of us who identify ourselves as humanists also deplore the fact that the schools neglect the great existential questions, ignore the great religious traditions, and fail to address metaphysical longing in constitutionally acceptable ways. But it will not do to trace all the bad things that occur in public schools to secular humanism, and if critics really believed that secular humanism is a religion, they would not make such a move.

What Might Be Done

Baer and other critics of public schools want "to get the state out of the business of operating schools."[26] As part of their campaign, they refer to public schools as *government* schools. This change in language is deeply disturbing, first, because the designation "public" applied to schools has long been a term of some approbation, in contrast to anything associated with government and government control. Even more disturbing is the implication that the schools no longer serve a recognizable public and therefore that citizens need no longer concern themselves with education as a public good. Even if it is true that the schools are in a period of unparalleled struggle to serve many publics, the continued search for a solid public must remain a high priority. Dewey recognized a problem that has only grown more complex since he wrote this:

> We have the physical tools of communication as never before. The thoughts and aspirations congruous with them are not communicated, and hence are not common. Without such communication the public will remain shadowy and formless, seeking spasmodically for itself, but seizing and holding its shadow rather than its substance. Till the Great Society is converted into a Great Community, the Public will remain in eclipse. Communication can alone create a great community. Our Babel is not one of tongues but of the signs and symbols without which shared experience is impossible.[27]

What I am arguing here is that we should maintain the search for a Great Community, that we should keep trying to communicate across the lines created by different worldviews. In the continued search for a Great Community, the public school plays a central role.

Baer and Carper (and many others in the broad-based campaign to reduce the hegemony of the public schools) recommend a voucher system that would enable parents to choose their children's schools. It is beyond the scope of this chapter to address the many problems with vouchers, but two are pertinent here.

First, vouchers are sometimes recommended in response to the "double taxation" argument. Countless speeches at public meetings have begun with the words, "Why should I pay for . . ." after which the speaker identifies something about public schooling that does not affirm her or his beliefs. The answer to such questions must be that we all pay for public schools, whether we use them personally or not, because education is a public good, and we care about the education of all children, not just our own. Parents who believe that public schooling undermines the free exercise of their religion must either work together to finance alternative schooling or, better, work with the schools to find a satisfactory compromise. If they purchase private education as they would any other consumer good, they may still rightly be held responsible for their share in supporting education as a public good.

There is a parallel here to tax-supported health plans. Some people argue strenuously against these too, not only on the grounds that such plans tax many citizens for services they will never use but that state-run medicine leads inevitably to mediocrity. This widely expressed objection to "socialized medicine" echoes Mill's early concern about state-run schools. The claim about mediocrity in medicine is an empirical one and seems, based on the available evidence, to be false, but pursuing the matter here would take us too far afield. Few would argue that a healthy citizenry is not a common good, but many differ on how this goal is to be achieved.

Similarly, most people agree that education is a public good—that is, that an educated citizenry benefits everyone. But why can't individuals be left free to choose forms of schooling consonant with their own deepest beliefs? The answer here has to be that public schooling serves the best interests of a liberal democracy and its individual members. It provides the sites for demonstration of democratic life in miniature; it brings together people and views that might otherwise remain outside the domain of public communication.

There is another way in which public schools serve the public good. In purpose at least, they are committed to the fullest education of every individual. Speaking of the purpose of public institutions, Dewey wrote:

> That purpose is to set free and to develop the capacities of human individuals without respect to race, sex, class or economic status. And this is all one with saying that the test of their value is the extent to which they educate every individual into the full stature of his possibility. Democracy has many meanings, but if it has a moral meaning, it is found in resolving that the supreme test of all political institutions and industrial arrangements shall be the contribution they make to the all-around growth of every member of society.[28]

I will return to this important theme.

But what if the public schools do not live up to the purpose Dewey described? Rejection of the double taxation argument does not imply rejection of all voucher plans. A means-tested program that would allow poor parents to escape demonstrably bad schools might still be entertained.[29] But all able citizens would have to pay for this. The good achieved would be a public, not a private, good. The need to provide such plans should be taken as a heavy reproof of the existing public schools and should trigger serious reform.

A second set of arguments that must be rejected is ideological. Parents who object to the worldview projected by public schools must avail themselves of alternatives already available. Even this method of escape from public schools has been questioned in the past, but the right of parents to choose nonpublic schools (at their own expense) was firmly established in 1925.[30] However, it is still appropriate to ask on what grounds this should be allowed. Amy Gutmann has argued that a "democrat must reject the simplest reason for sanctioning private schools—that parents have a 'natural right' to control the education of their children."[31] She believes, as I do, that education is a task for both parents and state. The state, parents, and children all have interests that must be protected. The interests of children are too often overlooked. This is the concern raised by Justice William Douglas in the *Yoder* decision. Excusing Amish children from secondary schooling might well help to maintain the Amish religious community, but what of the children's right to choose? If secondary education would increase their options, should they not participate in it? Again, we are looking for a balance—for an institution, really—that will consider the interests of parents, state, and children. Parents do not own their children. They have no "natural right" to control their education fully.

However, even if the claim to a "natural right" is rejected, a recognition that many citizens believe in this natural right cannot be brushed aside. In a community composed of people with many differing beliefs, no majority or powerful minority should ignore the deeply held beliefs of others unless they are so harmful that the community must be protected against them. Gutmann would protect against the loss of democratic values by insisting that all schools—public and private—teach these basic values, but ensuring that this is done requires careful supervision, and we may predict a new round of outraged complaints if government begins to monitor private schools in this way. Instead of intruding heavily in the conduct of private schools, we might do better to stem their proliferation.

There may be ways in which the public schools could be more responsive to the concerns of parents who have religious objections to some of what is taught. Baer and Carper, while expressing a preference for separation of school and state, suggest a "released time" plan that might be workable. Under such a plan, children would be taught during school day released time some of the ethically charged subjects (for example, sex education, values, and worldview) by religious leaders in groups chosen by their parents. This kind of plan would be very like one that seems to work in much of Europe. Children might elect a secular ethics course or a religious one. There should be a way to work out such a plan, and its great merit would be to keep as many children as possible in public schools.

Keeping as many children as possible in the public schools is in the interest of a liberal democracy; allowing the inclusion of explicitly religious worldviews in public education (strictly by choice) might satisfy the legitimate concern of parents who want to take primary responsibility for the education of their children. But the needs and rights of the children must also be considered. This is the concern I expressed at the outset and again in quoting Dewey on the purpose of public education—one that is too often overlooked in liberal thinking.

Public education has served as a check on the power of parents, and this is another powerful reason for maintaining it. Feminists are right to be concerned about the deprivation of rights many girls would suffer if they were schooled entirely in some religious settings. Furthermore, by its very nature, a liberal democracy depends for its legitimacy on the continuing and voluntary affirmation of a critical citizenry. This means, and Dewey was clearly right on this, that students must be encouraged to inquire, to object, to think critically.[32] Thus, the state has a compelling interest to enforce forms of education that will produce such a citizenry. It also has an obligation to see that all of its young citizens are well informed about their rights as well as their responsibilities.

In exploring ways in which a liberal state might accommodate illiberal groups, William Galston has acknowledged that the state must educate for tolerance: "The state may establish educational guidelines pursuant to this compelling interest. What it may not do is prescribe curricula or pedagogic practices that require or strongly invite students to become skeptical or critical of their own ways of life."[33]

This rather extraordinary recommendation has to be rejected. The whole notion of liberal democracy requires that we "strongly invite" students to examine their ways of life, but it also requires that they have a fair chance to understand both their own and other ways of life. The publicly controlled part of schooling need not engage in the explicit criticism of religious belief, but it must promote critical thinking, and it would be disingenuous on the part of advocates to deny that critical thinking might spill over into areas not explicitly addressed. Of course, it might. Such spillover is the great hope of liberal education, and too often we are disappointed that it does not occur.

It need not, and should not, be the purpose of schooling in a liberal democracy to support some groups and undermine others (assuming the legitimacy of all), but as Will Kymlicka has suggested, it is not a violation of neutrality if some practices, chosen for compelling reasons, have the unintended effect of weakening some groups.[34] Critical thinking widely adopted at the secondary school level might indeed weaken some religious groups. But without it, the public schools really will have given up their central mission in a democracy. That mission has long been to support the health of democratic communities and to do so by promoting the "all-around growth of every member of society."

Responsible educators, together with parents, should decide at what ages critical thinking will be strongly encouraged. My own sense is that children of all ages, engaged in age-appropriate discussions, should be encouraged to ask, "How, why, and on what grounds?"[35] Serious discussion of the great existential questions should probably occur at the secondary school level—probably in grades 10 through 12. By then students should have a fair understanding of the basic teachings in their own religious or secular framework, and if they have been educated earlier to ask for reasons on less controversial matters, they should be ready to join the "immortal conversation."

It is important for both educators and students to understand that critical thinking does not involve only analysis and criticism or, if it is so limited, it is not enough. If we are committed to a search for community, then the best thinking must also include appreciation and caring. The purpose of critical thinking need not be destructive. Students should learn about commitment that survives criticism and doubt and come to appreciate well-considered positions very different from their own.[36]

Concluding Comments

In conclusion, I think public school advocates can concede much to religious dissenters. The schools have largely abdicated their role in examining the great existential questions, and they do not give fair and appropriate respect to our religious traditions as powerful answers to existential questions. I would, of course, favor a curriculum that presents a full range of responses to existential questions. It is important that nonreligious students learn something about the religious traditions that have influenced American social and political life. It is also important that children raised in sectarian traditions learn that many humanists have been moral exemplars and humanism has made significant contributions to moral thought. These dual aims can best be met in public schools. Discussion should continue on ways to reconcile secular and religious views without denying the very differences that separate them.

Indeed, our open and vigorous efforts to do this will set an example for the students we teach. Thorough discussion of competing views (with all their passion) may not persuade anyone to join the other side, and this sort of persuasion should not be the goal of teaching the conflicts. Instead, when we understand and appreciate those who hold very different views, our tactics change. We no longer feel comfortable (or righteous) about calling names, attributing evil motives, or scorning or mocking our fellow citizens. We have, in short, learned something about democratic character. Finally, any plans advanced to accomplish reconciliation should provide adequate protection not only for state and parents but also for children. Children should not be consigned like property to either their parents or the state. That is a powerful reason for keeping children in the public schools and teaching them to think critically.

NOTES

1. See John Stuart Mill, *On Liberty* and *Utilitarianism* (New York: Bantam Books, 1993). In *On Liberty,* Mill contends that the harm principle does not apply to children. He also says that the liberal state has a right to insist on education, but he expresses concern about state-run schools. The Socratic happiness/wallowing pig comparison appears in *Utilitarianism,* p. 148. In contrast to Mill, Bertrand Russell expressed great reservations about compulsory education and felt that liberalism probably could not justify such coercion. See Alan Ryan, *Bertrand Russell: A Political Life* (New York: Hill and Wang, 1988), p. 13.

2. See Nancy Fraser, "Social Justice in the Age of Identity Politics: Redistribution, Recognition, and Participation," Tanner Lecture on Human Values, Stanford University, 1997; and Nel Noddings, *Caring: A Feminine Approach to Ethics and Moral Education* (Berkeley: University of California Press, 1984).

3. Jacob G. Hornberger, "Introduction," in Sheldon Richman, *Separating School and State* (Fairfax, Va.: Future of Freedom Foundation, 1994), p. xii.

4. Alan Peshkin, *God's Choice: The Total World of a Fundamentalist Christian School* (Chicago: University of Chicago Press, 1988), p. 127.

5. Peshkin, *God's Choice,* p. 150.

6. Peshkin, *God's Choice,* p. 298.

7. *Mozert* v. *Hawkins County Public Schools,* 827 F.2d 1058 (6th Cir. 1987). For a comprehensive discussion of this case and its effects on a community, see Stephen Bates, *Battleground: One Mother's Crusade, the Religious Right, and the Struggle for Our Classrooms* (New York: Poseidon Press, 1993).

8. Quoted in Louis Fischer, David Schimmel, and Cynthia Kelly, *Teachers and the Law,* 5th ed. (New York: Longman, 1999), p. 444.

9. *Wisconsin* v. *Yoder,* 406 U.S. 205 (1971). For a thoughtful discussion of both this case and *Mozert,* see Stephen Macedo, "Liberal Civic Education and Religious Fundamentalism: The Case of God v. John Rawls?" *Ethics* 105 (April 1995): 468–496.

10. See John Dewey, *Democracy and Education* (1916; New York: Free Press, 1966), p. 87 and passim.

11. Justice William Douglas's dissent in *Yoder* is an exception. For a discussion of his dissent, see Macedo, "Liberal Civic Education."

12. *School District of Abington* v. *Schempp*, 374 U.S. 203 (1963).

13. See the discussion in Leonard W. Levy, *The Establishment Clause: Religion and the First Amendment* (New York: Macmillan, 1986). See also Fischer, Schimmel, and Kelly, *Teachers and the Law.*

14. Quoted in Gilbert J. Sewall, "Religion and the Textbooks," in James T. Sears with James C. Carper (eds.), *Curriculum, Religion, and Public Education* (New York: Teachers College Press, 1998), p. 76.

15. Sewall, "Religion and the Textbooks," p. 74.

16. Sewall, "Religion and the Textbooks," p. 74.

17. W. Warren Wagar, *The City of Man: Prophecies of World Civilization in Twentieth-Century Thought* (1963; Baltimore: Penguin Books, 1967), p. 163; quoted in John I. Goodlad, "Democracy, Education, and Community," in Roger Soder (ed.), *Democracy, Education, and the Schools* (San Francisco: Jossey-Bass, 1996), p. 102.

18. See Nel Noddings, *Educating for Intelligent Belief or Unbelief* (New York: Teachers College Press, 1993).

19. I have discussed the metaphysical longing shared by believers and unbelievers in Joan Montgomery Halford, "Longing for the Sacred in Schools: A Conversation with Nel Noddings," *Educational Leadership* 56 (December 1998–January 1999): 28–32.

20. Richard A. Baer and James C. Carper, "Spirituality and the Public Schools: An Evangelical Perspective," *Educational Leadership* 56 (December 1998–January 1999): 34.

21. Baer and Carper, "Spirituality and the Public Schools," p. 34.

22. Rodney Stark and William Sims Bainbridge, *The Future of Religion: Secularization, Revival, and Cult Formation* (Berkeley: University of California Press, 1985), p. 3.

23. John Dewey, "A Common Faith," in Jo Ann Boydston (ed.), *The Later Works, 1925–1953*, vol. 9, *1933–1934* (Carbondale: Southern Illinois University Press, 1989), p. 20.

24. Dewey, *Common Faith*, p. 35.

25. Richard A. Baer, "A Functional View of Religion," in Sears and Carper (eds.), *Curriculum, Religion, and Public Education*, pp. 108–109.

26. Baer and Carper, "Spirituality and the Public Schools," p. 35. The same call is made by Richman in *Separating School and State*. For an earlier argument along the same lines, see Stephen Arons, *Compelling Belief: The Culture of American Schooling* (New York: McGraw-Hill, 1983).

27. John Dewey, *The Public and Its Problems* (Chicago: Swallow Press, 1927), p. 142.

28. John Dewey, *Reconstruction in Philosophy*, in Jo Ann Boydston (ed.), *The Middle Works, 1899-1924*, vol. 12 (Carbondale: Southern Illinois University Press, 1982), p. 186.

29. For a discussion of democratically defensible voucher plans, see Kenneth R. Howe, *Understanding Equal Educational Opportunity* (New York: Teachers College Press, 1997).

30. *Pierce v. Society of Sisters*, 268 U.S. 510 (1925). See the discussion in Fischer, Schimmel, and Kelly, *Teachers and the Law*.

31. Amy Gutmann, *Democratic Education* (Princeton, N.J.: Princeton University Press, 1987), p. 116.

32. Dewey was not alone in this recommendation. Countless philosophers, including Socrates, Cicero, John Stuart Mill, Israel Scheffler, and Harvey Siegel, have argued for self-examination and critical thinking.

33. William Galston, "Two Concepts of Liberalism," *Ethics* 105 (April 1995): 529.

34. See Will Kymlicka, *Liberalism, Community, and Culture* (New York: Oxford University Press, 1989).

35. See the discussion of "manner" in teaching in Israel Scheffler, *The Language of Education* (Springfield, Ill.: Thomas, 1960).

36. For an excellent and moving example (the commitment of a Mormon feminist), see Judith Dushku, "The Mormon Caregiving Network," in Suzanne Gordon, Patricia Benner, and Nel Noddings (eds.), *Caregiving* (Philadelphia: University of Pennsylvania Press, 1996), pp. 278–291.

9

CHOICE, THE AMERICAN COMMON SCHOOL, AND DEMOCRACY

Julie Underwood

HAS THE SEDUCTIVENESS of school choice programs obscured the fundamental purposes for which the common public schools were created in the United States? Can and will the values of a democratic society be taught in a private school setting, as they are taught in public schools? School choice, which generally refers to ideas such as the increasingly popular voucher plans that allow for public funding of private school tuition charges, has captured the attention of the American public and policymakers. But important questions seem to get lost in the rhetoric.

The notion of funding private schools through public payment of tuition gained attention in 1955 through the writings of economist Milton Friedman.[1] To introduce competition and free market forces into the educational system and thereby improve quality, Friedman advocated a system in which parents would receive a tuition voucher that they could redeem at any participating private school.[2] Although this notion has had support of long standing, it did not catch fire until the past few years.[3] Now it has been called "the most prevalent reform idea of the 1990s"[4] and "the panacea" for educational reform.[5] Moreover, it is a cornerstone of many state and national political platforms.

Special thanks to Edwin C. Darden and Julie Lewis from the Office of General Counsel, National School Boards Association, for their thoughts on and assistance in the preparation of this chapter.

The rhetoric of choice is powerful stuff. The concept of improving schools through privatization fits well into the current mood of the country. For many people, choice sounds much like freedom. For parents, it represents the freedom to send their children to any school and have the government pick up the bill. For students, it represents the freedom to escape from any troubled public school. And for private educators and many critics of public schooling, it represents an escape from the public educational bureaucracy.

Choice seems to many people to represent the ultimate school reform, a quick and easy solution to the problems of public education. This rhetoric has not been lost on American politicians. Many have been quick to jump on the bandwagon and make school choice a political tool. But the rush to embrace school choice ignores a fundamental question: Can such programs operate within the basic concepts of public schooling and the common school, which have been traditionally valued in American education and have taught democratic citizenship and plurality along with basic educational skills?

Education's Role in a Democratic Society

A strong public educational system is a prerequisite for a strong democratic society. That a public educational system is necessary to bequeath democratic values to the young has been an enduring tenet in the United States. Early advocates of public schools believed that the American people had a duty to provide a basic education for all children in order to achieve certain basic democratic goals: preparing people to become responsible citizens, protecting individual liberties, upholding civic values, and ensuring social harmony, which has come to mean promoting tolerance and respect for racial, ethnic, gender, cultural, and other forms of human diversity.

Many educators have thought seriously about the curriculum required to prepare students for citizenship in a democracy, which is really the crux of the first of these four responsibilities. But one must also consider education from the policy perspective: the structure and organization necessary for this great experiment to yield its desired results. Can that responsibility be met through other systems of education? Supporters of private schools argue that those institutions can deliver improved results on measures of student performance. Private voucher schools could probably provide a curriculum on U.S. government that would fulfill the duty to prepare students for citizenship. Can private schools deliver improved results in that task as well? I contend that they cannot.

Preparing People to Become Responsible Citizens

The founders of the United States believed that the success of American democracy depended on the development of an educated citizenry who would vote wisely, protect its own rights and freedoms, rout out political corruption, and keep the nation secure from internal and external threats to democracy. Strong character and moral virtue were considered an essential part of good citizenship. Early leaders generally endorsed Thomas Jefferson's statement that "a people who mean to be their own Governors must arm themselves with the power which knowledge gives."[6] More than any others, Jefferson's words express the "common school" philosophy that swept the nation in its development. An often-cited passage on this point comes from a letter that Jefferson wrote to George Wythe, one of his teachers and mentors:

> I think by far the most important bill in our whole code is that for the diffusion of knowledge among the people. No other sure foundation can be devised for the preservation of freedom, and happiness. . . . Preach, my dear Sir, a crusade against ignorance; establish and improve the law for educating the common people. Let our countrymen know . . . that the tax which will be paid for this purpose is not more than the thousandth part of what will be paid to kings, priests and nobles who will rise up among us if we leave the people in ignorance.[7]

This theme is also set forth in another of Jefferson's writings, the preamble to his Bill for the More General Diffusion of Knowledge:

> Whereas it appeareth that however certain forms of government are better calculated than others to protect individuals in the free exercise of their natural rights, and are at the same time themselves better guarded against degeneracy, yet experience hath shewn, that even under the best forms, those entrusted with power have, in time, and by slow operations, perverted it into tyranny; and it is believed that the most effectual means of preventing this would be, to illuminate, as far as practicable, the minds of the people at large. . . . And whereas it is generally true that that people will be happiest whose laws are best, and are best administered, and that laws will be wisely formed, and honestly administered, in proportion as those who form and administer them are wise and honest; . . . and that they should be called to that charge without regard to wealth, birth or other accidental condition or circumstance; but the indigence of the greater number disabling them from so educating, at their own

expence, those of their children whom nature hath fitly formed and disposed to become useful instruments for the public, it is better that such should be sought for and educated at the common expence of all, than that the happiness of all should be confided to the weak or wicked.[8]

And in his Farewell Address, George Washington exhorted: "Promote then as an object of primary importance, Institutions for the general diffusion of knowledge. In proportion as the structure of a government gives force to public opinion, it is essential that public opinion should be enlightened."[9]

This is not to say that the early states adopted the notion of free public schools wholesale and immediately funded quality education for all children. That struggle continues today in state legislatures, and it has been a perennial theme. One example is this narration delivered by Governor Gabriel Slaughter of Kentucky to the state legislature in 1819:

> Our government depends for its perpetuity upon the virtue and wisdom of the people; virtue is the offspring of wisdom. To be virtuous, the people must be wise. But how shall they be wise, unless the appropriate means are employed? And how shall the appropriate means be extended to the bereaved and destitute, otherwise than by legislative provision? Education is more vitally important in a republican than in any other form of government; for there the right to administer the government is common to all, and when they have the opportunity of administering the government, the means of obtaining the wisdom requisite for its administration should be accessible to all. The wealthy are never without the means of obtaining education; the poor never, or rarely possess them. But the capacity for the acquisition of knowledge, and the display of virtue, is not confined to the wealthy. It is often, and perhaps more frequently found amongst the poor. Instances are not rare in which genius has emerged from poverty, surmounted the difficulties and privations inseparable from that condition, and like the sun burst through a cloud, illumined the social and political horizon by its benignant irradiations. The ornaments and benefactors of society have not unfrequently arisen when but very slight helps were afforded, from the humblest walks of life.[10]

Protecting Individual Liberties

Public schools are subject to all of the restrictions and restraints placed on the state through federal and state constitutions, statutes, and regulations. In other words, public schools are places where individual rights are guaranteed: the free exercise of religion,[11] freedom of expression,[12] freedom of association,[13] freedom against unreasonable search and seizure,[14] equal protection under the law,[15] and due process.[16] As the Supreme Court put it, children should not be forced to "shed their rights at the school house gate."[17] Defenders of such rights for school children believe that students who experience them in the public schools learn to exercise, respect, and value them responsibly. Yet it is just these liberties that private voucher schools want to be freed from, on grounds that they are largely the cause of the chaos and turmoil that parents want to leave behind.

Merely to teach about the responsible exercise and protection of constitutional rights is not enough. To equip students with the civic skills they need to be effective participants in a representative democracy, they must be given opportunities to practice those skills within institutions that protect their constitutional rights and offer democratic opportunities. Guaranteeing students due process rights, for example, slows the disciplinary process when the administration wants to expel a student. And providing students even a limited open forum within a student publication can lead to uncomfortable situations for administrators when students exercise those rights to express views that may be in conflict with or critical of the school or its adult stewards. But the benefits outweigh the costs. Students who have an opportunity to learn to exercise these constitutional rights responsibly are likely to appreciate and respect the democratic institutions that are the pillars of our democracy.

Upholding Civic Values

Historically, one of the missions of American public schools has been to instill moral virtues in students that will help to make them good neighbors and good citizens. American educator Horace Mann explained in 1846:

> In regard to the extent of the education to be provided for all, at the public expense, . . . under a republican government, it seems clear that the minimum of this education can never be less than such as is sufficient to qualify each citizen for the civil and social duties he will be called to discharge; such an education . . . as is indispensable for the civil functions of a witness or a juror; as is necessary for the voter in municipal affairs; and finally, for the faithful and conscientious discharge of all those duties which devolve upon the inheritor of a portion of the sovereignty of this great republic.[18]

During the 1960s and 1970s, the schools' ability or willingness to fulfill this role waned a bit. Today, however, many public schools are returning to the promotion of civic values, incorporating them into the curriculum or into requirements for service on the part of students. In addition, many are establishing rules for student conduct that promote such virtues as civil discourse, individual responsibility, respect for the rights of others, respect for the law, open-mindedness, and tolerance—behavior required of citizens in a democracy. Furthermore, during the past decade, the courts have recognized this role of public schools and have reinstated schools' ability both to teach students to value good citizenship and to impose related requirements on them.[19]

Promoting Tolerance and Respect for Diversity

In this process of developing a strong, educated citizenry, public schools have a particularly vital role that has no equal in private education: teaching tolerance and respect for diversity. The U.S. Supreme Court has recognized this role, articulating as one purpose of public education the teaching of fundamental values essential to a democratic society, including "tolerance of divergent political and religious views" and "taking into account consideration of the sensibilities of others."[20] Justice John Paul Stevens observed that respect for diversity is "one of the most important lessons that the American public schools teach. . . . It is one thing for a white child to be taught by a white teacher that color, like beauty, is only 'skin deep'; it is far more convincing to experience that truth on a day-to-day basis during the routine, ongoing learning process."[21]

Attending public schools is one of the few experiences that Americans of different backgrounds share. Every state constitution mandates the establishment of public schools and requires that those schools make education available to all of the state's children. By far, the majority of all children in the United States are educated in public schools. And because public schools must educate all comers, they offer all young people the opportunity to build their citizenship skills, thereby helping to ensure that future voters and leaders will come from all walks of life. In public schools with diverse student populations, students have the opportunity to hear different points of view, to disagree amicably, and to reach livable compromises. In other words, public schools are the places where we learn to get along with one another.

Not all public schools live up to this ideal. Many are racially and economically isolated. Nevertheless, this role of public schools in creating social harmony is becoming more essential as the nation becomes more diverse. In 1999, 82 percent of the U.S. population was white, 11 percent Hispanic, 13 percent black, and 4 percent Asian or Pacific Islander. The

U.S. Census Bureau projects that in 2050, the country will be 75 percent white, 24 percent Hispanic, 15 percent black, and 9 percent Asian or Pacific Islander.[22] During earlier waves of immigration, the public school was the institution responsible for building a common culture; it was the melting pot. More recently, public schools have helped to promote progress in civil rights by bringing together children of different races during their formative years, before prejudices have taken hold.

Bolstering the sense of plurality are the numerous federal constitutional and statutory prohibitions on discrimination and requirements of accommodation and fairness. When states, and state departments of education, are recipients of federal funds, they incur an obligation to comply with a number of federal statutes and regulations. The Department of Education's regulations, to pick but one example, require the state's compliance with Title VI of the Civil Rights Act of 1964, Title IX of the Education Amendments of 1972, the Age Discrimination Act, Section 504 of the Rehabilitation Act of 1973, and the Individuals with Disabilities Education Act,[23] among other laws. These are the antidiscrimination provisions that all public entities must respect. For example, Section 504 of the Rehabilitation Act of 1973 states: "No otherwise qualified handicapped individual . . . shall, solely by reason of his handicap, be excluded from the participation in, be denied the benefits of, or be subjected to discrimination under any program or activity."[24] This provision holds two guarantees for disabled children in public schools. First, a public school may not exclude a person from participating in or benefiting from a program that it implements. Second, a public school must ensure that all disabled students who are in publicly funded schools are provided an opportunity to a free, appropriate education as defined by the Individuals with Disabilities Education Act.[25] Private voucher schools, not being public, are not held to these requirements for recipients of federal funds and generally do not want to adhere to them.

In the area of educating disabled children, although participating voucher schools may not blatantly discriminate on the basis of the disabling condition, neither have they been required to make substantial adaptations to accommodate disabled students or to provide an appropriate education for disabled students who wished to enroll. If one looks at this type of program from the perspective of a disabled student, the covert discrimination becomes apparent. A student and parent must choose. Do they want to participate in the voucher program, enroll the student in the private school, and face potential academic failure for lack of appropriate accommodations, or do they enroll the student in the public school, where the necessary special education services are guaranteed? Some choice.

If voucher students have no rights to accommodations or additional necessary educational services in the program, the dilemma is clear. The discrimination against the child and the effect on the public school are obvious. A program that truly offers choices broadens alternatives; it does not limit educational opportunities. Limited opportunities discriminate against the child who needs additional educational services in order to be successful.

More than 10 percent of public school enrollments are children with disabilities. In any district, there also are children who have other special needs—bilingual education, remedial language skills, counseling, and others. If the design of a voucher program does not take into consideration how to meet these needs in voucher schools, the schools will become segregated; few disabled or at-risk students will be served in the private voucher schools.

Perhaps more important is the question of racial, religious, and ethnic diversity. Public schools are not permitted to discriminate on the basis of race, religion, national origin, or language. Voucher schools have not been so obligated under the law.[26] Without a guarantee against these types of discrimination, schools—reflecting our other social and religious patterns—would likely be insular and homogeneous. Our predilection to a homogeneous retreat is seen in the construction of charter and magnet schools—not to mention neighborhoods—that focus on and attract people from similar backgrounds. How many groups will seek their own schools, promote their own cultures, and isolate their children from those with different backgrounds? The cohesion of our communities and nation depends on reaching consensus about solutions to problems of the day. That is the heart of democracy. People of diverse backgrounds must be tolerant and respectful of each other, or we run the risk of great social and political upheaval. Without a common institution like public schools to bring people together, the nation would become more divided and people more fearful of those different from themselves. The United States will pay a dear price if we allow ourselves to be thus divided along racial, ethnic, religious, or economic lines.

Public schools were created as places where a diverse nation of immigrants could come together to learn how to be a democracy. Common schools were conceived as places where civic virtue was passed on to the next generation. Continuing to play that role is the public schools' niche in American society. The opposing forces of the school marketplace—evidenced by voucher programs, charter schools, and home schooling—will not teach children how to set aside their differences and celebrate those things that can draw them together. In fact, most of these innovations exacerbate the problems of separation.

Public schools are uniquely positioned to provide an education to all children, to equip students with the skills they need to participate in a democracy, and to be an instrument of harmony in society. The public school has been and continues to be the most important institution for maintaining freedoms and democracy. Without public schools, the United States would become more divided and less devoted to the democratic process, and the nation's leaders would be less representative of all segments of the U.S. population.

As the nation continues its rapid journey toward even greater diversity and people struggle to find better ways to live harmoniously with each other, the dream of Horace Mann and Thomas Jefferson is the only antidote to a potential national nightmare. We must learn to get along with each other, and that can happen only through exposure to those who differ from us. We cannot afford to let the United States become a nation of separate, warring tribes and gangs. Yet the only way to prevent that is by celebrating those things we share—our dreams, our common values, and our national legacy of powerful ideas.

Public schools need to improve—not because they are not as good as they used to be but because they are not as good as they need to be to take the nation into an uncertain future. They must be affirmed by this nation in their critical mission.

Common Schools, Not Choice, for the Future of Democracy

A choice or voucher program, by publicly funding private schools, creates a new form of public education. State legislatures have traditionally funded public education by creating and funding the common school. As presented by Horace Mann, such a school was to be common not in the traditional European sense of a school for common people, but in the sense of common to all people—held in common, owned, controlled, and used by all. It is available and equal to all children, rich and poor alike. Its doors are open to all, no matter how easy or difficult their educational tasks might be. Not only are these schools free of charge, but they provide a minimal substantive level of education. That minimal educational level is necessary for the common school to fulfill its central purpose: the development of informed and productive citizens who can actively participate in a democratic society. This notion has also been enshrined in many of the individual state constitutions that create a compact between the state government and the governed. The common school has educated its citizens for active roles in society through instruction and interaction with others. In this common school, children of all creeds, classes, and backgrounds come together. It is the tool that turns the individual members in a diverse, pluralistic society into citizens who are respectful of all and dedicated to the preservation of its democratic form.

Because public education and public schools hold a special place in our republic, the reform of public education must be approached deliberately. The adoption of vouchers as a state educational reform is in essence the abandonment of the common school. A private school voucher program permits—in fact, in some ways encourages—the abandonment of the social institution best able and most likely to preserve our commitment to diversity and pluralism. Without a societal commitment to diversity, the tendency may be for people to flee one another in search of their own isolated educational repose. This places us back to the days before *Brown v. Board of Education,* when separate was considered equal but was, in fact, quite the opposite.

Public education has served us all well. It is in need of improvement— in some cases, desperately in need. First, a major investment is needed in the infrastructure that supports children and families. How does a voucher program alone resolve the problems of a low-income urban community like Milwaukee? It will not change the lives of children overnight, nor will it guarantee their educational success. In fact, it will create additional stresses on an already overextended educational enterprise. Over time we will see how a voucher system resegregates the public schools and requires them to do difficult additional tasks with less and less money.

Professionals in the field of education have seen quick fixes and educational fads come and go. Choice, too, may come and go. However, this reform du jour has the potential of creating significant costs to the resident public school districts and lasting harm to the nation's educational enterprise. Rather than the quick fix or the silver bullet, the reform that public education needs now is more active support and public involvement. The United States cannot afford to turn its back on public education as an institution. Public education cannot cure all of society's problems, but it should not be penalized for failing to meet that impossible goal. Neither should we be so naive as to believe that changing to an unregulated delivery system for education will cure all of those problems. Choice is no panacea.

NOTES

1. Milton Friedman, "The Role of Government in Education," in Robert A. Solo, *Economics and the Public Interest* (New Brunswick, N.J.: Rutgers University Press, 1955). See also Milton Friedman, *Capitalism and Freedom* (Chicago: University of Chicago Press, 1962).

2. Friedman, *Capitalism,* p. 89.

3. See John E. Coons and Stephen D. Sugarman, *Education by Choice: The Case for Family Control* (Berkeley: University of California Press, 1978). The tuition tax program that received attention in the 1980s was upheld in *Mueller v. Allen,* 463 U.S. 388 (1983).

4. John F. Witte, "Public Subsidies for Private Schools: What We Know and How to Proceed," *Educational Policy* 6 (June 1992): 206.

5. John E. Chubb and Terry M. Moe, "America's Public Schools: Choice Is a Panacea," *Brookings Review* 8 (Summer 1990): 4–12.

6. Quoted in Kern Alexander and M. David Alexander, *American Public School Law,* 3rd ed. (St. Paul, Minn.: West, 1992), p. 20.

7. Julian P. Boyd (ed.), *The Papers of Thomas Jefferson,* vol. 10 (Princeton, N.J.: Princeton University Press, 1954), pp. 244–245.

8. Julian P. Boyd (ed.), *The Papers of Thomas Jefferson,* vol. 2 (Princeton N.J.: Princeton University Press, 1950), pp. 526–527.

9. Washington's Farewell Address may be found in any number of publications. One of the most accessible is in the Library of America collection, *George Washington: Writings,* selected by John Rhodehamel (New York: Literary Classics of the United States, 1997), pp. 962–977. This quotation is from p. 972.

10. Quoted in Alexander and Alexander, *American Public School Law,* p. 22.

11. *West Virginia v. Barnette,* 318 U.S. 624, 63 S. Ct. 1178 (1943).

12. *Tinker v. Des Moines Independent School District,* 393 U.S. 503, 89 S. Ct. 733 (1969).

13. *Healy v. James,* 408 U.S. 169 (1972).

14. *New Jersey v. T.L.O.,* 105 S. Ct. 733 (1984).

15. *Brown v. Board of Education,* 347 U.S. 483 (1954).

16. *Goss v. Lopez,* 419 U.S. 565, 95 S. Ct. 729 (1975).

17. *Tinker v. Des Moines Independent School District,* 393 U.S. 503, 89 S. Ct. 733 (1969).

18. From Horace Mann's *Tenth Report* (1846), quoted in Alexander and Alexander, *American Public School Law,* p. 25.

19. *Bethel School District No. 403 v. Fraser,* 478 U.S. 675 (1986); *Hazelwood School District v. Kuhlmeir,* 484 U.S. 260 (1988); *Herndon by Herndon v. Chapel Hill–Carrboro City Board of Education,* 899 F. Supp 1443 M.D.N.C. 1995 (ruled that a community service program did not violate

the Thirteenth Amendment or the right to privacy); *Immediato* v. *Rye Neck School District,* 73 F.3d 454 (2d Cir. N.Y. 1996) (mandatory community service program was not impermissible involuntary servitude and did not violate parents' liberty interest in the upbringing of their children).

20. *Bethel School District No. 403* v. *Fraser,* 478 U.S. 675 (1986).

21. *Wygant* v. *Jackson Board of Education,* 476 U.S. 267, 315 (1986) (Stevens, dissent).

22. Percentages total more than 100 because "persons of Hispanic origin may be of any race" and may therefore be counted twice. U.S. Census Bureau, "National Population Projections: II. Detailed Files" (NP-D1-A, Middle Series), available at http://www.census.gov/population/www/projections/natdet.html. Accessed 14 July 2000.

23. 20 U.S.C. 2001.

24. 29 U.S.C. 793(a).

25. 20 U.S.C. 2000.

26. *Beaufort* v. *Lighthouse,* S.C. Court of Common Pleas 97-CP-7–794 2000.

EDUCATION FOR DEMOCRACY

THE FOUNDATION FOR
DEMOCRATIC CHARACTER

Roger Soder

IT IS OFTEN SAID that the first words of a character in a novel or play tell us much about the context, the underlying meaning, and what is to come. Hamlet's first words, "A little more than kin, and less than kind," tell us much about his character, his sense of humor and irony, his puns, his bitterness. We think too of Martha's opening line in the movie version of *Who's Afraid of Virginia Woolf?*: "What a dump!" Thus we can attend to the opening line of the main character in that great icon of American movies, *The Godfather,* expecting to mine considerable ore, and we will not be disappointed. The movie is about gangsters, an early version of the Mafia. But the movie is also a running commentary about civil society and the failures of a particular kind of civil society, the failures of democracy. The movie is thus about what this book is about: what it takes to create and sustain a democratic civil society.

The main theme of *The Godfather* is thrust at us during the opening two minutes. On the day of his daughter's wedding, Don Corleone listens to the sad tale of the undertaker. The undertaker's daughter has been brutalized by thugs. The undertaker, being a good American, goes to the police. The case is thrown out of court, the thugs laughing at the undertaker. Now he has come to Don Corleone for justice. The don sets the scene for the whole with two short questions: "Why did you go to the police? Why didn't you come to me first?" There are at least two civil societies, the don implies. When the official one does not work, you either choose to come to me, or you opt out and suffer the consequences. The world of Don Corleone works, in some respects: the thugs who terrorized the undertaker's daughter are dealt with in a rough form of rough justice: an eye for an eye. The undertaker wants Don Corleone to have the thugs killed. But the don objects: the undertaker's daughter was not murdered, so the thugs cannot be murdered. Even in this undemocratic civil society, there are rules, some definition of what is just. But this model of a civil society is not one that should appeal to us. For all of its talk about honor and justice, it is a model of violence, of amorality, of an unwillingness to consider the welfare of others in noninstrumental ways. The world of the Godfather is a gated community. Don Corleone lives in a gated compound (although this does not protect him from an almost-successful assassination attempt). His son, as shown in the movie sequel, lives in a gated community near Lake Tahoe. He too comes close to being killed by an assassin's bullets fired into his bedroom: gated communities do not seem to provide much beyond the formalities of security. And in our own time and in the real world, gated communities are being offered with assurances of security—the kind of security, it is implied, that the regular municipalities and their police departments are unwilling or unable to provide.[1]

A similar kind of civil society, with similar circumstances, is found in another movie, another cultural icon, *The Magnificent Seven*. The opening scenes are a staple: the peasants in a small village in Mexico are being terrorized by a gang. The Mexican government is far away. The peasants heed the advice of a wise man in the village: hire gunfighters. And thus the peasants seek out Yul Brynner and his colleagues, who in time mete out a kind of justice to the gang. An earlier version of the same situation is found in the Japanese film *Yojimbo*. At the end of this magnificent Kurosawa production, our samurai hero has wiped out both warring factions in a village. As the poor peasants peer out from behind the few remaining huts, the samurai strides away, saying, "Now maybe there will be some peace and quiet around here." Stability, peace, and quiet, to be sure, but to what extent was the village destroyed in the process of saving it?

The motif of the failure of democratic civil society is played out repeatedly in American television and movie dramas. As crime rates rise or are perceived to be on the rise, the popular culture turns to alternative ways, alternative civil societies, to get the job done. One thinks of such television fare as *Have Gun, Will Travel* from the 1950s (a lax sheriff will not seek justice); *Mission Impossible* (government cannot do the job, so extralegal forces are needed); and *The Equalizer* (equalizing the struggles of victims against criminals, making a level playing field when the police fail to do so); as well as such movies as *Death Wish* (in its many forms, starring Charles Bronson as the revenge seeker) and *Star Chamber* (with Michael Douglas as a judge who engages in extralegal efforts to mete out justice because the courts cannot do the job).

Another kind of civil society that we can consider and reject is exemplified by the exchange, not in a movie but in "real life," between a London businessman and his agent in Belarus. The agent calls London with a problem. It seems that the local truck drivers are refusing to transport company merchandise. The trucks won't move until the drivers are bribed with huge sums. What are we to do? asks the businessman in London. Easy, says his agent. We shoot all the truck drivers. That way we not only don't have to pay their bribes, but we can also get all the trucks. And what's the alternative plan? Well, the agent says, we'll beat them up so badly they'll be afraid to try to blackmail us again. The third alternative? London agreed to pay the money. The civil society in Belarus as exemplified here surely lacks appeal.

Here is one final example of a civil society we would find repugnant: at his first meeting with Hitler at Berchtesgaden in November 1937, Lord Halifax was talking about England's problems with India. Hitler said the solution was simple. "Shoot Gandhi," he said. Lord Halifax apparently did not know quite what to make of this.[2] I trust that we do.

As these examples suggest, there are civil societies that are unappealing, ones that violate any reasonable sense of decency, fair play, and humanity. And there remains a kind of civil society, a kind of political and social democracy, that is more in keeping with our sense of what we want, what we think is right. It is not just any civil society that we want; what we want is a democratic civil society. But what is it that we want when we say we want a democracy or a democratic society? Again, we might start with what we do not or should not want. When we say we want democracy, we are talking about more than democracy as participation and majority rule. If that were all democracy involves, then all sorts of unlikely and unwanted group structures will qualify. A lynch mob can have lots of participation, with a majority in favor of the lynching, but what of that? We sometimes conflate democracy with collaboration, cooperation, and working well together, as if getting along and having good interpersonal relationships are all that matter. But again, a lynch mob can exhibit collaboration, cooperation, and good intragroup relationship skills. The mob in *The Ox-Bow Incident* worked together just fine.

What we must have in mind when we say we want democracy is more than participation or majority rule or some version of laissez-faire in the Old West. And what we must have in mind is necessarily difficult to achieve and to sustain. As Edmund Burke points out, government is easy to establish. Freedom is easy to have. Free government, on the other hand, is hard to accomplish.[3] In like manner, Alexander Hamilton argues that the great question is whether we can establish good government on the basis of reflection and choice, or whether we are condemned to have government on the basis of accident and force. It is good government, Hamilton reminds us,[4] that is at stake: good government that is in effect a liberal, constitutional, democratic republic. Such government has the features delineated by Robert Dahl:

1. Elected Officials. Control over government decisions about policy is constitutionally vested in elected officials.

2. Free and fair elections. Elected officials are chosen in frequent and fairly conducted elections in which coercion is comparatively uncommon.

3. Inclusive suffrage. Practically all adults have the right to vote in the election of officials.

4. Right to run for office. Practically all adults have the right to run for elective offices in the government, though age limits may be higher for holding office than for the suffrage.

5. Freedom of expression. Citizens have a right to express themselves without danger of severe punishment on political matters broadly defined, including criticism of officials, the government, the regime, the socioeconomic order, and the prevailing ideology.

6. Alternative information. Citizens have a right to seek out alternative sources of information. Moreover, alternative sources of information exist and are protected by laws.

7. Associational autonomy. To achieve their various rights, including those listed above, citizens also have a right to form relatively independent associations or organizations, including independent political parties and interest groups.[5]

For the sake of brevity, I will use the term *democracy* to denote this broader sense of a political regime that is characterized by freedom, constitutionality, and democracy (in the sense of self-rule by the people rather than rule by the one or the few) in a republican state (in the sense of elected representatives chosen from parties presenting viable and significant alternative philosophies and programs).

Democracy: Do We Want It?

We say we want a democracy. At least we think that is what we want. Francis Fukuyama argued that we were at the end of history, that democracy had indeed emerged as the great desideratum of political and social life.[6] For many reasons, critics assailed Fukuyama's position. One of the fundamental questions still being asked is whether people do indeed want a democracy and the responsibilities that go with that territory. This is not an idle question. Throughout many parts of the world, democracy is seen not as something to be desired but rather as something to be avoided. Dostoevsky's Grand Inquisitor insists that people do not want freedom, cannot handle freedom, and will do anything they can to avoid the responsibilities of freedom. At most, the Grand Inquisitor says, people want some sort of benevolent dictatorship or oligarchy, with the few telling the many what to do and what to believe. In our own time, the Grand Inquisitor's notions remain popular, with countries such as Singapore declining the adoption of democratic institutions in favor of security and economic development.[7]

When we talk about wanting a democracy, we have to talk about more than what it takes to establish a political regime. We need to understand that it is often more difficult to sustain a democracy than it is to create it.[8] As Dankwart Rustow reminds us, "The factors that keep a democracy stable may not be the ones that brought it into existence."[9] In trying to sustain a regime, it is easy to get sidetracked. There is a tendency to do "big things" for show rather than for real sustenance. As Tocqueville warned, France and England should not compensate for national malaise "by making railroads."[10] A regime can do more than build railroads. In 1958, the U.S. government conducted a study of the feasibility of exploding an atomic bomb on the moon. Officials apparently thought this would be a good way to compensate for our being behind in the space race with the Soviet Union. Another way to get sidetracked is to engage in various imperialistic campaigns. The costs can be considerable. Edward Gibbon could well be speaking of our own time as well as speaking of Rome:

> There is nothing perhaps more adverse to nature and reason than to hold in obedience remote countries and foreign nations in opposition to their inclination and interest. A torrent of barbarians may pass over the earth, but an extensive empire must be supported by a refined system of policy and oppression: in the centre an absolute power, prompt

in action and rich in resources: a swift and easy communication with the extreme parts: fortifications to check the first effort of rebellion; a regular administration to protect and punish; and a well-disciplined army to inspire fear, without provoking discontent and despair.[11]

It is not an easy task to sustain a democracy.[12] To sustain a regime necessarily involves questions of succession. Note that the first four characteristics of good government outlined earlier in this chapter deal specifically with how new leaders are to be selected. Beyond mere questions of procedure and orderly succession, we must consider how, in a democracy, we are to get the best leaders—those who will be not only effective but also good and wise. The succession issue is difficult and complex, particularly because of the threat posed by the highly ambitious. In a provocative and disturbing speech, "Perpetuation of Our Political Institutions," the young Abraham Lincoln describes the danger to the Republic posed by the ambitious man, the new Caesar, who, if he cannot be accorded recognition by building things up, will be just as likely to seek recognition by tearing things down. For this kind of man, Lincoln tells us, mere perpetuation will not do: "Towering genius disdains a beaten path."[13]

And the regime is threatened by apathy, the kind of apathy that Tocqueville described so movingly near the conclusion of *Democracy in America*. He speaks of how people respond to the "immense, protective" power of government:

That power is absolute, thoughtful of detail, orderly, provident, and gentle. It would resemble parental authority if, fatherlike, it tried to prepare its charges for a man's life, but on the contrary, it only tries to keep them in perpetual childhood. It likes to see the citizens enjoy themselves, provided that they think of nothing but enjoyment. It gladly works for their happiness but wants to be sole agent and judge of it. It provides for their security, foresees and supplies their necessities, facilitates their pleasures, manages their principal concerns, directs their industry, makes rules for their testaments, and divides their inheritances. Why should it not entirely relieve them from the trouble of thinking and all the cares of living? . . .

Having thus taken each citizen in turn in its powerful grasp and shaped him to its will, government then extends its embrace to include the whole of society. It covers the whole of social life with a network of petty, complicated rules that are both minute and uniform, through which even men of the greatest originality and the most vigorous temperament cannot force their heads above the crowd.

It does not break men's will, but softens, bends, and guides it; it seldom enjoins, but often inhibits, action; it does not destroy anything, but prevents much from being born; it is not at all tyrannical, but it hinders, restrains, enervates, stifles, and stultifies so much that in the end each nation is no more than a flock of timid and hardworking animals with the government as its shepherd.[14]

In addition to ambition and apathy, political regimes are threatened by the plain fact that things go wrong. The successful maintenance of a regime depends to some extent on the successful functioning of the day-to-day activities, but as any planner will acknowledge, things are more likely to go wrong than to go right. The challenge in human affairs is not to have things go perfectly. The challenge is how to maintain equilibrium while things are falling apart. Just as the maintenance of individual relationships depends on knowing how to recover and reconstitute when things go wrong, so does the maintenance and improvement of a regime depend on processes for recovery and reconstitution. And when we think of reconstitution, we need to remind ourselves of Tocqueville's shrewd admonition:

The most perilous moment for a bad government is one when it seeks to mend its ways. Only consummate statecraft can enable a King to save his throne when after a long spell of oppressive rule he sets to improving the lot of his subjects. Patiently endured so long as it seemed beyond redress, a grievance comes to appear intolerable once the possibility of removing it crosses men's minds. For the mere fact that certain abuses have been remedied draws attention to the others, and they now appear more galling; people may suffer less, but their sensibility is exacerbated.[15]

There is a further challenge. We do not—or should not—want merely to create, sustain, and recover. We need also to focus on improving the democratic regime and not be content with maintaining or recovering the status quo, holding frozen in amber a now-distant past.[16]

Conditions for Democracy

Let us assume that despite the challenges, we want democracy. And let us assume that we want to sustain it and improve it. Then the next question we must ask is: Are there conditions necessary for the functioning of a healthy democracy, or can a democracy somehow exist without recourse to context?

The notion of conditions is critical. Consideration of conditions tells us what is necessary for proper functioning of systems and helps us understand relationships among elements of systems. John Goodlad has reminded many of us of what analysis of conditions means through his example of what to do about mosquitos. If you want to get rid of mosquitos, you do not go after individual mosquitos. You go after the pond. The pond is a necessary condition for the mosquitos.

Consideration of conditions also points us toward the normative. An example of conditions defining a desired good can be found in the world of Islam. By Koranic law and cultural tradition, five conditions are specified for a village to be considered a village: (1) bakery, (2) fountain, (3) mosque, (4) *hammam,* or public bath, and (5) elementary school. A village needs bread. It needs clean water. People must be clean, they must involve themselves with a sense of the sacred (rather than pure self-interest), and they must assume the responsibilities of enculturation of the young. Without these five things, a village might be some sort of village, but it would not be a good and virtuous place, an authentic and productive Muslim village. In like manner, we might specify conditions of our own towns and villages in the United States that will help us understand what is necessary for a good life and how we are to sustain it.

Conditions do not automatically appear. As Dewey reminds us:

> If we want individuals to be free we must see to it that suitable conditions exist:—a truism which at least indicates the direction in which to look and move. It tells us among other things to get rid of the ideas that lead us to believe that democratic conditions automatically maintain themselves, or that they can be identified with fulfillment of prescriptions laid down in a constitution.[17]

Democracy does not simply exist in some sort of pure sense, unconnected to conditions in its environment. We need to delineate the necessary conditions. From these, we can develop a reasonable sense of the kind of character we as a people must have in order to sustain the kind of democratic regime we want to have.[18]

Assuming that there are such conditions, what are they? Elsewhere, I have in brief suggested eleven conditions.[19] I present them here in expanded form.

Trust

If there is no trust, people will not be able to enter into the kinds of long-term relationships necessary for political and social interaction in a democracy.[20] It is necessary to establish trust. Without trust, we find ourselves no further along than the people at Corcyra whom Thucydides described so compellingly:

> Oaths of reconciliation, being only proffered on either side to meet an immediate difficulty, only held good so long as no other weapon was at hand. . . . Religion was in honour with neither party; but the use of fair phrases to arrive at guilty ends was in high reputation. . . . The ancient simplicity into which honour so largely entered was laughed down and disappeared; and society became divided into camps in which no man trusted his fellow. To put an end to this, there was neither promise to be depended upon, nor oath that could command respect; but all parties dwelling rather in their calculation upon the hopelessness of a permanent state of things, were more intent upon self-defence than capable of confidence.[21]

An equally important question deals with the recovery of trust. Given that trust is probably going to be violated, a question of critical importance focuses on recovery: how do you reconstitute trust once it has been violated?

Exchange

People must be able to exchange goods and services in order to survive in a democracy. The act of exchange is a way of building and sustaining relationships.[22] It is often difficult to maintain balanced exchange relationships. Montaigne reminds us of the dangers of unbalanced relationships:

> When some years ago I read Philippe de Commines, certainly a very good author, I noted this remark as uncommon: That we must be very careful not to serve our master so well that we keep him from finding a fair reward for our service. I should have praised the idea, not him; I came across it in Tacitus not long ago: "Benefits are agreeable as long as they seem returnable; but if they go much beyond that, they are repaid with hatred instead of gratitude." And Seneca says vigorously: "For he who thinks it is shameful not to repay does not want the man to live whom he ought to repay." Q. Cicero, in a weaker vein: "He who thinks he cannot repay you can by no means be your friend."[23]

In considering exchange, then, we must be aware not only of the functions of giving, receiving, and repaying but also of the dangers of unbalanced exchange, and we must be adept at finding ways to redress the unbalance.

Social Capital

People need to have social and political skills in order to work together to understand problems and create solutions—as opposed to simply accepting orders.[24] Social capital seems to work within the bounds of the "Matthew effect," with the rich getting richer. Thus, a difficulty in a democracy is how to secure and sustain social capital for all rather than for a select few.

Respect for Equal Justice Under Law

If there is no justice, we have no recourse other than self-interest, which is ultimately self-defeating.[25] Incorrigible self-interest reaches its apotheosis with Faust. His bet with Mephistopheles makes little sense from the perspective of group (as well as individual) interest or from an ecological perspective. Faust's proposition—if you can ever satisfy me, you can have my soul—is not a proposition that makes sense, not even, in the end, to Faust. What happens when justice loses to self-interest is described by Thucydides in the Melian dialogue. The Athenians, in their struggle against Sparta during the Peloponnesian War, have lost their sense of justice and are now defining themselves solely in terms of self-interest. They prepare to invade the neutral island of Melos. Why are you invading us? ask the Melians. Because we are stronger than you are, say the Athenians (in language similar to that used by Thrasymachus in *The Republic*, that is, justice is whatever is in the interests of the stronger). But, say the Melians, what of our rights? The Athenians laugh, replying that "rights are only in question between equals in power, while the strong do what they will, and the weak suffer what they must."[26] In our own time, we have problems in trying not only to secure but to sustain equal justice under law.[27]

Respect for Civil Discourse

If people cannot talk to each other, advance ideas, adduce evidence, and weigh and consider options without resorting to physical or verbal violence, democracy will have difficulty surviving.[28] As Goodlad notes, "We are not born knowing the art of conversation that is central to the moral art of democracy."[29] Respect for civil discourse is difficult to sustain, especially given campaign financing practices and pervasive corporate control of the media.[30]

Recognition of the Need for E Pluribus Unum

The American democracy is not experienced simply by isolated groups, each celebrating its own peculiar identity. There must be some sort of glue that holds the whole together. But there must also be respect for individual and group differences. The trick here is to acknowledge and deal with the constant tension between the *unum* and the *pluribus*.[31] In our own time, we seem to place considerable emphasis on the *pluribus,* resulting in self-limiting politics of identity and group self-calculation.[32]

Free and Open Inquiry

This condition is central to a democracy. People will not be able to participate in any thoughtful way in a democracy unless they have the ability and inclination to inquire into all aspects of the workings of society.[33]

Knowledge of Rights

If we do not know what our rights are, we will have difficulty exercising them. A people without knowledge of its rights can hardly participate effectively in a democracy.[34] In his First Annual Address to Congress, George Washington speaks of the need to teach "the people themselves to know and to value their own rights; to discern and provide against invasions of them; to distinguish between oppression and the necessary exercise of lawful authority."[35]

Freedom

As many have said, you have to have the power to exercise freedom and the insight to value it. Both conditions are necessary.[36] Herodotus gives us an early sense of what is at stake in his account of the Spartan envoys' meeting with Hydarnes, a Persian satrap, during a lull in the war between Persia and Greece. Hydarnes advises the Greeks to surrender, telling them that the king "knows how to honor merit." "Hydarnes," they answer, "you are a one-sided counsellor. You have experience of half the matter, but the other half is beyond your knowledge. A slave's life you understand, but never having tasted liberty, you do not know whether it be sweet or no. Had you known what freedom is, you would have bidden us fight for it, not with the spear only, but with the battleaxe."[37]

Recognition of the Tension Between Freedom and Order

Leo Strauss reminds us that we have to deal with the "freedom that is not license and the order that is not oppression."[38] If we maximize freedom and ignore order, we end up with anarchy. But if in our desire for order, we move beyond reasonable order to oppression, then we are no better off. The tension between freedom and order is a constant. We have to distinguish, as George Washington reminds us, "between burthens proceeding from a disregard to their convenience and those resulting from the inevitable exigencies of Society."[39]

Recognition of the Difference Between a Persuaded Audience and a More Thoughtful Public

We must know this ourselves, and we must demand that our leaders know it too.[40] As Ralph Lerner notes, "As sure as 'a great empire and little minds go ill together' [from Burke, "On Conciliation with America"], so too might it be said more generally that the conduct of the public's business demands enlarged views both from the few charged with that business and from the many empowered to select them. An electorate that expects its representatives to behave like lapdogs will get what it deserves—creeping servility— not what it most needs."[41] A thoughtful public is difficult to sustain, especially in times of stress. When things are not going well, we have a tendency, as said earlier, to build railroads—or to succumb to demagoguery.

Ecological Understanding

The unit of survival is the organism plus its environment.[42] The organism that destroys its environment destroys itself. As John Goodlad, Stephen Goodlad, and Paul Theobald and Clif Tanabe have noted in their respective chapters in this book, the only way for democracy to survive is for the larger environment to survive.

The Conditions Considered

Some of these conditions could be applied equally to a dictatorship. Survival of a dictatorship depends on respect for law (although what might motivate the respect is fear of the secret police as opposed to a thoughtful understanding of the relationship among freedom, order, and law). But just because a condition might be useful to a dictatorship as well as a democracy does not mean that we should reject it as a condition for a democracy. There are, on the other hand, conditions that are peculiar to a democracy. Civil discourse or deliberation, for example, is critical to a democracy (and critically threatening to a dictatorship).

It should be noted that these are postulated conditions. One might well come up with a variation of this set or an entirely different set.

Nonetheless, once we accept the notions that we want a democracy and that a democracy has necessary conditions, we are obligated to come up with a set of conditions.

Assuming that we agree that conditions are necessary for a healthy democracy, and assuming that we either accept the conditions postulated here or reject them and construct a different set, the next question is: Are people born knowing about these conditions and how to create and maintain them, or do they have to learn about them?

Let us assume that there is no genetic programming that enables us to know about such matters as justice and law and freedom from the time of birth, and let us assume that we choose learning. The next question, then, is obvious. Where are people to learn these things? The response to this question depends in part on the kind of regime you want to have. If you want a democratic regime, then you will want all people, as a matter of principle, to have a working knowledge of the conditions necessary to creating and maintaining the regime. So we have to determine where it is most likely that the greatest proportion of the people will be able to gain that working knowledge. Mary Ann Glendon indicates a similar concern: "Where do citizens acquire the capacity to care about the common good? Where do people learn to view others with respect and concern, rather than to regard them as objects, means, or obstacles? Where does a boy or girl develop the healthy independence of mind and self-confidence that enable men and women to participate effectively in government and to exercise responsible leadership?"[43]

Some might argue that the conditions I have set out (or an alternate set) can and should best be learned at home. Others will say that such matters are best dealt with in community organizations such as the Boy Scouts or Camp Fire Girls. Others might argue that much of what matters in dealing with these conditions stems from religious character, and thus young people should learn about the conditions in religious places of learning and worship. All of these sources for learning about the conditions may seem appealing. But in considering any of them, the question still must be addressed: Where will the greatest proportion of people in a democracy be likely to learn about these conditions? It is in response to this question that many have concluded that the public schools remain the most likely place that most people will be able to learn about what is necessary to establish and sustain and improve our democracy. The fundamental purpose of schools, on this view, is to teach children their moral and intellectual responsibilities for living and working in a democracy. This is the public function of schools.[44] If this public function is paramount, then there are significant implications for schools and those who teach and learn in them. Schools must be structured in ways that reflect the teaching of the conditions necessary for a democracy, and the curriculum in the schools must focus both directly and indirectly on the teaching of these conditions. Moreover, if teachers are to teach children moral and intellectual responsibilities, then the teachers themselves must have gained, through their own education in the liberal arts and professional preparation programs, a reasonable, subtle, and extensive understanding of just what those moral and intellectual responsibilities entail.

Characteristics of a Democratic People

Let us recapitulate. We have acknowledged the desire for a democracy, we have set forth twelve conditions (and, again, there could be some variation of the twelve) necessary to secure and sustain a democracy, and we have argued that public schools represent the most likely source of learning about these conditions. But our task is not yet complete. Learning or talking about conditions for a democracy is necessary but hardly sufficient. We have to act. *Conditions are created by people.* Therefore, we must ask, What must be the character of a people such that it can create and sustain the conditions necessary for a democracy? We must recognize that, as Ralph Lerner suggests, "In the last analysis, what matters is the character of the people. Those who prize liberty only instrumentally for the externals it brings—ease, comfort, riches—are not destined to keep it long."[45] Here Lerner is close to Tocqueville: "I am quite convinced that political societies are not what their laws make them, but what sentiments, beliefs, ideas, habits of the heart, and the spirit of the men who form them, prepare them in advance to be, as well as what nature and education have made them."[46]

Accordingly, we have to talk about characteristics of a democratic people, about democratic character, if you will. It might be tempting to talk about democratic character in general terms. But if we say we want a democracy and postulate the necessary conditions, then we are bound at least to begin our discussion within the framework of the postulated conditions. The question, still, is: If conditions are created by people, what kind of characteristics in a people are necessary to achieve the greatest likelihood that the conditions will indeed be created? Let us turn, then, to a brief exploration of characteristics in terms of these conditions.

Trust, Exchange, and Social Capital

These three conditions are closely related, as are the dispositions necessary to secure them; as such, they are considered here as one. First, we must encourage as a disposition a general willingness to trust. As with all other dispositions, moderation is the key. Thus, a general willingness must be tempered by a prudent skepticism (perhaps, as was said about disarmament, "trust, but verify"). Given the frequency of trust violation, we must also encourage people to be willing to recover trust and help others with the struggle of trust recovery. Second, we must encourage people to engage in exchange, honor the obligations exchange implies, and be mindful of the dangers of unbalanced exchange. We must encourage the desire to create opportunities for exchange, especially among individuals and groups of individuals traditionally left out of the process. Third, we must encourage understanding of social capital as a tool, skill, and process open to all. We must encourage patience to allow others the opportunity to learn how to exercise newly found social capital.

Respect for Equal Justice Under Law

We must encourage respect for the law, even when decisions go against perceived self-interest. We must encourage the rejection of temptations to take the law into our own hands.

Respect for Civil Discourse

We must encourage people to be willing to entertain propositions, consider evidence, and accept ambiguity as inevitable. They must embrace the sentiments of Pericles: "Instead of looking on discussion as a stumbling-block in the way of action, we think it an indispensable preliminary to any wise action at all."[47]

Recognition of the Need for E Pluribus Unum

We must encourage a willingness to accept the tension between the *pluribus* and the *unum* as a positive good rather than a problem to be solved. People need to reject the tendency to resolve the tension by trying to choose either one or the other.

Free and Open Inquiry

We must encourage critical inquiry as a personal and civic virtue. We must therefore encourage a willingness to be a minority of one and acceptance of democracy as a manifestation, in the words of Dewey, of the "capacity of the intelligence of the common man to respond with commonsense to the free play of facts and ideas which are secured by effective guarantees of free inquiry, free assembly, and free communication."[48]

Knowledge of Rights

We must encourage a willingness to believe that human rights are essential and that rights are natural rather than positive. We must encourage a willingness for a democratic people to be "alert, assertive, and mindful of its honor, interest, and happiness."[49]

Freedom

We must encourage people to recognize freedom as an inherent part of what it means to be a human being. We must encourage a willingness to consider—but to reject—the claims that all or even some people do not want or cannot deal with freedom.

Recognition of the Tension Between Freedom and Order

We must encourage a willingness to accept and support the enduring tension between the two goods of freedom and order. The strength of character needed here is, as with recognition of the need for e pluribus unum, a willingness to understand and act on the need to balance the tension rather than to seek an either-or solution.

Recognition of the Difference Between a Persuaded Audience and a More Thoughtful Public

We must encourage a willingness to select and support leaders and representatives who will not pander to ephemeral public tastes or the immediately gratifying. Frederick Douglass argued that "the limits of tyrants are prescribed by the endurance of those whom they oppress."[50] In like manner, if we have venal, calculating, servile, or otherwise unprincipled leaders, we must look to our own character and not transfer the blame to those who take advantage of our ignorance and lack of virtue. Moreover, given the threats to a democracy posed by at least some of the highly ambitious, we must be able to distinguish between those who value their reputations for probity and ability to benefit the community—for such valuation will temper their ambitions—and those who want only to benefit themselves.

Ecological Understanding

We must encourage a willingness to look beyond the immediate horizon and change our time frame accordingly.[51] We must encourage a willingness to look for the patterns that connect and a willingness to understand the connectedness of the ecology of mind.[52] And along these lines, we must encourage acceptance of the notion that, as Wendell Berry put it, "To think better, to think like the best human beings, we are probably going to have to learn again to judge a person's intelligence, not by the ability to recite facts, but by the good order or harmoniousness of his or her surroundings."[53]

Concluding Comments

Perhaps these characteristics or traits or dispositions deemed necessary to ensure creation and sustenance of the conditions necessary for our democracy are best summed up by Thomas Jefferson in the Rockfish Gap Commission Report. Jefferson argued that what is needed is to enable the citizen

> To improve, by reading, his morals and faculties;
> To understand his duties to his neighbors and country, and to discharge with competence the functions confided to him by either;
> To know his rights; to exercise with order and justice those he retains, to choose with discretion the fiduciary of those he delegates; and to notice their conduct with diligence, with candor, and with judgment;
> And, in general, to observe with intelligence and faithfulness all the social relations under which he shall be placed.[54]

We can derive overlapping core elements from the characteristics outlined here. For example, a recurring motif in our listing of conditions and related characteristics is the notion of contradiction, tension, and dilemma. Thus, it would seem that one overlapping element centers on patience, on tolerance for ambiguity, and an unwillingness to leap to either-or "solutions" because of discomfort with problems that in fact are not problems. A second element is a willingness to act on the basis of reasoned probabilities rather than to refrain from action until one has ultimate and absolute truths. A third element focuses on the notions of conflict between individual and group, and on how to satisfy individual needs while helping to meet the needs of the larger community. A fourth element deals with keeping the idealistic desire to improve within bounds of reason and prudence: citizens need to avoid intemperate actions destructive of the very democratic republic that provides succor for improvement in the first place.[55] Perhaps in reflecting on the characteristics needed for the conditions offered here, I am left in the end with a notion of modesty, of moderation, in keeping Talleyrand's wise cautions of not too much zeal, and in keeping with the wise observation in the *Tao Te Ching*: "If you know when you have enough, you will not be disgraced. If you know when to stop, you will not be endangered."[56]

Others might well derive a different set of characteristics or common elements of characteristics from the conditions offered here. The argument nonetheless still stands. There must be conditions in place for democracy to be created, sustained, recovered, and improved. Conditions are created by people. People must have a given set of dispositions or characteristics that will most likely lead to the creation of those conditions.

These dispositions or characteristics are taught and reinforced in homes, churches, private associations, street corners—and schools. I continue to believe that it is to the schools that we must look for sustained attention to the development of the character of a democratic people. Keeping in mind the conditions and characteristics offered here, we might then be able to address more thoughtfully issues of school structure and curriculum and the preparation of teachers. That thoughtful attention must be our focus in the years to come if we are indeed to deserve and sustain a free society.

Notes

1. Theodore White tells us of what he learned in 1930s China about civil society, government, and protection in his *In Search of History: A Personal Adventure* (New York: Harper & Row, 1978):

   "What I learned was that people accept government only if the government accepts its first duty—which is to protect them. This is an iron rule, running from bombed-out Chungking to the feudal communities of the Middle Ages to the dark streets of New York or Rome where the helpless are so often prey. Whether in a feudal, modern, imperial or municipal society, people choose government over nongovernment chiefly to protect themselves from dangers they cannot cope with as individuals or families. . . .

   "I had learned the first real lesson of politics, government and history: governments are instituted among men in the first instance, and accepted by men gratefully, to protect them from random violence and killing. I had begun to observe that when the central government replaced the local government of Chungking after the bombings. But I had not seen what government meant in the hills of Shansi, where the Communists, not yet calling themselves government, were becoming government. They offered protection" (pp. 83, 101).

For a current useful discussion of the privatization of protection, see Diego Gambetta, *The Sicilian Mafia: The Business of Private Protection* (Cambridge, Mass.: Harvard University Press, 1993).

2. William Manchester, *The Last Lion* (Boston: Little, Brown, 1988), p. 243. According to Manchester, Chamberlain was amused by Halifax's report of Hitler's advice: "It occurred to neither of them that the Führer had been serious."

3. Edmund Burke, *Reflections on the Revolution in France* (New York: Penguin Books, 1986), p. 374.

4. Alexander Hamilton, "Federalist No. 1," in Garry Wills (ed.), *The Federalist Papers* (New York: Bantam Books, 1982).

5. Robert A. Dahl, *Democracy and Its Critics* (New Haven, Conn.: Yale University Press, 1989), p. 221.

6. Francis Fukuyama, *The End of History and the Last Man* (New York: Free Press, 1992). See also Fukuyama, "Second Thoughts," and Harvey Mansfield, E. O. Wilson, Gertrude Himmelfarb, Robin Fox, Robert J. Samuelson and Joseph S. Nye, "Responses to Fukuyama," *National Interest* 56 (Summer 1999): 16–44.

7. See Fareed Zakaria, "The Rise of Illiberal Democracy," *Foreign Affairs* 76 (November–December 1997): 22–43, and responses by John Shattuck and J. Brian Atwood, and Marc F. Plattner, *Foreign Affairs* 77 (March–April 1998): 167–181; Gordon P. Means, "Soft Authoritarianism in Malaysia and Singapore," *Journal of Democracy* 7 (October 1996): 103–117; and Marcin Krol, "Where East Meets West," *Journal of Democracy* 6 (January 1995): 37–43. For an interesting debate, see Fareed Zakaria, "Culture Is Destiny?: A Conversation with Lee Kuan Yew," *Foreign Affairs* 73 (March–April 1994): 109–126, and the response by Kim Dae Jung, "Is Culture Destiny: The Myth of Asia's Anti-Democratic Values," *Foreign Affairs* 73 (November–December 1994): 189–194. For a larger perspective, see Samuel P. Huntington, *The Clash of Civilizations and the Remaking of World Order* (New York: Simon & Schuster), 1996.

8. The careful student can ask for no better guide to the questions of sustaining a regime than Ralph Lerner's, *Revolutions Revisited: Two Faces of the Politics of Enlightenment* (Chapel Hill: University of North Carolina Press, 1994).

9. Dankwart A. Rustow, "Transitions to Democracy," *Comparative Politics* 3 (April 1970): 346.

10. Tocqueville to John Stuart Mill, March 18, 1841, in Roger Boesche (ed.), *Selected Letters on Politics and Society,* trans. James Toupin and Roger Boesche (Berkeley: University of California Press, 1985), pp. 150–151.

11. Edward Gibbon, *The Decline and Fall of the Roman Empire,* vol. 2 (New York: Modern Library, 1932), chap. 49, p. 627.

12. See, for example, Jean-François Revel, *How Democracies Perish* (Garden City, N.Y.: Doubleday, 1983), and *Democracy Against Itself: The Future of the Democratic Impulse* (New York: Free Press, 1993). See also Robert D. Kaplan, *The Coming Anarchy: Shattering the Dreams of the Post Cold War* (New York: Random House, 2000), especially chap. 2, as well as Adam Przeworski and others, "What Makes Democracies Endure?" *Journal of Democracy* 7 (January 1996): 39–55.

13. See Abraham Lincoln, "Address to the Young Men's Lyceum of Springfield, Illinois: The Perpetuation of Our Political Institutions," in Don E. Fehren-bacher (ed.), *Speeches and Writings,* vol. 1 (New York: Library of America, 1989), pp. 28–36. For a detailed commentary on this most disturbing speech, in which, at least for me, Lincoln delineates a fundamental problem (the designs and threats of the highly ambitious) while eschewing any ready solution other than an apparent reliance on cold reason, see Harry V. Jaffa, *Crisis of the House Divided: An Interpretation of the Issues in the Lincoln-Douglas Debates* (New York: Doubleday, 1959), especially chap. 9.

14. Alexis de Tocqueville, *Democracy in America,* vol. 2, trans. George Lawrence (New York: Harper & Row, 1966), part iv, chap. 6, p. 692.

15. Alexis de Tocqueville, *The Old Regime and the French Revolution,* trans. Stuart Gilbert (New York: Anchor Books, 1955), pp. 176–177. Frederick Douglass made a similar point in his *Narrative of the Life of Frederick Douglass, An American Slave* (New York: Penguin Books, 1986), p. 135: "I have observed this in my experience of slavery—that whenever my condition was improved, instead of its increasing my contentment, it only increased my desire to be free, and set me to thinking of plans to gain my freedom. I have found that, to make a contented slave, it is necessary to make a thoughtless one. It is necessary to darken his moral and mental vision, and, as far as possible, to annihilate the power of reason. He must be able to detect no inconsistencies in slavery; he must be made to feel that slavery is right; and he can be brought to that only when he ceases to be a man."

16. Readers will likely have their own notions of where improvements need to come. One of many recent and compelling suggestions can be found in

David Cole, *No Equal Justice: Race and Class in the American Criminal Justice System* (New York: Free Press, 1999).

17. John Dewey, *Freedom and Culture* (New York: Putnam, 1939), pp. 34–35.

18. For further discussion of conditions, see Dahl, *Democracy and Its Critics,* p. 7.

19. Roger Soder, "To Ourselves and Our Posterity," in Wilma F. Smith and Gary D Fenstermacher (eds.), *Leadership for Educational Renewal: Developing a Cadre of Leaders* (San Francisco: Jossey-Bass, 1999), pp. 49–71.

20. Of the extensive literature on trust, the following have been particularly useful to me: Diego Gambetta (ed.), *Trust: Making and Breaking Cooperative Relations* (New York: Blackwell, 1988). See also Francis Fukuyama, *Trust: The Social Virtues and the Creation of Prosperity* (New York: Free Press, 1995), as well as his *The Great Disruption: Human Nature and the Reconstitution of Social Order* (New York: Free Press, 1999); Adam B. Seligman, *The Problem of Trust* (Princeton, N.J.: Princeton University Press, 1997); Barbara A. Misztal, *Trust in Modern Societies: The Search for the Bases of Social Order* (Cambridge, Mass.: Polity Press, 1996); and Bernard Barber, *The Logic and Limits of Trust* (New Brunswick, N.Y.: Rutgers University Press, 1983).

21. Thucydides, *The Peloponnesian War,* book 3 (New York: Modern Library, 1951), chap. 10, par. 82, p. 190.

22. For a useful discussion of exchange, see Peter Blau, *Exchange and Power in Social Life* (New York: Wiley, 1964); Marcel Mauss, *The Gift: Forms and Functions of Exchange in Archaic Societies* (New York: Norton, 1967); John Davis, *Exchange* (Buckingham: Open University Press, 1992); and Alfred North Whitehead, *Adventures of Ideas* (New York: Free Press, 1967), chap. 5.

23. Michel de Montaigne, "On the Art of Discussion," in *The Complete Essays of Montaigne,* trans. Donald M. Frame (Stanford: Stanford University Press, 1958), p. 718.

24. In *Making Democracy Work: Civic Traditions in Modern Italy* (Princeton, N.J.: Princeton University Press, 1993), Robert Putnam and his colleagues argue that the three conditions so far stated (trust, exchange, and social capital) are critical to a healthy democracy. For additional considerations of the notion of social capital, see James Coleman, *Foundations of Social Theory* (Cambridge, Mass.: Belknap Press, 1990), chap. 12.

25. Useful here is James Boyd White, *The Legal Imagination* (Chicago: University of Chicago Press, 1987), as well as his *Acts of Hope: Creating Authority in Literature, Law, and Politics* (Chicago: University of Chicago Press,

1994), and *Justice as Translation: An Essay in Cultural and Legal Criticism* (Chicago: University of Chicago Press, 1990).

26. Thucydides, *Peloponnesian War,* book 5, chap. 16, pp. 330–337. See also James Boyd White, *When Words Lose Their Meaning: Constitutions and Reconstitutions in Language, Character, and Community* (Chicago: University of Chicago Press, 1984), especially chap. 3.

27. See Cole, *No Equal Justice.*

28. See, among others, Mary Ann Glendon, *Rights Talk: The Impoverishment of Political Discourse* (New York: Free Press, 1991).

29. John I. Goodlad, "Democracy, Education, and Community," in Roger Soder (ed.), *Democracy, Education, and the Schools* (San Francisco: Jossey-Bass, 1996), p. 105.

30. See, for example, Robert W. McChesney, *Rich Media, Poor Democracy: Communication Politics in Dubious Times* (Urbana: University of Illinois Press, 1999).

31. Conversations about these matters might best begin (and end) with Tocqueville, *Democracy in America.*

32. See Daniel Patrick Moynihan, *Pandaemonium: Ethnicity in International Politics* (New York: Oxford University Press, 1993); see also Arthur Schlesinger Jr., *The Disuniting of America: Reflections on a Multicultural Society,* rev. ed. (New York: Norton, 1998).

33. For this matter of free and open inquiry, Socrates and Galileo come to mind. Of the many texts useful and inspiring, I keep returning to Herbert J. Muller, *The Uses of the Past: Profiles of Former Societies* (New York: Oxford University Press, 1952), chap. 3.

34. A most useful discussion is found in Philip B. Kurland and Ralph Lerner (eds.), *The Founders' Constitution: Major Themes,* vol. 1 (Chicago: University of Chicago Press, 1987), chap. 14.

35. George Washington, *The Writings of George Washington,* vol. 30, ed. J. C. Fitzpatrick (Washington, D.C.: Government Printing Office, 1939), p. 493.

36. See Donald Treadgold, *Freedom: A History* (New York: New York University Press, 1990). See also Herbert J. Muller's trilogy, *Freedom in the Ancient World* (New York: Harper, 1961), *Freedom in the Western World: From the Dark Ages to the Rise of Democracy* (New York: Harper & Row, 1963), and *Freedom in the Modern World* (New York: Harper & Row, 1966), as well as his *Issues of Freedom: Paradoxes and Promises* (New York: Harper, 1960). Also useful is Orlando Patterson, *Freedom: Freedom in the Making of Western Culture* (New York: Basic Books, 1991); Isaiah

Berlin, *Four Essays on Liberty* (New York: Oxford University Press, 1968); and Ruth Nanda Anshen (ed.), *Freedom: Its Meaning* (New York: Harcourt, Brace, 1940). For a discussion of the connection between economic freedom and political freedom, see Amartya Sen, *Development as Freedom* (New York: Knopf, 1999). Robert Nisbet's *The Present Age: Progress and Anarchy in Modern America* (New York: Harper & Row, 1988) presents a useful analysis of threats to freedom; see especially chap. 2 on the growth of invasive government. Also useful for its discussion of threats to freedom by invasive government is James C. Scott's *Seeing Like a State: How Certain Schemes to Improve the Human Condition Have Failed* (New Haven, Conn.: Yale University Press, 1998).

37. Herodotus, *The Persian Wars*, book 7, trans. George Rawlinson (New York: Modern Library, 1942), chap. 135, p. 547.

38. Leo Strauss, *Persecution and the Art of Writing* (1952; Chicago: University of Chicago Press, 1988), p. 37.

39. Washington, *Writings*, vol. 30, p. 493.

40. For the notion of the distinction between the two, see Lerner, *Revolutions Revisited*, p. 59.

41. Lerner, *Revolutions Revisited*, p. 67.

42. See Gregory Bateson, *Steps to an Ecology of Mind* (New York: Ballantine, 1972; reissued with an introduction by Mary Catherine Bateson, Chicago: University of Chicago Press, 2000). For an exceedingly useful explication of Bateson's thought, see Peter Harries-Jones, *A Recursive Vision: Ecological Understanding and Gregory Bateson* (Toronto: University of Toronto Press, 1995).

43. Glendon, *Rights Talk*, p. 129.

44. See John I. Goodlad and Timothy J. McMannon (eds.), *The Public Purpose of Education and Schooling* (San Francisco: Jossey-Bass, 1997), and John I. Goodlad, *In Praise of Education* (New York: Teachers College Press, 1997) for discussions of the distinction between public and private purpose.

45. Lerner, *Revolutions Revisited*, p. 127.

46. Tocqueville to Claude-François de Corcell, September 17, 1853, in *Selected Letters*, pp. 293–294.

47. Thucydides, *Peloponnesian War*, p. 105.

48. John Dewey, "Creative Democracy—The Task Before Us," in Jo Ann Boydston (ed.), *The Later Works, 1925–1953*, vol. 14, *1939–1941* (Carbondale: Southern Illinois University Press, 1988), p. 227.

49. Ralph Lerner, *The Thinking Revolutionary: Principle and Practice in the New Republic* (Ithaca, N.Y.: Cornell University Press, 1987), p. 25.

50. Frederick Douglass, "West India Emancipation," speech delivered at Canandaigua, New York, August 4, 1857, in Philip S. Foner (ed.), *The Life and Writings of Frederick Douglass,* vol. 2, *Pre–Civil War Decade, 1850–1860* (New York: International Publishers, 1950), p. 437.

51. For a telling discussion of the need for longer time frames, see Stewart Brand, *The Clock of the Long Now* (New York: Basic Books, 1999).

52. See Gregory Bateson, *Mind and Nature: A Necessary Unity* (New York: Dutton, 1979); Gregory Bateson and Mary Catherine Bateson, *Angels Fear: Towards an Epistemology of the Sacred* (New York: Macmillan, 1987); and Gregory Bateson, *A Sacred Unity: Further Steps to an Ecology of Mind,* edited by Rodney Donaldson (New York: HarperCollins, 1991).

53. Wendell Berry, *Standing by Words* (San Francisco: North Point, 1983), p. 77.

54. Thomas Jefferson, "Report of the Commissioners Appointed to Fix the Site of the University of Virginia, &c.," quoted in Gordon C. Lee (ed.), *Crusade Against Ignorance: Thomas Jefferson on Education* (New York: Teachers College Press, 1961), p. 117.

55. For insightful, if depressing, discussions of the dangers of improvement based on utopian schemes, massive social engineering, and ideologies of perfection, see Robert Conquest, *Reflections on a Ravaged Century* (New York: Norton, 2000), and Tony Judt, *Past Imperfect: French Intellectuals, 1944–1956* (Berkeley: University of California Press, 1992).

56. *Tao Te Ching,* no. 44, trans. Thomas Cleary (New York: HarperCollins, 1993), p. 36.

INDEX